NIGHTMARE
OVERHANGING
DARKLY

NIGHTMARE OVERHANGING DARKLY:

ESSAYS ON AFRICAN AMERICAN CULTURE AND RESISTANCE

ACKLYN LYNCH

THIRD WORLD PRESS

Chicago

Nightmare Overhanging Darkly

Published by Third World Press, P.O. Box 19730, Chicago, IL 60619.

ISBN: 0-88378-142-5

Library of Congress Number: 91-65325

Cover Illustration by Patrick Hill
Cover Design and Color Separations by Angelo Williams

Manufactured in the United States
93 94 95 96 97   1 2 3 4 5

DEDICATION

To my mother, Ms. Esmee Lynch, whose faith and vision
pointed the way.

We are not a people of stagnant waters,
we are rememberers of the way.
- Ayi Kwei Armah, *Two Thousand Seasons*

TABLE OF CONTENTS

FOREWORD

The fire that burns in spite of torrential rains casts hope in the hearts of those who must make "a way out of no way." It conjures an energy that transcends the padlocks of despair, bringing forth memory and action for tomorrow. The voice of the flame issues a command: thou shall not be a member of the living dead, ignorant of the truths, the promises, and the possibilities of your lot. The command can be heard in the message of Acklyn Lynch, son of Shango, god of fire.

The fire spits ancient truths that knock naked against modern lies, which have been written and painted for generations of children. These truths are best comprehended in the eye of the storm, through music, poems, dances, and stories that gather in the whirlwind to sustain us. They find common ground in individuals who, like Lynch, make a life's commitment to act upon and spread "the Word" and inspire a better tomorrow.

The flame of the fire has branded steel and made possible the teachings of Lynch, who walks with us as griot, poet, activist, teacher, orator, writer, organizer, man of the mountains and fields, companero, father extraordinaire, brother, friend and loved one. Sugar cane alley. City brown. A man molded by the hands, souls, and spirits of those who once danced with the sparks and traversed the path, issuing strength to those born and yet to be. A man who consciously calls upon Conchise, Cinque, Toussaint, Turner, Tubman, Truth, Garvey, Dubois, Butler, Ida B., Padmore, James, Malcolm, Nkrumah, Che, George Jackson, Coltrane, Billie, Duke, Mingus, Marley, and more — many, many more — giants of our history, chained and unchained.

The very persona of Acklyn Lynch is like that of the fire — blazing, brilliantly, consistent, filled with dedicated energy, informed. He exudes trust and creativity combined with a sincere desire to learn from others while teaching. Even his moments of silence emerge like granite, listening and offering enormous statements in words not said, the rooted, the touched, the connected.

All praises for his works, which offer the open eye a point of discovery, an opportunity to be better informed, a chance to understand the reasons for our most frightening nightmares, our most significant dreams, and our most compelling actions.

All praises for this son ...

All praises for the fire that burns...in spite of "the nightmare over-hanging darkly."

Zala Chandler, ED.D.
Medgar Evers College, CUNY
Brooklyn, New York
April 1992

Introduction

Controversy has never deterred Acklyn Lynch from conveying truth to the people and, simultaneously, offering us alternative ways of seeing the human condition. Two decades ago, Afrocentricity, multiculturalism and cross-cultural comparative study encompassing oppressed peoples' quests for self-determination and autonomy were controversial in higher education. Lynch, not surprisingly, was at the forefront of orienting thousands of students to these methods of intellectual inquiry before they had coined names and entered the domain of public debate. He has remained committed to this quality of instruction, with a level of depth still uncommon in academia, for more than twenty years.

In the wake of the Civil Rights Movement that occurred in tandem with post-World War II, anti-colonial struggles in Africa, Asia, and Latin America, I was fortunate to find myself in the Black Studies courses of Acklyn Lynch. "Fortunate" because Lynch, a first-generation immigrant from the Caribbean who had received his post-secondary education in the United States, helped to make sense of our times. The early '70's were bearing witness to a multitude of power movements, and Lynch, with his knowledge of U.S. people of color's cultures and experiences, linked our realities to events in the outside world — that "other," known as the Third World, deemed inconsequential by the controllers of institutions of higher learning. In this respect, he offered us a holistic understanding of the political, economic, social and cultural forces at work and influencing our lives.

Over dinner, en route to a rally, at a community forum, at one of his countless artistic productions, as well as in the classroom, Lynch continues to stimulate the minds, to challenge the spirits, and to help forge the moral wills of those who come in contact with him. A social theorist and cultural worker, he discusses Middle East politics with as much mental agility as he dialogues about Latin American poetry. He lectures on the relevance of theoretical writings by late psychiatrist and spokesperson for the Algerian revolution Frantz Fanon with as much passion as he treats the social meaning of urban city rappers RUN DMC, Boogie Down Production, or Public Enemy. Just as earnestly, he analyzes the crisis in human values that has led to new peaks of infamy in violence against individuals, women, children, ethnicities, nations, and Earth. And with the insightfulness of a renaissance man, Lynch readily expounds upon radical changes the decade of the '90s has thus far produced: the dissolution of the Soviet Union; the economic ascendancy of Japan; the unification of Germany and the European Community; the sociopolitical tenacity of China; the international repercussions of the liberation struggle in South Africa; the deadly competitions for natural resources; and the real possibility of a global, ecological holocaust.

In addition, Lynch probes vigorously the dynamics of transition in the United States. He characterizes as a "cold war" the government's increasing reliance upon violence and repression to compensate for economic and social contradictions. Fallen warrior George Jackson likened it to "nightmare overhanging darkly," a fascist state of centralized authoritative power upon us in this fifth century of Black resistance.

In *Nightmare Overhanging Darkly: Essays on African American Culture and Resistance*, a literary concerto in three parts, Acklyn Lynch incisively and eloquently dissects the Black experience in "the belly of of the beast." "Black Culture and Consciousness," part one, resonates as a blues tribute to the legacies of African American warriors, radical thinkers, and cultural icons who have confronted the social injustice of their eras with courageous challenges to the status quo: W.E.B. DuBois, Marcus Garvey, Claude McKay, Langston Hughes, Alaine Locke, Paul Robeson, A. Philip Randolph, Margaret Walker, Richard Wright, Medgar Evers, Rosa Parks, Martin Luther King, Jr, Nina Simone, Fannie Lou Hamer, Malcolm X, Erika Huggins, George Jackson, Angela Davis, Assata Shakur, and Sandy Smith, among others.

Lynch imparts the significance of major personages, events, and ideas in the twentieth century to contemporary Black America, tracing the evolution and dialectic of Black culture and consciousness. He examines the artistic and political representations of this culture and consciousness in urban cities, the nation's chambers of power, and international arenas with incisive journeys into the bowels of the American nightmare — the "dream" exploded!— prison movements, Black-on-Black homicide, the mental casualties of imperialist wars, the plight of the Black "underclass," and the rage of Black youth. Removing the "rose colored glasses" that the late James Baldwin contended African Americans needed to keep from going mad, Lynch gives us unadulterated clearsightedness about our wretchedness while shoring up our sanity with equal clarity about the continuity of Black struggle.

"Art and Resistance," the second section of *Nightmare Overhanging Darkly*, has the impact of a jazz rendition. Lynch sets before us the agents for change who preserve the collective memory and interpret the collective consciousness. These essays about African American artists constitute drumtalk, invoking the spirit world that has historically impelled Black struggle: the gods, orishas, ancestors. In the creative genius of our artists, such as musicians Max Roach and Archie Shepp or writers Sonia Sanchez and Toni Morrison, we locate the spiritual well for cultural regeneration, for wholeness. Eschewing technological gimmicks or material incentives for polluting the souls of Black people, the artists examined in this collection seek accurate renderings of Black life, culture, and aspirations in song, dance, music, visual image, and the word. Dr. Lynch demonstrates that such artists have assumed their necessary "duty" of being a "guerilla fighter," of being "blk/and ready." Drumtalk, for certain.

Part three of *Nightmare Overhanging Darkly*, "The Educational Imperative: Toward the Reconstruction of The Black World," has the energy and urgency of hip hop, rap, and reggae. Calls to action, these essays are reverent yet biting, reminding us that commitment *is* foremost "an action." Without apology, Lynch critiques the political order, market economy, technologies, and popular culture of Western society. He elucidates the crippling effects of silence and false images, and the futility of social integration and uncritical faith in dehumanizing institutions as means of rectifying the Black condition. Lynch does not ignore formidable obstacles to achieving justice and freedom. But he insists that collecting the debt due for the exploitation of "our talents, creativity, and heavy labor" requires Black people's development of new "structures, systems and codes." Nothing short of reconstructing the Black world. Arguing that "it is the liberated individual who undertakes to build the new society," he underscores the importance of the educational process with a "blueprint for change."

Nightmare Overhanging Darkly contains the penetrating analyses needed for our era. Absent of illusion, accommodationist rhetoric, and fear, these essays on African American culture motivate the reader to appreciate his/her role in shaping the cultural matrices of American society and the world community.

Andree Nicola McLaughlin
Professor of Humanities
Medgar Evers College, CUNY
Brooklyn, NY
April 1992

PART ONE

BLACK CULTURE
AND CONSCIOUSNESS

I. BLACK CULTURE AND CONSCIOUSNESS

INTRODUCTION

BEYOND LOVE AND DEATH: A TRIBUTE TO THOSE WHO LIVE ON IN OUR MEMORIES

I will always remember Sandy Smith, a friend and former student, who was assassinated while protecting little children in Greensboro, North Carolina. Yet, when martyrs fall, one never talks of love in sentimental tones. Rather, one reaches deeper into one's soul for commitment because our struggle against capitalist exploitation demands disciplined love.

The manipulative horrors of racism and global oppression must be passed on to present and future generations. The Klu Klux Klan and the White Citizen's Council are repressive para-military arms of the nation state, working in cohesion with those reactionary elements that attempt to terrorize the ordinary citizen. They try to paralyze the powerless, who are seeking justice, by using intimidation, fear, murder, beatings and lynchings. At one level, these actions compel people to remain silent, praying behind closed doors. But history never sustains this paralysis, for at another level, there is the indomitable courage of ordinary folks, who possess the will to fight back. The latter is always prepared to organize and confront the cowards.

Sterling Brown writes beautifully about this in his poem, "An Old Woman Remembers," as he refers to the Atlanta Riot of 1906.

> Her eyes were gentle; her voice was soft for singing
> In the stiff-backed pew, or on the porch when evening
> Comes slowly over Atlanta. But she remembered
> She said: "After they cleaned out the saloons and the dives

3

The drunks and the loafers, they thought that they had better
Clean out the rest of us. And it was awful.
They snatched men off of street-cars, beat up women.
Some of our men fought back, and killed too. Still
It wasn't their habit. And then the orders came
For the milishy, and the mob went home,
And dressed up in their soldiers' uniforms,
And rushed back shooting just as wild as ever.
Some leaders told us to keep faith in the law,
In the governor; some did not keep that faith,
Some never had it: he was white too, and the time
Was near election, and the rebs were mad....

And the police they helped the mob, and the milishy
They helped the police. And it got worse and worse....

The newspapers named us black brutes and mad dogs,
So they used a gun butt on the president
Of our seminary where a lot of folks
Had sat up praying prayers the whole night through.

"And then," she said, "our folks got sick and tired
Of being chased and beaten and shot down.
All of a sudden, one day, they all got sick and tired.
The servants they put down their mops and pans,
And brooms and hoes and rakes and coachman whips,
Bad niggers stopped their drinking Dago red,
Good Negroes figured they had prayed enough,
All came back home – they'd been too long away –
They sat on their front stoops and in their yards,
Not talking much, but ready; their welcome ready:
Their shotguns oiled and loaded on their knees.

"And then
There wasn't any riot any more."

Whenever brave leadership is prepared to challenge the cowardly
pack, then the collaboration between the state apparatus and the para-
military right-wing elements must be set in motion. Here, the state
assumes the responsibility to arrest, imprison and assassinate that leadership in order to break the people's will. The right wing elements are given

the fullest protection and they become public executioners. We see that phenomenon clearly today in El Salvador, Guatemala and South Africa. They perform their historical function in the service of the state, without realizing that they, too, are victims of its manipulative design. However, by their actions, they bring clarity to the people, who quietly resolve to deepen the struggle against oppression and corruption. In this way, the fallen workers become heroes, and new leadership is infused with a deeper sense of commitment.

Greensboro, North Carolina has become the signal for the decade of the Eighties, in very much the same way it sparked the Civil Rights movement of the Sixties after the Woolworth lunch counter sit-ins. Today we are confronted with the real task of furthering the revolutionary process, at a time when the nation state faces a profound crisis of leadership and vision. Since there are neither alternatives nor solutions to the current problems of the bourgeois state, then the historical confrontation between reactionary and progressive forces becomes inevitable. The state apparatus will now have to suppress, destroy and liquidate all serious radical opposition, while at the same time, removing its deformed liberal mask.

The mass of the population knows clearly that there are no solutions to the present economic crisis and social malaise. The ordinary citizen understands the bankruptcy of the existing order. There are no "friends" on Wall Street, in the World Bank or the IMF (International Monetary Fund), in the White House, in Congress, in the Pentagon, and in the J. Edgar Hoover Building. There are only political opportunists who subscribe to injustice and chicanery. There are only propagandists who consciously manipulate the truth in order to postpone the day of reckoning. There are only assassins who execute their victims (here and around the world) after they have met in their conference rooms and secret hallways.

From Attica to Watergate, from Greensboro to Iran-Contragate, we have been exposed to the direct machinations of the imperial state as it intensifies its repressive order. The linkages between increasing umemployment, the expansion of the prison population, the drug epidemic, low intensity warfare and hi-tech offensives have scarred the globe from the West Bank to the Persian Gulf, from Central to South America, from the South Bronx to South Africa. Like Greensboro, North Carolina, these are the explosive centers of the most brutal and inhumane exploitation. However, they have also become the locations of untapped and organized courage, where ordinary people have had a long history of struggle for justice.

Now we must come face to face with our determination to carry forward the ideals of our fallen comrades, because we recognize that they stood bravely for peace, justice, freedom and democracy. We know those who have died because we understand what they stood for. We love those who have died because we believe in the principles and ideals for which they fought. We respect those who have been wounded because we recognize their courage to fight. We care for the loved ones of the fallen because we, too, celebrate the strength of their love.

As conscious participants in the struggle for justice and human dignity, we also will be marked as victims. As the repression heightens, many of us will be singled out in a far more brutal way than during the Sixties and Seventies. There will be betrayals, but we will grow stronger, qualitatively reshaping our lives for this historic struggle. We will live beyond death, for we believe in freedom and justice far beyond the alienating contours of a bankrupt social order. We know the enemy and we know the truth. Let us, then, go forward and quietly build a new tomorrow.

BEYOND SURVIVAL

The need to discuss "Beyond Survival" at this juncture in our history certainly must be applauded. At this time, we are confronted with the dynamic of internal contradictions in the North American political ethos, the changing character of international politics through the recent success of progressive forces in Africa and Asia, and the latter's determination to correct the imbalances created by colonial domination. The world, in the remainder of this century, will provide cataclysmic changes as peoples of color seek to redress their undifferentiated character so aptly described by Frantz Fanon as "The Wretched of the Earth." By their heroism, they have marched into contemporary history with weapons of truth, liberating not only their territorial space, but — in the process of struggle — chiselling out the integrity of their national culture and bringing into existence new values that speak to equality, dignity and justice.

The focus here is the survival of Black people in North America as expressed on two fronts: (1) the literature behind the barricades which deals with the harsh reality of prison life and (2) the search for an idea that could embrace our external reality both nationally and globally. It is a task of tremendous significance because historically our cultural workers have been broadcasters of a unique experience as we have attempted to carve out a niche in this alien environment. Our survial has been predicated on that historical struggle, which is not only defined by the nation state, but which challenges categorically the philosophical underpinnings of the North American socius. Consequently, there have been appeals to the efficacy of constitutional law in our struggle for Civil Rights, as well as revolutionary alternatives as predicates for our present and future survival.

Away from the outside world
Exists a cold hard lonesome void
A people oppressed without individuality
Not knowing who they are, where they are going
Their minds made to become a prison
Low minded they have become.

Confusion in the worshipping of many gods
That,
With drunken jealously has turned an oppressed people
against itself
Rough and ready they have become
Fighting wars for reasons unknown
Flaming hearts crying
Crying, in a terrific comic of hate
Corruption is like magic
And,
Still away from the outside world
The day will come
Expel Black Prison
Men [1]

When Robert Rice, one of the Harlem Six, wrote this poem in Rikers Island prison, he was still a teenager. Yet, he recognized that his struggle for survival was historically linked to that of the Scottsboro Boys.

To see a healthy, intelligent and able-bodied man stoop to a position, where he abandons all sense of his humanity is really an unpleasant sight. Jessie Lang, Haywood Patterson, and George Jackson have all graphically attested to this demoralization of the human spirit in the prison experience. Since the Civil War, prison has been used as an institution to disenfrancise Blacks politically, to terrorize Blacks with abnormal and inhumane treatment, and to provide a cheap labor supply in rural economies. Historically, it has had a tremendous impact on deforming certain sectors of the Black community, more specifically, Black youth. And yet, in the recent past, we have seen Blacks use these institutions as centers of learning and revolutionary political education, thereby, opening up new possibilities for creative, intellectual and spiritual development among the prisoner class.

George Jackson, Malcolm X and others began to study history, religion, philosophy, economics, military science, literature, linguistics, genetics, etc. while they were in prison. They examined carefully the important modern writers and had a profound thirst for knowledge about contemporary affairs. They were immersed in the great issues of their times. George Jackson writes in his prison letters from *Soledad*,

Later, when I was accused of robbing a gas station of seventy dollars, I accepted a deal — I agreed to confess and spare the court costs in return for a light county jail sentence. I confessed, but when the time came for sentencing they tossed me in the penetintiary with one to life. That was in 1960. I was eighteen years old. I have been here ever since. I met Marx, Lenin, Trotsky, Engels and Mao when I entered prison and they redeemed me. For the first four years I studied nothing but economics and military ideas. I met Black guerillas, George "Big Jake" Lewis and James Carr, W.L. Nolen, Bill Christmas, Terry Gibson and many, many others. We attempted to transform the Black criminal mentality into a Black revolutionary mentality. As a result each of us has been subjected to years of the most vicious reactionary violence by the state. [2]

Malcolm X also recognized the value of his search for knowledge during the time he was incarcerated. He states in his autobiography,

I don't think anybody ever got more out of going to prison than I did. In fact, prison enabled me to study far more intensively than I would have if my life had gone differently and I had attended some college. I imagine that one of the biggest troubles with colleges is there are too many distractions, too much panty-raiding, fraternities, boola-boola and all of that. Where else but in prison could I have attacked my ignorance by being able to study intensely sometimes as much as fifteen hours a day. [3]

Now, the issue at hand here is not that Malcolm or George had "time on their hands," or that they are justifying prison as ideal, but, rather, that under the most brutal and inhumane conditions, they were able to find the motivation to seek knowledge, organize a program of study, and eventually teach others what they had learned. As leaders, they developed a critical consciousness, thereby, enhancing their fullest creative potential, because this was important to survival and the liberation of new time and space. Thus, they made intellectual advances in their early twenties far beyond many of their contemporaries, who were receiving university education; their insights were sharper, clearer and more directly focused on the critical issue of freedom.

George wrote to his father saying that "I spend what you have sent me on books." He read extensively the works of Mao Tse Tung and Dr. W.E.B. Dubois and considered this to be an education in itself. He maintained,

> It is difficult, very difficult to get any facts concerning our history and our way of life. The lies, half-truths and propoganda have won total sway over the facts. We have no knowledge of our heritage. Our economic status has reduced our minds to a state of complete oblivion. The young Black who comes out of college or the university is as ignorant and unlearned as the white laborer. For all practical purposes he is worse off than when he went in, for he has learned only the attitudes and ways of the snake and a few well-worded lies. The ruling culture refuses to let us know how much we did to advance civilization in our lands long ago. It refuses to recognize and appreciate our craft and strength and allow us some of the fruits of our labor; all of this has left an emptiness in our lives, a void, a vacuum that must be filled by hostilities. [4]

In an earlier epoch, one would find Richard Wright, a poor disenfrancised Mississippian having the same thirst for knowledge. As a teenager, he forged library cards in order to discover a new world which completely overwhelmed him and nurtured his creative sensibilities. In *Black Boy,* he writes,

> I grew silent wondering about the life around me. It would have been impossible for me to have told anyone what I derived from these novels, for it was nothing less than a sense of life itself. All my life had shaped me for the realism, the naturalism of the modern novel and I could not read enough of them. [5]

Richard Wright had delved into a new world of thought. Survival had brought these men to the discovery of ideas that propelled in them a creative force as well as desire to explore perceptions, which they had grasped intuitively. Chester Himes, James Baldwin and Bob Kaufman write passionately about this experience and their drive to push beyond the boundaries of despair and hopelessness. Charlie Parker and John Coltrane also discovered this urgency in their music and what they blew left everyone in a state of shock. They were always biting into that reality which escapes us everyday, but remains vital to the essence of our will to survive.

Education, at all levels, must stimulate and guide young minds to discover their tremendous creative capacities through discipline, patience and hard work. Our schools must nurture these possiblities rather than become way-stations of mediocrity. These prisons have produced the Malcolms and the Georges, who, out of the objective necessity for survival, have discovered alternatives to their negative environment. But these spaces have been closed recently through physical lobotomy, behavior modification and drug experiments on serious young prisoners. This situation, therefore, demands new strategies to protect the lives and creative work of those who are behind the barricades.

Jesse Lang, who was assassinated by prison authorities in 1974, after his penetrating analysis "Inside Missouri State Penitentiary" which was published by the Institute of the Black World, wrote,

> The policy of the prison officials is to harass beat or even kill Muslims and Marxist-Leninists here. They fear that these two beliefs will engulf the prison and bring an end to its white racist rule. The followers of the Honorable Elijah Muhammad and Marx are a threat to homosexual rapes and racist murders which go on here. They are a driving force for unity and for an end to the racist and inhumane abuse in this prison - an end to prison exploitation. Prison policy is therefore to destroy them. [6]

These were the two organizations which provided the leadership in the Attica revolt of September, 1971. L.D. Barclay, who was brutally murdered at Attica called the events "the sound before the fury." On this point George Jackson maintains,

> These men in prison live like there is no tomorrow. And for most of them there isn't. Somewhere along the way they have sensed this life on the installment plan, three years of prison, three months on parole, then back to start all over again, sometimes in the same cell. The holds are being fast broken. Men who read Lenin, Fanon and Che don't riot, they mass, they rage, they dig graves. [7]

As a result of this reality, George makes a sweeping denunciation of North American society, when he writes,

> Black men born in the U.S.A. and fortunate enough to live pass the age of eighteen are conditioned to accept the inevitability of prison. For most of us, it simply looms as the next phase in a sequence of humiliations. Being born a slave in a captive society and never experiencing any objective basis for expectation and the effect of preparing me for the progressively traumatic misfortunes that led so many black men to the prison gate. I was prepared for prison. It only required minor psychic adjustments. [8]

One could make the same argument for Bigger Thomas (*Native Son*), Alonzo Hunt (*If Beale Street Could Talk*), Bob Jones (*If He Hollers Let Him Go*), or Berry and Joe Hamilton (*Sport of the Gods*), since the authors locked these protagonists into a spiral of circumstances that made them helpless victims. But, how were they prepared for prison and the dehumanizing experience of being placed behind bars? Malcolm X states,

> Any person who claims to have a deep feeling for human beings should think a long, long time before he votes to have other men behind bars caged. Behind bars, a man never reforms. He will never forget. He will never get completely over the memory of bars.
>
> After he gets out, his mind tries to erase the experience, but he can't. I have talked with numerous former convicts. It has been very interesting to me to find that all of our minds had blotted away many details of years in prison. But in every case, he will tell you that he can't forget those bars. [9]

The creative writings, which have come out of prison have spoken precisely to the outmoded conditions that exist and the brutality that prisoners encounter daily. Many of us have been entertained by the Academy Award winning movie, *One Flew Over the Cookoo's Nest*, but we must look more closely at the fact that this represents a cultural justification for lobotomy. If we could only imagine a young Black man or woman in the lead role, the graphic reality would drown out all the laughter. But this is precisely what is taking place today at Vaccaville, Chino, Joilet and many other Adjustment Centers around the nation. The movie validates this experimentation, which produces human vegetables in the prison system. There is a need for a public outcry against these policies and the implications suggested by the cultural apparatus. To date, Carole Byard, a young graphic artist living in New York City, has made the most critical statement in her *Lobotomy Series*, as she demonstrates the stark reality outlined by this experience.

George Jackson writes movingly about Fred Billingslea after his return to San Quentin from Vaccaville, but it is Ethridge Knight who captures graphically this brutal nightmarish experience in his poem, "Hard Rock Returns to Prison from the Hospital for the Criminal Insane."

> Hard Rock was "known not to take no shit / from nobody"....and he had the scars to prove it.... / The word was that Hard Rock wasn't a mean nigger / anymore, that doctors had bored a hole in his head, / Cut out part of his brain, and shot electricity / Through the rest / When the prison guards shook him down and barked / in his face, Hard Rock did nothing/ "Just grinned and looked silly... / His eyes erupting like hot holes in a fence" / And after we discovered that it took Hard Rock / Exactly three minutes to tell you his first name, / We told ourselves that he had just wised up, / Was being cool; but we could not fool ourselves for long. / And we turned away, our eyes on the ground. Crushed. / He had been our destroyer, the doer of things / We dreamed of doing but could not bring ourselves to do. / The fear of years, like a biting whip / Had cut grooves too deeply across our backs. [10]

When we move outside the barricades of the prison experience, we begin to find another dimension of survival as literary figures search for an ideal to embrace our reality. They turn to the dominant themes in contemporary politics in order to examine Nationalism, Pan Africanism, Marxism-Leninism, violence and non-violence. A careful examination of their writings indicate that the tendencies expressed by these thinkers are reflections of their social formation — as they attempt to sift through the alternatives for survival in the North American ambience.

However, as one views or defines oneself in the second half of the twentieth century, the fundamental question is one of power. In Africa,

Asia and the Americas, there has been a tremendous struggle waged for independence and national liberation and in that struggle the coordinates of power have shifted. Small countries, which challenged successfully the military and material domination of metropolitan centers, have eroded the power of the imperial order in the decades of the sixties and seventies. They have been able to manipulate the political space created by super power rivalries, thereby, pushing armed liberation struggle to its logical conclusion. But today, we began to witness the closing of that space....that liberated free zone....as the disintegration of the Soviet Union and the radical push for democracy and the free market system in Eastern Europe, have dramatically altered the balance of power in global relations.

In the 19th century, as the European colonial empires consolidated their gains with agreements at the Berlin Conference, and the American empire emerged victoriously in the Spanish-American War (giving it control over Puerto Rico, Cuba and the Phillipines in 1898), African peoples had to find solutions to this conquest and its subsequent domination and terror. For example, it was a struggle in 1897 between the Matabele and the British settlers over the question of land in Zimbawbe that led to the formation of the African Association and the First Pan African Congress organized by Henry Sylvester Williams and Dr. W.E.B. Dubois in 1900. It was also the Niagara Conference of 1905 that led to the formation of the National Association for the Advancement of Colored People in 1909. The Urban League was formed in 1911 and the African National Congress in 1913.

Dr. W.E.B. Dubois first wrote in 1903 that "the problem of the twentieth century is the problem of the color line." However, fifty years later, he argued:

> But today, I see more clearly than yesterday that back of the problems of race and color, lies a greater problem which both obscures and implements it: and that is the fact that so many civilized persons are willing to live in comfort and ease even if the price of this is poverty, ignorance, and disease of the majority of their fellowmen, that to maintain this privilege men have waged war until today war tends to become universal and continuous and the excuse for this war continues largely to be color and race. [11]

Dr. Dubois' thinking on Pan Africanism evolved from 1900 through 1945 in a series of conferences in which he played a leading role. In his earliest formulations, he was trying to link the North American question of cultural autonomy and authenticity with the need for political sovereignty in colonized Africa. Some of his earliest arguments were: (1) In 1900, as author of the Declaration to the nations of the World, he wrote,

Let the Congo Free State become a great Central Negro State of the World and let its prosperity be counted not simply in cash and commerce, but in the happiness and the advancement of its people.

(2) In November 1917, he published an article in *The Negro's Fatherland* as a response to the Balfour Declaration. It reads,

Africa is today held by Negro troops trained under European white officers during the period of World War I. These Negro troops have served France, conquered Germany, and their American Negro Brothers are helping to save Belgium. It woud be the least that Europe could do in return and some faint reparation for the terrible world history between 1441 and 1861 to see that a great free Central African State is created out of German East Africa and the Belgium Congo. I trust therefore that among the new relations to start out after this war will be a new Africa and a beginning of culture for the Negro race.

Here is obviously one important key. DuBois saw a vital connection between the emergence of an African nation state and the cultural regeneration of Black people, even before the end of World War I and the conclusion of the Bolshevik Revolution in Russia. He was fifty years ahead of his time. It was not until the decade of the Sixties that we witnessed the merger between the decisive move for independence on the African continent and the nationalist response evoked by Black culture in North America and the Caribbean. (3) In November 1918, he presented to the Board of the NAACP his famous memorandum on the Future of Africa. Points 9 and 10 state,

> If the world after the war decided to reconstruct Africa in accordance
> with the wishes of the Negro race and the best interest of civilization,
> the process might be carried out as follows: 1) the former German
> colonies with one million square miles and 12.5 million inhabitants
> could be internationalized, 2) to this could be added by negotiation the
> 800,000 square miles and the 9.0 million inhabitants of Portugese
> Africa, 3) and it is not impossible that Belgium could be persuaded to
> add to such a state the 900,000 square miles and 9.0 million inhabitants
> of the Congo — making an International Africa with over 30.0 million
> inhabitants. This reorganized Africa could be under the guidance of
> organized civilization. The governing international commission
> should represent not simply government, but modern culture that is
> science, commerce, social reform and religious philantrophy. [12]

Here Dr. DuBois has suggested the formation of a strategic African nation
state, which would have territorial and cultural autonomy, while political
jurisdiction would have remained in the hands of an international commission like the League of Nations. During this period, he was also
attempting to work out a niche for the flowering of Black culture in the
North American ethos, while the tenets of national sovereignty would
remain firm. He was, therefore, concerned about cultural coexistence or
cultural pluralism on one hand, and a sovereign political system regulating
its constituent parts in economics, law, language, politics and citizenship
on another level. This obviously fits into his notion of separating culture
from sovereignty for he writes,

> If in America it is to be proven for the first time in modern history that
> not only are Negroes capable of evolving great figures like Frederick
> Douglass but are a nation stored with wonderful possibilities of culture
> and their destiny is not a servile imitation of Anglo Saxon culture but
> a stalwart orginality which shall unswervingly follow Negro ideals.
> That is to say that Negro ideals would be retained and assured by the
> group through the development of Negro genius, of Negro literature
> and art and of Negro spirit. [13]

Thus, for Dr. DuBois, culture could be particular or national, while
sovereignty represents the amalgam of broader categories of jurisdiction.
Transferring this to the African continent, his argument insists on

nationality for the Africans but sovereignty for an international commission, which — acting as a supervising organism — will permit Africans to modernize while building the necessary infrastructure for economic development and political independence. The raison d'etre for internationalizing this new Central African State was that "This Africa would supply the missing political authority for a new beginning of culture for the Negro race." Dr. Dubois' Pan Africanism was, therefore, a way to help him work out a political deficiency in the relationship of Blacks to the American nation state as he struggled with this problem in the Niagara Movement and the N.A.A.C.P. Marcus Garvey disagreed with him fundamentally on this question. Mr. Garvey argued for a united Africa under African control and without the presence of imperial powers.

Today, as we examine this aspect of Dr. DuBois' thought today, we must recognize the incisiveness of his tactics and of his political vision. He was involved in the real politique of international diplomacy. He did not challenge French and British hegemony in Africa, he did not tackle the question of Southern Africa, nor did he demand independence for colonial territories like the Fifth Pan African Congress of 1945. Yet, he was suggesting an intermediary ploy based on the tactics of survival and the probabilites of change. He looked at the former German colonies and the overseas terrritories of Portugal and Belgium on the geopolitical sphere. He then suggested a gradualist approach to national independence and sovereignty. Dr. Martin Luther King argued for this gradual approach to the Montgomery Bus Boycott in its early phases. In a sense these strategies would be viewed as similar to those of Duke Ellington who used the Cotton Club as an extended workshop facility and an opportunity to develop his creative genius, while playing so-called "Jungle Music" for a white clientele in Harlem, New York.

Malcolm X, at a later period, comes to the question of Pan Africanism from a different angle. After his visits to Africa and the Middle East, he began to understand the international implications of our struggle and he turns to two solutions, 1) orthodox Islam as an instrument of brotherhood and universalism, and 2) the unity of African peoples

under the geopolitical umbrella of Pan-Africanism. With regard to the
latter, he states in Accra, Ghana in 1964,

> Upon close study, one can easily see a gigantic design to keep Africans
> here and the African-Americans from getting together. Unity between
> the Africans of the West and Africans of the fatherland will change
> the course of history. Just as the American Jew is in harmony
> (politically, economically and culturally) with world Jewery, it is time
> for all African-Americans to become an integral part of the world's
> Pan-Africanists, and even though we might remain in America
> physically while fighting for the benefits the Constitution guarantees
> us, we must "return" to Africa philosophically and culturally and
> develop a working unity in the framework of Pan Africanism. [14]

Paul Robeson, in founding the Council on African Affairs in 1941,
was also deeply concerned with the independence of Africa as well as the
promotion of unity among African peoples. However, like Malcolm X
and Dr. W.E.B. Du Bois, his concern was for a unity of progressive forces
in Africa and not the blind support for feudalistic, reactionary and corrupt
elements in African nation states that seem wedded irrevocably to the
imperial matrix through neo-colonial manipulations. These men were
never narrow thinkers as some ideologues might suggest: Their lives and
work were always in the service and support of progressive peoples.

George Jackson, however, does not have Dr. Du Bois' or Malcolm's
dilemma. He argues that a protracted revolutionary struggle must take
place in the U.S.A. before there can be any adjustment to the inequities
that presently exist in the society. For him, the transformation process
cannot take place unless there is a violent revolutionary struggle with the
progressive forces emerging victorious. He maintains that we must
develop the capacity to raise the consciousness of the people to the nature
of their exploitation and to the need for revolt. He writes,

> To postpone our liberation with the excuse that the people aren't ready
> is to underestimate them; in effect it's like saying they don't have the
> mentality to act in their defense. We can only be repressed if we stop
> thinking and stop fighting. People who refuse to stop fighting can
> never be repressed — they either win or they die — which is more

attractive than losing and dying. The primacy of politics remains but we must prepare for armed confrontation. By no stretch of imagination can we hope to overthrow so determined an enemy without force. [15]

George sees our struggle in North America as taking place at the same time as other liberation movements around the world. Survival for him is based on struggle, "a struggle to change the character of scientific capitalism." But this remains a difficult task, because the major obstacle to a united front of progressive tendencies in this country is white racism. Furthermore, he argues, that the old left has failed to understand the true nature of fascism and the vanguard elements have been crushed, thereby, removing the threat they once posed. Thus, he claims,

...that the violence of the ruling class of this country in the long process of its trend toward authoritarianism and its last and highest state, fascism, cannot be rivaled in its excesses by any other nation on earth or in history. The capacity of the state for violence terrorizes and sometimes immobilizes us — and yet, intellectuals still argue whether America is a fascist country. This concern is typical of the American left's flight from reality, from any truly extreme position. This is actually a manifestation of the authoritarian process seeping into its own psyche. At this stage, how can one question the existence of a fascist arrangement? Just consider the awesome centralization of power in the hands of a few people. [16]

The Communist Party U.S.A. and Angela Davis have been very critical of George Jackson's analysis of the nature of fascism in North America. George has been labelled as adventuristic or anarchistic, while Johnathan Jackson's daring act at the Marin County Court on August 7, 1970, when he said, "All right gentlemen, I'm taking over now," has been considered revolutionary suicide. Today, neither Black educators nor political activists feel it necessary to analyze critically or even discuss George's political tract, *Blood in My Eye*. Actually, they feel much more comfortable invoking El Hajj Malik El Shabazz than George and Johnathan Jackson.

Historically, from Gabriel Prosser, Denmark Vessey, David Walker and Nat Turner to Malcolm X and George Jackson the dialogue on revolutionary violence as an alternative to the status quo has been a very sharp and bitter one. In some cases, Black writers have argued for armed self-defense, while rejecting any offensive strategies. Dr. W.E.B. Du Bois in his *Basic American Negro Creed* writes,

> We do not believe in lynching as a cure for crime; nor in war as a necessary defense of culture; nor in violence as the only path to economic revolution. Whatever may have been true in other times and places, we believe that today in America, we can abolish poverty by reason and the intelligent use of the ballot, and above all by that dynamic discipline of soul and sacrifice of comfort which, revolution or no revolution, must be the only path to economic justice and world peace. [17]

Richard Wright wrote in *Black Boy*,

> I could fight the Southern whites by organizing with other Negroes as my grandfather had done. But I knew that I could never win that way; there were many whites and there were but few blacks. They were strong and we were weak. Outright black rebellion could never win. If I fought openly I would die and I didn't want to die. News of lynching were frequent. I could submit and live the life of a genial slave, that was impossible. All my life had shaped me to live my own feelings and thoughts. [18]

This problem haunts him and it is sharply focussed in *Uncle Tom's Children*, his book of brilliant short stories. In one story, "Long Black Song," Silas decides to stay and fight. He sends Sarah away with the child, saying,

> It don make no difference....Fer ten years, ah slaved mah life to git mah farm free.... Now, it's all gone. Gone. Ef Ah run erway, Ah ain got nothin. Ef Ah stay n' fight, Ah ain got nothin. It don' make no difference which way Ah go. The white folks ain never gimme a chance. They ain never give no black man a chance! There ain nothin in yo' whole life yuh kin keep from 'em. They take yo'lan! They take 'yo freedom! They take yo' women! 'N then they take yo' life. Ahm

gonna be hard like they is. When they come fer me Ahm gonna be here! But Lawd Ah don' wanna be this way! It don' mean nothing. Yuh die if yuh fight. Yuh die if yuh don' fight! Either way yuh die. It don' mean nothin. [19]

Silas had killed as many whites as he could, and stayed on to be burned alive in his house. He died without a murmur, in the heroic tradition of Sterling Brown's *Ole Lem, Break of Day* and *The Ballad of Joe Meek*. But in "Bright and Morning Star," Richard Wright has Johnny Boy brutally tortured and lynched for his political organizing, while Mama will shoot Booker, the agent, and die heroically in the presence of her son.

Malcolm X comes to the question of violence in a rather interesting way. After arguing for armed self-defense and analyzing the character of revolutionary struggle, he states that,

America is the first country on this earth that could actually have a bloodless revolution. But America is not morally equipped to do so. Why is America in a position to bring about a bloodless revolution: Because the Negro in this country holds the balance of power, and if the Negro is given what the Constitution say he is supposed to have, the added power of the Negro in this country would sweep all of the racists and the segregationists out of office. It would change the entire political structure of the country. It would wipe out the Southern segregationists who now control America's foreign policy as well as domestic policy.

And the only way without bloodshed that this can be brought about is that the Black man has be given full use of the ballot in everyone of the fifty states. But if the Black man doesn't get the ballot then you are going to be faced with another man, who forgets the ballot, and starts using the bullet. [20]

Malcolm X, like Martin Luther King, is making here one last plea to the political leadership of the country to avert the inevitable historical confrontation. But one gets a sense that Malcolm X, unlike George Jackson, is not prepared to posit a revolutionary agenda. He does not believe that Blacks have the infra-structure or leadership to wage a protracted revolutionary struggle. And today, we still do not have the capability. (Furthermore, opportunism, "snitching" and betrayal have gained respectability).

Malcolm stands for violence as a catalyst for social change and he argues that effective change can be produced through organized violence. In essence, he condemns critically the American political system, but he recognizes that "the Negro revolt merely insists on justice within the system."

The literary work that presents this problem dramatically is Charles Chestnutt's classic, *The Marrow of Tradition*. Written at the turn of this century, it was a response to the Wilmington race riots of 1898, during the November elections. In the novel, Josh Green, Dr. Miller and Mr. Watson present different arguments on the question of the community's response to Sandy's lynching and armed self-defense. Sandy Campbell, the trusted servant, is accused of the ghastly murder of Mrs. Ochiltree, which he did not commit and Josh Green knows it. Josh Green appeals to Dr. Miller and Mr. Watson, two successful Negro professionals in the community, to protect Sandy's life, for the latter is about to be lynched by a white mob. Dr. Miller is terrified by the murder and its consequences. He says,

> The whole thing is profoundly discouraging. Try as we may to build up the race in the essentials of good citizenship and win the good opinion of the best people, some black scoundrel comes along, and by a single criminal act, committed in the twinkling of an eye, neutralizes the effect of a whole year's work. [21]

Dr. Miller is concerned with the threat to his class position and his work in building up a small Black hospital. He does not deal with Sandy's innocence or guilt, but presumes that a "Black scoundrel" committed the horrendous act, when in reality it was Mr. Delamere's son. Josh Green, on the other hand, is not only concerned about justice but "dis way er pickin up de fus' nigger dey comes across an' stringin' 'im up regardless ought ter be stop, an' stop right now." Josh is prepared to confront the white folks, say "No" to their method of justice and revolt against their conditions of exploitation and oppression. The slave and the peasant revolt, but the educated professionals see their revolt not only as futile, but, more importantly, dangerous. Dr. Miller is prepared to go to the

Mayor, the Judge and even the President in order to avert the explosion and to obtain redress. However, he knows that his actions will be useless, because the whole state machinery is in the hands of fanatical white men, elected partly by Black votes, but bent on suppressing or liquidating Black discontent.

In the international arena, the imperialist power structure initiates the same "big stick diplomacy" on Third World People, who dare to fight for their national liberation and sovereign integrity. The National Security argument justified the coup in Chile and the assasination of Salvador Allende, the South East Asian holocaust and the Mayaguez incident. The military incursions into Grenada and Panama have been most disturbing. The Persian Gulf War followed the same security logic. Like Josh Green, George Jackson argues, "These actions must stop....Gun boat diplomacy has to go." But then the explosions in Southern Africa remain a historical eventuality lurking on the horizon of twentieth century politics.

Our survival and beyond survival strategies demand that we consider seriously the alternatives for meeting the challenges of tomorrow. With the rise of fascism and racism among white youth, with the continuing hostilities in Southern Africa, with the absence of an adequate infrastructure for facing the challenges of global politics, with the traumatizing of the minds of Black youth through urban miseducation, drugs, AIDS, homicide and crass consumption, with the absence of wise and courageous leadership to chart our national and international destiny, there will be serious problems of liberating the Black world by the year 2001.

Our writers must examine this changing reality to which our musicians have alluded. George Jackson maintains, "That strength comes from knowledge, knowing who you are, where you want to go, what you want, knowing that you are alone on this spinning, tumbling world. " [22] Our destiny is in our hands. We must confront it as we infuse Black youth with hope, creative energy, tenacity, courage, and a determination to change the course of American history by the year 2001. Finally, George also insists, "When I revolt, slavery dies with me. I refuse to pass it down again. The terms of my existence are founded on that." [23] This is not an adulation of death or even revolutionary suicide, but, rather, an applause for the refusal to accept either slavery or neo-slavery, and, more importantly, an understanding that because many thousands have gone, there will be "no more auction bloc for me." According to Max Roach, the drum signals: We insist, Freedom, Now!

NOTES

1. Robert Rice, "Expel Black Prison Men," *Drum* (Fall 1972), p.14.

2. George Jackson, *Soledad Brother: The Prison Letters of George Jackson*, p. 21.

3. *The Autobiography of Malcolm X* (New York: Grove Press, Inc., 1964), p. 180.

4. George Jackson, p. 56.

5. Richard Wright, *Black Boy* (New York: Harper and Row Publishers, 1944) p. 274.

6. Jesse Lang, "Inside Missouri State Penitentiary," Institute of the *Black World Review*, (Winter 1973), p. 11.

7. *Soledad Brother*, p. 31.

8. Ibid., p. 9.

9. *Autobiography of Malcolm X*, p. 152.

10. Ethridge Knight, *Black Voices From Prison*, p. 122.

11. Dr. W.E.B. Dubois, *Souls of Black Folk.* (New York: Penguin Group, 1969) p. xiii.

12. Dr. Robert Hill, "Dr. W.E.B. Dubois and the Pan African Ideal," *Institute of the Black World Monograph* (Fall 1974), p. 16.

13. Dr. W.E.B. Dubois, ed. Daniel Walker, *The Crisis Writings.* p.181.

14. *Malcolm X Speaks*, (New York: Grove Weidenfeld, 1990) p. 62.

15. George Jackson, *Blood In My Eye.* (Baltimore: Black Classic Press, 1990) p. 111.

16. Ibid., p. 119 and 120.

17. Dr. W.E.B. Dubois, *Dusk of Dawn.* Transaction Publishers, 1991) p. 34.

18. *Black Boy.* p. 276.

19. Richard Wright, *Uncle Tom's Children.* (New York: Harper Collins, 1989) pp. 124-125.

20. *Malcolm X Speaks*, pp. 56 and 57.

21. Charles Chestnutt, *The Marrow of Tradition*. (Ann Arbor: University of Michigan Press, 1969) p. 190.

22. *Soledad Brother*, p. 184.

23. Ibid., p. 189.

NIGHTMARE OVERHANGING DARKLY

BLACK ON BLACK HOMICIDE:
A MENTAL HEALTH CRISIS

I have taken my lesson from the past and attempted to close it off.

I have drunk deeply from the cisterns of gall, swam against the current in the Blood Alley, Urban Fascist Amerika, experienced the nose rub in shit, armed myself with a monumental hatred and tried to forget and pretend. A standard Black male defense mechanism.

It hasn't worked. It may just be me, but I suspect that it is part of the pitiful black condition that the really bad moments record themselves so clearly and permanently in the mind, while the brief flashes of gratification are lost immediately, NIGHTMARE OVERHANGING DARKLY.

My recall is nearly perfect, time has faded nothing. I recall the very first kidnap, I have lived through the passage, died on the passage, lain in the unmarked shallow graves of the millions who fertilized the Amerikan soil with their corpses; cotton and corn growing out of my chest, "unto the third and fourth generation", the tenth, the hundredth. My mind rages back and forth through the uncounted generations, and I feel all that they have ever felt, but double. I can't help it; there are too many things to remind me of the 23 1/2 hours that I am in this cell. Not ten minutes pass without a reminder. In between, I am left to speculate on what form the reminder will take. [1]

This statement is written by someone who is a statistic — being charged with armed robbery, homicide, assault with intent to commit murder — and who was incarcerated in the California Penal System with an indeterminate sentence: one year to life at eighteen years of age (after he had entered into a plea bargaining arrangement in order to spare the county court costs in return for a light county jail sentence). Here is a careful examination of the Black historical experience, through the eyes of a high school dropout. Despite his youth and limited formal education, George Jackson recognized the cell of insanity, that many have confronted inside and outside the barricades.

In 1989, the annual homicide rate for whites was 5.6 per 100,000 persons, a rate lower by almost four times all the deaths due to automobile accidents. In sharp contrast, the homicide rate within the Black community has escalated in the past twenty years. Homicide accounted for 21.9 deaths per 100,000 within the Black population in 1960, 35.5 deaths in 1970, 40.7 deaths per 100,000 in 1974, and 64.6 per 100,000 in 1989. A Black male growing up in New York City, for example, has a one in twenty chance of being murdered. One out of twenty-two Black men alive in 1986 will at some time become a Black homicide victim.

Twenty percent of Black married women of child-bearing age are sterilized, many without knowing the facts of the procedure, some without even knowing that the operation has taken place. In Cook County Jail in Illinois, 40 percent of the women inmates are charged with murdering or assaulting their husband or lover. In many cases, the victims called the police several times to report that they were being beaten by the man who they eventually killed or hurt.

In 1984, Blacks in the U.S. accounted for 54 percent of all murder victims, and homicide is now the leading cause of death for Black people between the ages of 25 and 34. Almost half of all the prisoners in the U.S. are Black. fifty-one percent of the entire prison population is below 29 years of age and 30 percent between the ages of 20 and 24. Fifty-six percent of the prisoners have never completed high school, and over 25 percent have less than an eighth grade education. About one-third of those arrested were unemployed and 60 percent earned less than $6,000 per year.

In 1975, whites constituted 87.8 percent of all persons arrested as runaway youths, 84 percent of all persons charged for driving under the influence of liquor, 88.6 percent of all those who violated state laws, and 83 percent of all vandals. Blacks, on the other hand, comprised more than half of all Americans charged with murder and non-negligent homicide at 54.4 percent, prostitution 53.6 percent, armed robbery 58.8 percent, gambling, 72.2 percent, forcible rape 45.4 percent, aggravated assault 39.5 percent, and 41.4 percent of those carrying or receiving illegal weapons.

We should always remember the brutal murder of defenseless prisoners at Attica on 13 September 1971. On that day, Governor Nelson Rockefeller sent in the troops to quelch the prison revolt. Flip Crowley, as he read the prisoner's demands, stated, "Attica is all of us. If we must live like dogs, let us at least die like men." After the state troopers stormed the A-block yard and took control of the facility, some prison inmate leaders like L. D. Borclay were brutally murdered by the guards, while lying face down on their stomachs and with their arms outstretched.

It is important to understand the events of Attica. H. Rap Brown placed these events into perspective when he said, "Violence is as Amerikan as apple pie." In saying this, he was reflecting not only on the political rebellions and urban unrest of the sixties, but the murder cum assassinations of Black men like Medgar Evers, Emmett Till, Mack Parker, Malcolm X, Li'l Bobby Hutton, James Cheyney, Albert Ayler, Henry Dumas, Marc Clark, Ralph Featherstone, Che Payne, Martin Luther King, Fred Hampton, Sammy Younge, James Carr, Jonathan Jackson, George Jackson, Jesse Lang and the countless others who were murdered, leaving the scars of these experiences etched on our psyche.

Are we then looking at a contemporary local or national problem? Are we looking also at a global problem as we see people of color being exterminated around the world (in South Africa, in the Middle East, in Central and South America and in Asia)? When we refer to Black on Black homicide are we also talking about genocide? What are the implications of these devastating experiences on our psyche, and on those future generations that we had hoped for?

What represents homicide or murder? Is homicide a mental health problem or is it a political and economic problem? Is it something that one should relate to the individual or to society in general? Is homicide consistent with our lifestyles and traditions as (1) Africans, (2) colonized people, and (3) urban people? These three categories demand closer critical analysis as it relates to the origins and manifestations of violence. We should, therefore, examine if these categories have complementary or diverse characteristics, value structures, and modes of cultural expression. Who kills Whom? Where? When? How? Under what circumstances? As I raise these questions in order to deal with the subject matter at hand, I find I am confronted with alarming statistical data which indicate that things are getting worse in our fratricidal race, and that never before have Black people experienced this level of Black on Black crime viz homicide. Furthermore, our situation vis-a-vis whites, Asians and Hispanics would suggest that we are threatened by a social disease of alarming dimensions. Sometimes, comparative figures are used boldly to support these arguments, and the media, backed by social scientists, politicians, jurists and penologists, often dramatize a sense of urgency to correct this public health crisis. Furthermore, this data also has been used to affirm and confirm historical stereotypes of Blacks as violent, criminal, irrational, emotional, murderous and cancerous in the body politic, whose only redress should be LAW AND ORDER.

Another important question is, where are people killed? Are they killed in jails, on the street, at home, at a party, in a store, at the work place, at the bank, in a car? Are they killed in urban settings or rural settings. It is essential to know this information, for it will help us to deepen our analysis. Further, we must ascertain such specifics as the neighborhood setting of the act. We must sift through such factors in Black homicide as income, class, location and housing. We must distinguish when Black homocide is an individual act or gang decision, and when it is a political or an apolitical act? We must seek the answers to the following: under what conditions are people killed? Do people kill when they are sane or insane, drunk or sober, high or spaced? Does the killer represent himself or an organization? Is it rational or irrational? How was the person killed? Was he shot, cut, choked, burned alive, gassed, whipped, bludgeoned, hacked to pieces, pushed off of a building, or did the person take an overdose? We must approach the specifics! For example, is someone responsible for Lenny Bias' death, and if so, would that be considered Black on Black homicide? What about the drugs provided by people like the Baronness to Bird and Monk? Do we consider that murder? Was the person killed as an individual or in a mass murder? Is the MOVE situation considered Black on Black homicide? (Some people in Philadelphia may feel that way, while others might look at it as administrative expediency). When a person is acquitted in a case, do we still consider the act to be Black on Black homicide? How do we feel personally in our neighborhood where the incident occurred? How is it reflected in the statistics? How does Wayne Williams show up in the statistics on Black on Black homicide? Do we believe that he killed 26 people in Atlanta?

The ultimate question that I am raising is, what do the figures that we have really represent? One may say that I am being absurd and merely grasping at straws. The bottom line is that there has been a continuing increase in Black on Black homicide between 1946 and 1990, and there is substantial data to indicate that the increase has reached crisis proportions. We continue to question Black on Black homicide because we are alarmed; the entire Black community should be alarmed. At this juncture, the HARD COLD FACTS overwhelm us and cause us to fear our brothers and sisters both on and off the streets. It has become difficult to trust one another. Our existence has become precarious, especially in the urban centers. Black folks, especially poor Black youth, have become crazier, freakier and more desperate — and our moral outrage, as well as personal well-being, demand that we STOP BLACK ON BLACK MURDER.

IMPACT OF VIETNAM WAR

If our information indicates that the large majority of persons who commit murder in the Black community are young (ages 15 through 30) and poor, then it might be useful to discuss the impact of the Vietnamese war on the present levels of violence. Firstly, a twenty year old "brother" born in 1966, during the high point in the escalation of the war, may have a father who fought in Vietnam. Likewise, his father may have been a veteran who returned from World War II in 1946. My speculative concern is that between 1966 and 1976 large numbers of Black G.I.'s returned from "the Nam," where they had been 40 percent on the frontline and 50 percent in the stockades.

Malik Edwards, Private First Class, Rifleman, 9th Regiment, U.S. Marine Corps, reflects on his experiences at Danang in 1965, in Wallace Terry's *Bloods.*

> I mean we were crazy, but it's built into the culture. It's like institutionalized insanity. When you are in combat, you can do basically what you want as long as you don't get caught. You can get away with murder. [2]

The "Bloods" returned home as young men trained in violence and with knowledge of the use of all types of sophisticated weapons as well as techniques for killing a person (who was faceless and counted as a statistic). Human life had been depreciated as they killed men, women, children, elders, pregnant women and even some of their friends. These young men had been moved from the narrow confines of their urban neighborhoods and rural southern hamlets into an international conflict against Third World people. There was a severe rupturing of the psyche as a result of this war, as they fought against a people whom they did not know or even understand. The terrain was unfamiliar and the enemy was unreal. This was a different kind of experience from World War I and II. The "Bloods" came back home confused and devastated.

We have heard horror stories from Black families about the tragedies of their sons who lost their minds in "the Nam," and who are now languishing in jails or insane asylums. Many of them met violent deaths after their return, like Mark Essex in New Orleans. These brothers came back to a troubled society, a recessionary economy, the political demise of President Lyndon B. Johnson in 1968, the assassinations of Martin Luther King and Robert Kennedy and the Watergate scandals of the early seventies. They were not welcomed home as heroes like their fathers and uncles of earlier wars. The anti-war sentiment, which swept the nation, left them psychologically devastated and morbid. Black Vietnamese veterans have been scattered in prisons all over the country. Because there were no real programs to reintroduce them into society, they sat around the house brooding, looking at T.V., and being observed by their younger brothers, nephews, and neighborhood kids. Neither the U.S. government, the Urban League, the NAACP, SCLC, SNCC, the Black Panther Party, CORE or the Nation of Islam had a broad based program for them. With two major economic recessions in the Seventies, they found themselves unemployed and unemployable. They had been looked upon as social outcasts, and Marvin Gaye was singing prophetically — "What's Going On, Makes Me Wanna Holler!" He saw the implications of what was taking place in the early Seventies.

As the economy collapsed in 1979, the country was faced with "stagflation," which brought about double digit inflation, unemployment and high interest rates. By 1980, Black people had already felt the depressing results of this stagnant growth. Black unemployment remained permanently double that of the national rate between 1972 and 1990, and unemployed Black youth remained over 35 percent. Many young Black people have never been gainfully employed during the seventies and eighties. By 1980, when Jimmy Carter was ready to leave the White House, Black male unemployment was about 32 percent, and Black youth unemployment was as high as 65 percent. In 1991, under the Bush Administration, Black youth unemployment still remains alarmingly high as the economy suffers from recessionary trends. The impact of the Savings and Loans and banking crisis , the high cost of the Persian Gulf War and increasing budget deficits have placed serious strains on the national economy.

During this period of permanent structural unemployment, caused by the decline in manufacturing, steel, automobiles, and mining, major sectors in the U.S. economy where Blacks had been employed, felt the strain of instability, retrenchment and negative growth. As thousands of workers were thrown out of work, the social fabric inside the Black community became tenuous. Alcoholism, crime and drugs began to eat away at the center of community life. The family unit became fragile, and the institutions, which had sustained the community's ethos, began to give way to a new street culture — a type of urban frontier existence. An illegitimate culture developed alongside legitimate institutions, and an underground economy expanded to meet the demands of survival. It was not only a market economy of "hot goods" and "drugs," of buying and selling, of reciprocity and greed, but there developed a cultural modality for understanding the dictates of urban uprootedness and survival. Those who lived within the framework of organized society, co-existed with and, even depended on, the expansion of the underground economy, so that there developed a certain level of tolerance for this lifestyle. The immediate concern was neither morality nor legitimacy, rather it was pure survival. There was no socialization process for these brothers from "the Nam" who joined forces with the unemployed out-laws. In essence, we left them as out-laws. No one taught them how to exist and participate in a work ethic. Therefore, by the mid-seventies, they had formed powerful gangs on the West side of Chicago, West Philadelphia, The Watts section of Los Angeles and the South Bronx. Some of these gangs like the El Rukns, the Bloods and the Crips had thousands of members with a distinct hierarchy of responsibility and chain of command, both inside and outside the prisons. These gangs controlled prostitution, drugs, "hot goods," extortion, etc. They dealt with everyone from the little man on the street, to the police officer, to the public servant, to the corporate executive and the politician, as they became the "runners" who would take the risk to keep themselves and others in their community surviving. They supported the sister who could not pay her rent, the brother who needed bail money, the mother who needed money to give birth to her son, and the sister who had to pay her doctor bills. Their influence, touched the lives of many people. An indication of this was a funeral of one of these young brothers in Oakland; he had been stabbed to death in San Quentin. At the funeral, they sang "Smooth Operator" as the parting hymn. Thousands of people attended a kind of statesman-like funeral, as the horse-drawn carriage moved through the streets with pomp and circumstance.

These young people live on the edge of social destitution. It is marginality stretched to its logical extremes and they refuse to back down anymore. These brothers go in and out of jail like the revolving door process, like their counterparts go in and out of college, in and out of church, in and out of marital relationships. They live within the drama of recycled lives constantly reshaping modes of existence as they take risks. They understand poverty, racism and affirmative action. They understand the progress of the Black middle class and they know the price which has been exacted for that progress since Martin Luther King's death. They have listened carefully to Black leaders, especially Black mayors and they are not impressed. They do not belong to the corporate drug elite or even those who control finance capital. They are the lumpen who don't have transcendental values for they live in a warped time zone. They belong to the "warrior" class in society, and they must always be prepared to "throw down," for they live in a world of tangential experiences. There is no time for negotiation or conflict resolution and you can never back down to an adversary. It is worth the risk to a young Black male, unemployed and unemployable, to make upwards of $300 to $1000 per day hustling than to work at McDonald's for $4.25 per hour. When young veterans returned from the Vietnamese conflict, they were not inspired to work in the service industries for low wages, and they passed that on to younger people around them! It simply made no sense to them. They discovered a frontier world because they knew that their existence would be precarious, and so they became adept at doing a dance of death. Living and dying were coterminous, as Grand Master Flash raps "Don't push me, 'cause I am close to the edge."

Some of the young people today are also the children of those Vets who suffered from Agent Orange and napalm bombings. We have seen with horror *The Killing Fields* and *Apocalypse Now,* but no research study has been done on the children of these vets, or their psychological development in the past decade. I have not found any research related to this area, which could provide insight into the types of bizarre homicidal acts. While the crisis escalates, the nation is moving to reindustrialize in a way that was quite different from World War I and II and even Korea. When the brothers came back from World War I, they returned into a booming economy with automobiles, steel and manufacturing expanding at a tremendous rate between 1919 and 1924. When they returned after

World War II, the economy was also healthy as America became the leader of the Free World, assisting with the Reconstruction of Europe through the Marshall Plan. Even after the Korean conflict, the economy was growing and Black veterans got jobs with expanded opportunities. But after Vietnam, the country was moved into a new phase of post industrial development based on the expansion of hi-tech industries, communications, micro-processors, computer chips, and information storage and retrieval systems. They returned to an American economy that was undergoing serious transformation, as well as stiff competition at the international level from Japan and Germany. Here, the Black veterans began to realize that the government was prepared to support the Vietnamese refugees who came to the United States after the war, and to provide the Soviet Union with wheat and agricultural credits, during periods of production shortages.

There were no real programs in place to meet their needs. Therefore, they became outlaws. They recreated a mystique around the machismo of the earlier frontier as Kool Mo Dee rapped about the "Wild, Wild West." The eighties seem to project that image in popular culture and we hail RAMBO as a hero. These brothers looked around and saw that between 1976 and 1990, one out of three Black families lived in constant poverty. These are the persons whom Claude Brown wrote about in a *New York Times Magazine* article in 1985. They are the youth who are trapped in "New Jack City"....the "Boyz in the Hood" who really want to get "Straight Out of Brooklyn". These young people became street vendors and street hustlers. They developed a culture that was particular to the rhythms of the street. When we look at the stance of ICE CUBE, PUBLIC ENEMY, and NIGGERS WITH ATTITUDES, we can easily recognize an assertion of defiance and aggressiveness. It is "Welcome to the Terrordome" and "Straight Out of Compton."

CRIME, VIOLENCE AND SOCIO-ECONOMIC CONDITIONS

All crime can be traced to objective socio-economic conditions, viz socially productive or counter-productive activity. George Jackson ar-

36

gues that "men are brutalized by their environment and not the reverse."
In a 1965 letter to his mother, he writes:

> I realized how few of the pleasures of life I have tasted. Trouble,
> difficulties and sorrow have pervaded these twenty four years.
> Twenty four years without one moment of mental gratification. For
> us it is always tomorrow: tomorrow we'll have enough money to eat
> better, tomorrow we'll be able to buy this article of clothing, to pay
> that debt. Tomorrow, it never really gets here. "To everyone who has
> more will be given....but from him who has not, even what he has will
> be taken away." I do not like this life. I can never reconcile myself
> to it or rationalize the fact that I have been basely used, hated and
> repressed as if it were the natural order of things. Life is at best a
> nebulous shadow, a vague contingency, the merest possibilities to
> begin with. But men, in general being at best complete and abject
> fools have rendered even what small possibilities there were to love
> and learn null and void. [3]

George is speaking with the voice of that lumpen person inside and outside
the barricades. The statement reflects the careful analysis of a political
prisoner, a man who was accused of murder, a social statistic. Look
carefully at what he is staying about alienation and prison revolt,

> My life here is slowly becoming one of complete alienation....I talk to
> fewer and fewer convicts every day....The die is cast now though, I
> guess, thumbs down on me. My future is round as a three dollar bill.

> I was born knowing exactly, nothing, I had no one to teach me the
> things of real value. The school systems are gauged to teach you what
> to think, not how to think...[and I maintain that it is a one track road
> from urban public school systems to jails, as I have seen the results in
> many prisons where I have taught on a volunteer basis]....My father,
> Robert, never had time to say even hello (because he was working
> two....sometimes three jobs....and he always came home tired)....and
> neither of you really knew anything to give me anyway, because your
> parents knew nothing. Do you see where the cycle brings us, to the
> real source of the trouble....the alienation and abandonment....the
> pressure from without....the system and its supporters? Robert didn't
> know any better. I didn't know either. [4]

Bigger Thomas, Malcolm Little and George Jackson all ended up in jail. Richard Wright in *Native Son* began to forecast Malcolm as Bigger Thomas, who discovered himself in jail in a dialogue with Max, his lawyer. In this dialogue, Bigger discerns his awakened knowledge and an understanding of the events that pushed him to homicide. The early lives of Malcolm X and George Jackson should be useful to our research, because thousands of young Black men have followed their paths. Malcolm was so violent in his early life that they called him SATAN in prison. He, like George Jackson, was feared and respected. However, after Bimbi spoke to him and the Honorable Elijah Muhammad touched him, he channeled his energies into productive work as well as spiritual upliftment.

More than 34 million Americans are classified by the census bureau as living below the poverty level. That figure includes thirty six percent of Black American. If we deal with the high percentage of children who live in poverty, single mothers with children and senior citizens, the figures are astounding. At the sophisticated protest level, we can articulate our response to any unjust order; at present, these responses are generally in electoral politics. Nevertheless, we must recognize that the unemployed, undereducated young Black male also comprehends the injustices in the socio-economic order and the contradictions in the law. His deeping frustration is his inability to understand why others accept the unjust status quo. Therefore, he takes his life in his hands and he lashes out instinctively at those around him who accept it, as well as at himself, as a result of self hatred, frustration and powerlessness.

Malcolm X, reflecting on the Harlem of his youth, stated,

> Many times, I have thought about it, and about what it really meant. In one sense we were huddled in there bonded together in seeking security and warmth and comfort from each other and we didn't know it. All of us—who might have probed space, or cured cancer, or built industries—were instead Black victims of the white man's American social system. [5]

He understood clearly how his family had been broken up by state authorities after his father's murder and the implications of this experience on their future development. He states,

> I truly believe that if ever a state social agency destroyed a family, it destroyed ours. We wanted to and tried to stay together. Our home didn't have to be destroyed. But the Welfare, the courts, and the doctor gave us the one-two-three punch. And ours was not the only case of this kind. [6]

> I knew that I wouldn't be back to see mother again (she stayed 26 years in an insane asylum, and when he first saw her in 1952, she didn't recognize him)...because it could make me a very vicious and dangerous person...knowing how they had looked at us as numbers and as a case in their book, not as human beings. And knowing that my mother in there was a statistic and didn't have to be; that existed because of a society's failure, hypocrisy, greed, and lack of mercy and compassion. Hence, I have no mercy or compassion in me for a society that will crush people, and then penalize them for not being able to stand up under the weight. [7]

This frustration leads the young man to turn to "New Jack City" as an expression of his limitations.

In almost every large American city, Blacks are segregated in huge enclaves. There are tremendous disparities in the standards of living based on class and color. The world of the "Underclass" (Douglas Glasgow, *The Black Underclass*) is one of despair, poverty and broken promises. There is a dishonesty between the rhetoric of racial progress and the reality of its acquisition, especially for those who are pushed over the brink. Martin Luther King once said that "without opportunities of some kind, there is no equality of any kind." The same Martin Luther King who, in the last year of his life, was saying, "We must recognize that we can't solve our problem now until there is a radical redistribution of economic and political power." "America," he remarked in 1968 to an interviewer,

> is deeply racist and its democracy is flawed both economically and socially. The Black revolution is much more than a struggle for the

rights of Negroes. It is forcing America to face all its interrelated flaws — racism, poverty, militarism and materialism. It is exposing evils that are rooted deeply in the whole structure of our [American] society. It reveals systemic rather then superficial flaws and suggests that radical reconstruction of society itself is the real issue to be faced. [8]

King, in the eighties, has been turned into a man whose sole contribution is encased in a dream. He has become calcified and mummified as a civil rights reformer, when, in his last days, he said clearly,

> We have been in a reform movement...But after Selma and the 1965 Voting Rights Bill, we moved into a new era, which must be the era of revolution. I think we must see the great distinction here between a reform movement and a revolutionary movement. [9]

This is precisely what he meant when he spoke of going to the mountain top, of going to the Sierra Maestra in Cuba like Fidel Castro and Che Guevara, of going on the Long march into the hinterland in China like Mao Tse Tung and Chou En Lai, of going to the mountains like Carlos Fonseca and Tomas Borge in Nicaragua. It was not a metaphysical mountaintop. Martin Luther King had made a concrete commitment not only to join the sanitary workers who were on strike in Memphis, and the umbrella organization, Community on the Move for Equality (COME), but he was preparing to organize a Massive Poor People's Campaign, which would have been different in political character and intensity than the 1963 March on Washington. This new political posture made King a dangerous man in American culture and he had to be assassinated. He was arguing strongly at this time that,

> the whole structure of American life must be changed. We are engaged in a class struggle....We are in a sense dealing with class issues....we're dealing with the problem of the gulf between the haves and the have nots. [10]

Today, we have difficulty recognizing this voice of Martin Luther King, because it is his earlier work that we have chosen to preserve. When he stated in his famous "Mountaintop" speech, that he was no longer afraid, and that his eyes had seen the promised land, it reminded me of Tomas Borge's eulogy to Carlos Fonseca.

> Today, for us, for our people, dawn is no longer beyond our reach. Tomorrow, one day soon, an as-yet unknown sun will shine on that earth our heroes and martyrs promised us. An earth with rushing rivers of milk and honey, where human beings will be brothers and sisters, where love, generosity and heroism will be everyday events. At the door of our world a guardian angel will wield a fiery sword against the return of selfishness, arrogance, disdain, corruption, violence and the cruel and aggressive exploitation of a few over many. [11]

Martin Luther King had begun to understand, in 1968, not only the widening gap between the haves and the have nots in America, but also the great distance between the wealthier, powerful nations of the world and the poorer and depressingly impoverished nations. He finally understood the arguments that Malcolm X and George Jackson had been posing as they criticized the imperial order.

There is no opportunity available for 48 percent of Black youth who are unemployed and unemployable. In the eighties and nineties, we have been coerced into submission by the state apparatus. At one level, some have accepted the status quo and imitate white, middle-class American lifestyles and values, while others have been left outside the orbit of any economic and institutionalized progress. The latter has been identified as the underclass and their lives have been marginalized. What brought about this deadening of the senses in the Black psyche? Have we been traumatized permanently by the experiences of whippings, castrations, "nigger-breaking," lynchings and solitary confinements? What impact have these violent experiences had on our sensibilities?

What we are seeing at the community level is a volcanic fury, whose force is equal to the oppression that the lumpen has been experiencing. Yes, they understand nothing but violence, trauma, vertigo. Then, after disillusionment, they begin to make violence their own; it becomes a vital part of the ethos of estrangement. This violence is often thrown back at the Black poor in the community because we live there, closest to *them*; but it is also directed toward Asian storeowners, Hispanics, working class

Blacks and whites, and the Black petty bourgeois who are in striking distance. The lumpen will strike at anyone who is within the trajectory of their fury and anger. *Do the Right Thing* was only a graphic manifestation of what had been taking place in Liberty City, Florida.

One-third of all Black adults cannot find work; two-thirds of all Black youth are unemployed. The failure to find employment is not with the individual indigent person, but it is the consequence of a racially discriminatory and class based neoconservative political order. As tensions develop over the struggle for scarce resources in the community, the gangs and the lumpen begin to fight among themselves because they are not confronting the real enemy. The policies of the state institutions will allow them to fight themselves and each other within certain limitations of social peace. Thus, the lumpen rip off and kill off each other. Black life is cheapened and considered meaningless. The videos, like Michael Jackson's "Beat It," reflect the tensions in the dance and the music. The young man, who raises his knife at or blows away his "brother" thinks that he has destroyed, once and for all, the detested image of their common degradation. We are living in a war zone, in a warped time zone and everything is up for grabs. Frantz Fanon writes in *The Wretched of the Earth*,

> The native who decides to put the program into practice and become a moving force is ready for violence at all times. From birth, it is clear to him that this narrow world, strewn with prohibitions can only be called into question by absolute violence. [12]

George Jackson argues that in prisons, where many homicides are committed,

> inmates live like there was no tomorrow. And for most of them there isn't. Somewhere along the line they sensed this. Life on the installment plan, three years of prison, three months on parole; then back to start all over again, sometimes in the same cell"....The holds are fast being broken." Violence is an "unavoidable consequence" of this human condition. [13]

Examine the causes of homicide? Where it occurs and under what circumstances? There can be no metaphysical approach to these problems. We know concretely where they occur. The majority of Black homicide happens in Harlem, South Bronx, West Philly, the Westside of Chicago, Southeast D.C. and Prince George's County. You rarely find Black on Black homicide west of Rock Creek Park, Bethesda or Potomac, the elite neighborhood of Washington, D.C. Bloods can't find Sugar Ray Leonard since he left Palmer Park and went to live in Potomac. So many of us feel safer as we move from Washington D.C. to the suburbs of Montgomery County. The superstars move even further to Beverly Hills.

With the poverty of spirit that exists, there is no development of a social conscience. Malcolm, as Detroit Red and Harlem Hustler, is declared insensitive to ethics. He represents not only the absence of values, but the negation of values and in this sense he is the absolute evil (Satan!). He would kill anyone, including West Indian Archie, or even play Russian Roulette with his life in order to prove his warriorhood. He is the corrosive element, destroying everything that come near him. He is the deforming element, disfiguring all that has to do with beauty or morality. He is the depository of maleficent powers — the unconscious and unretrievable instrument of blind forces. It is only when Bimbi pulls his coat in jail, and the Honorable Elijah Muhammad rescues him, that he could turn in another direction. George Jackson said, that, when he went to prison at age 18, he joined with inmates, whose mission was to transform the Black criminal mentality into a Black revolutionary mentality. The task was awesome and most of them were assassinated as a result of their heroic efforts. John Clutchette, James Carr, Fleeta Domingo, and George Jackson were all murdered inside and outside the barricades. Many of them have been completely forgotten, except by a few isolated persons, who try to carry on that legacy.

When we look carefully at this period of Black on Black crime, we could recognize that there is an element of avoidance in this drama of collective self-destruction. However, at the same time, it is one of the ways in which the brother's muscular tension is set free (Richard Wright's *The Outsider* and *Native Son*). Did the gang warfare of the fifties, prepare the way for the urban rebellions of the sixties? Who rioted in the sixties? It is as if the plunging into a fraternal blood bath allowed them to ignore the obstacle, and put off until later, the choice, nevertheless inevitable, of armed resistance. The brothers in the Black Panther Party, RAM, DRUM, and The Young Lords might have reflected on this and recruited among those elements. Lil Bobby Hutton is a product of that cultural mode.

We should examine closely popular culture in the eighties as we deal with Chuck Brown and the Soul Searchers, Prince and the Revolution, RUN DMC, The Fat Boys, Doug E. Fresh, The Kid ("Free Me From These Chains"), and the Winans ("Let My People Go"). Rapping, Go-Go Music, and Breakdancing express a different cultural attitude than Whitney Houston, Sade and Lionel Richie on WHUR's QUIET STORM. On another level, we see the dance as a warrior's act releasing muscular tension. It implies aggressivity and the most impelling violence in a canalized, transformed and conjured away. The breakdance has reintroduced the circle of combat. It is an attempt to exorcise oneself—to liberate and explain the tension of young Black urban males. Rappin' and Breakin' are essentially Black male dominated art forms trying to scratch their way out of a fecund reality. It is an underground elemental force, which speaks to the urgency of the oppressive experience.

The existence of a masked discontent, like the smoking ashes of a burned down house after the fire has been put out, will always portend the danger of bursting into flames again. The MOVE image in Philadelphia remains graphically before Mayor Goode's seared conscience. Fanon argues that the colonized man finds his freedom in and through violence. We have seen an escalation of that violence in Soweto and Crossroads, South Africa. On the other hand, we have seen an increase in Black on Black violence in America, very similar to what happened in South Africa prior to Soweto, 1976. However, at another level of consciousness, the militants in the townships have been able to restructure and reorder that violence between 1982 and 1986. Does an undercurrent of pre-liberation and pre-resistance activity exist in our present levels of violence? Colonies of despair often create unusual leadership and spontaneous centers of organization.

On the other hand, social scientists, religious leaders, professionals, journalists, jurists, moralists and politicians tend to insist that we simply lock up all the undesirables. Many suggest that we warehouse, lobotomize and sterilize them. Therefore the meaningful socialization of the Black "underclass" represents the ultimate challenge of our times. Federal Judge David Bazelon of the District Court, wrote in the *New York Times:*

> The real roots of crime are associated with a constellation of suffering, so hideous that as a society, we cannot bear to look at it in the face. So we hand over our casualties to a system that will keep them from out of our sight. And if we manage through actions to keep up with the criminals, to match their frenzy with our own, we pretend to have solved the crime. [14]

The ultimate expression of law is not order, it is prison. It actually costs about $30,000 annually to keep someone in prison. Ninety percent of the D.C. inmates are repeat offenders, forty percent of whom have been convicted at least once on drug charges and seventy-five percent are serving sentences of five years or longer. ninety percent of the current inmates are serving felony sentences and ninety-four percent of those have committed at least one previous felony. Half of all the present inmates were sentenced for violent felony crimes. The Washington, D.C. government is planning to build a new prison there because of the serious disturbances at the overcrowded Lorton Penitentiary, where 37 percent of the prisoners have more than 10 convictions and 47 percent are serving terms of more than ten year.

Dr. Bobby Wright, in an article on violence and suicide in the Black community, argued that "to deliberately prevent a people from developing life sustaining options and to promote conditions of self destruction is an act of genocide." [15] He was discussing the pernicious aspects of oppressive control which impact on our lives, especially in response to B.F. Skinner's celebrated statement in his book, *Beyond Freedom and Dignity*, that "it is possible to 'delude' people into believing that they have the essence of life, namely freedom and dignity and still control them."

Between 1970 and 1989, the national prison population rose from less than 200,000 to 525,000 persons. There has been a general outcry for the expansion of prisons, as the overcrowding has created many problems. In California, they have approved a $1.2 billion prison expansion program to add 22,000 beds in 10 new prisons by 1989. The prison population in California is over 75,000 inmates. Today, private corporations are trying to run prisons, arguing the case for management efficiency and cost benefits. Corrections Corporation of America(CCA), a Nashville based company, is the largest company in the prison management business. CCA's chief financier is Jack Massey of Nashville, one of the wealthiest, men in the Southeast. He owns Kentucky Fried Chicken and Hospital Corporation of America, the nation's largest-for-profit hospital management company. Massey helped to put together a $250 million package for CCA to take over the state's prison system. Honey Alexander (the wife of Secretary for Education, Lamar Alexander) and the Tennessee speaker of the House, Ned Ray McWherter, were stockholders in CCA. The CCA officials, in submitting its proposal, said, "private prison management is just like private management of transportation or waste removal, which local and state governments increasingly have transferred to the private sector.

In Bullock County, Alabama, which is the 19th poorest county in the nation, with most people living below the poverty level and 67 percent of the population Black, the state authorities have decided to build its next prison facility (just as the toxic waste dump in Alabama). In fact, the school children in this county in the town of Union Springs have even been warned that unless a prison is built there, they will lose their school breakfast program. When construction began, the citizens protested and stood in front of the bulldozers everyday for more than a week. The Black folks were told that they will get more jobs as a result of the prison and there will be increased revenue for the county. The struggle continues.

Today, there is more than 30 percent overcrowding in Federal and State prisons. The U.S.A has the largest prison population in the industrial World. The Union of South Africa is second and the Soviet Union is third. About 10 percent of the persons imprisoned in the U.S. are under 17 years of age. Many of these children are locked up for status offenses or behaviors that would not result in imprisonment if the person were an adult. Victimless crimes accounted for nearly 30 percent of arrests in 1984. A victimless crime is legislatively declared morally condemned behavior which directly affects only the person or persons actively involved (e.g. alcohol, substance abuse).

When these persons are abused in prison do they become the murderers, who return as recidivists? Damu Smith points out, in an article in *Black Scholar* that of the 567 men and women who await execution, 40 percent of them are Black. [16] A recent *60 Minutes* report explained that there has been a growing number of people over 60 years who have been sent to prison. Police arrested nearly 580,000 persons over 65 years of age in 1988, mainly for shoplifting and minor offenses. Nearly 50 percent of those arrested had incomes of $6,000 or less. 30 percent of the older people in prison are first time offenders. What impact does this have on any aspects of violence in our society? Did a grandson commit a murder because his grandfather was "busted" and went to jail? When and where does the violent explosion take place?

The argument for building more prisons and incarcerating certain elements in the society is a costly delusion. Ellito Currie in an essay entitled "Confronting Reality," argues that "to triple the current prison population in hopes of reducing crime by 25 percent would cost about $70 billion just for construction and will require and additional $14 billion for operating costs. Such spending could also raise all the poor families above the poverty line and give a million young people jobs paying $7.00 an hour." He insists that crime arises from chronic unemployment, social pathology, and breakdown of the community infrastructure. The arguments, therefore, of prison-for-profit are projected as a means of relieving the state of the responsibility of raising taxes for the construction of new prisons. More people will be warehoused, but will homicide, violence or crime be abated?

The militants in South Africa are now putting "a collar" around the necks of Black informers and traitors. What will happen, if that comes to our community? It is only a step away from us, because that is the motion of violence and politics, and it will be frightening. We must always remember that when Africans were engaged in the liberation struggles in Algeria, Kenya, Congo, Ghana, Guinea, Guinea Bissau, Angola, Mozambique and Azania, we were fighting and marching in the streets for our freedom and dignity here. There is a constellation of cross-currents in political life. Therefore, if the brothers are destroying Black informers and traitors in Crossroads and Soweto, we should watch for similiar activity at this end. As Bob Marley sings, it may "Catch a Fire," in the same way that Black music, Black Power and Black consciousness ignited in 1966 and spread to the Caribbean, South America and South Africa by 1976.

In the world of conflict, we have developed deep and profound prejudices against violence, and have observed society's response to Malcolm's death and George Jackson's death. How would we respond to Minister Louis Farrakhan's, Reverend Jesse Jackson's, or Colonel Muammar Quadaffi's death? Would we response in the same way we did to Steve Biko or Walter Rodney or Maurice Bishop? Would we respond in the same way as we did to Jonestown? How have we dealt with the violence that caused the death of Quadaffi's children? How have we responded to the callous bombing of Grenada, Panama and Iraq, where thousands of ordinary people....non-combatants...have been killed? No, ATTICA is all of us.

Do we have different solutions for different constituencies? I say yes, we must have: for the middle class, for the working class, for the lumpen, for urban, for rural, for teenagers, for adults, for those in jail, for those in the streets, for those in the homes, for drugs, alcohol, hypertension and McDonald's fast foods that destroy us everyday. And what is the relationship between fast foods and homicide? Yes, what is the relationship between how we eat and how we kill?

Who will draw up the blue prints for action and what roles will the institutions in the superstructure play? And how will old and new values interface? These pressing issues will challenge us in the days ahead as we prepare to move into the 21st century.

Assata Shakur dramatically escaped from a New Jersey prison in 1981. For a while she lived underground as head of the Black Liberation Army and later she went into exile in Cuba. She has become the Harriet Tubman of our times, even though many of us don't know her. She has been wanted "dead or alive". Writing about women in prison, Assata states, "[over] 50 percent [of women in prison] are Black, and many of them have children; there have been discussions about allowing these mothers to raise their children in prison, the implications of which will be enormous." Many of these Black women are in prison for major crimes, including homicide, and many are on drugs as well as into lesbianism, in the same way the Black men are turned into homosexuals in prison and sometimes brutally raped. This degradation of the human spirit in prison could lead one further into the world of crime. The statistics on recidivism have shown this, and it has the most serious impact on the young offender, who has been brutalized by other inmates as well as the prison guards.

She writes in her essay "Black Women in Prison:"

The women at Riker's Island come from places like Harlem, Brownsville, Bedford-Stuyvesant, South Bronx and South Jamaica. They come from places where dreams have been abandoned like the buildings. Where there is no more sense of community. Where neighborhood is transient. Where isolated people run from one "rat" trap to another. The cities have removed us from our strengths, from our roots, from our traditions. They have taken away our gardens and our sweet potato pies and given us McDonald's and Kentucky Fried Chicken. They have become our prisons locking us into the futility and decay of pissy hallways that lead nowhere. They have alienated us from each other and made us fear one another. They have given us hype and television as culture. There are no politicians to trust; No roads to follow; no popular progressive culture to relate to. There are no NEW DEALS, no more promises of golden streets and no place to migrate. My sisters in the streets, like my sisters at Riker's Island see no way out.
"Where can I go," said one sister on the day she was going home. "If there is nothing to believe in," she said, "I can't do nothing except try to find cloud nine.

> Women can never be free in a country that is not free. We can never
> be liberated in a country where the institutions that control our lives
> are oppressive. Or while the Amerikan government and Amerikan
> capitalism remain in tact. [17]

When the socioeconomic conditions under which a people live are
not progressive, what do they do? When institutions that govern people's
lives are destructive and non-developmental, where do the people turn?
When the society socializes a people through oppression, what will bring
positive change in their lives? When the government and institutions that
govern their lives don't give a damn about their development, how do the
people respond? When a people, as a result of their failure to create
institutions, have no options toward sustaining life beyond a $4.25/hr job
at McDonald's where do they turn? And I conclude with a letter from
George Jackson, who writes to his mother.

> The men of our group have developed as a result of living under a
> ruthless system, a set of mannerisms that numb the soul. We have
> been made the floor mat of the world, but the world has yet to see what
> can be done by men of our nature, by men who have walked the path
> of disparity, of regression, of abortion and yet come out whole. There
> will be some special page in the Book of Life for the men who have
> crawled back from the grave. This page will tell of utter defeat, ruin,
> passivity and subjection in one breath, and in the next, overwhelming
> victory and fulfillment. So take care of yourself and hold on.

> My cell partner put it this way: Every sickness ain't death, every
> goodbye ain't gone, and every big man ain't strong. [18]

The jungle is still the jungle, be it composed of trees or Skyscrapers (Bob
Marley's *Concrete Jungle* or Duke Ellington's *Money Jungle*), and the
law of the jungle is bite or be bitten.

NOTES

1. George Jackson, *Soledad Brother: The Prison Letters of George Jackson*. p. 173.

2. Wallace Terry, p. 16, *Bloods*.

3. *Soledad Brother*, p.65.

4. Ibid., p.65.

5. Alex Haley, *The Autobiography of Malcolm X*. (New York: Grove Press, Inc., 1964) p. 90.

6. Ibid., p. 21.

7. Ibid., p. 22.

8. David Garrow, *The FBI and Martin Luther King Jr.* (New York: Viking Penguin, 1983) p. 214.

9. Ibid., p. 215.

10. Ibid., 215.

11. Tomas Borge, *Sandinistas Speaks*, p. 140.

12. Frantz Fanon, *The Wretched of the Earth*, translated by Constance Farrington. (New York: Grove Weidenfeld, 1988) p. 31.

13. *Soledad Brother*, p. 31.

14. David Bazelon, Op. Ed., *New York Times*, (16 March 1982) p. 26.

15. Bobby Wright, "Black Suicide," in *Black Books Bulletin* (Vol. 7, No. 2, 1981) p. 16.

16. Damu Smith, "The Upsurge of Police Repression: An Analysis" The *Black Scholar* (Vol. 12, No. 1, Jan/Feb. 1981) p. 16.

17. Assata Shakur, "Women in Prison: How We Are," The *Black Scholar* (Vol. 9, No. 7, April 1978) p. 56.

18. *Soledad Brother*, p. 75.

BLACK CULTURE IN THE EARLY FORTIES

The Depression was ending and World War II had already begun. It was 1940 and President Franklin D. Roosevelt understood that isolationist politics had ended, and it was inevitable that the United States would be caught up in the second major war of the twentieth century. Except this time the ball game would be slightly different; this war would usher in a new order, for the political character of the world had changed drastically since World War I. The New Deal agenda had shifted to the left of center and the government had been intervening in major aspects of national life. Socialism had become an ideological reality in global politics. It had consolidated itself in the Soviet Union. It had expanded among the working classes, intellectuals and artists of Europe as an alternative to laissez-faire monopoly capitalism. It had spurred the nationalist sentiments of Asia, Africa, and Latin America. It had provided an attractive alternative to radical thinkers, workers and Blacks in the North American matrix.

Furthermore, Blacks, who had borne the brunt of the Depression as "the first fired and last hired," had developed a nationalistic posture, which was reflected politically and culturally. The "New Negro," as Alaine Locke so aptly called Blacks, had become urbanized as he shifted from the rural south to the Northern metropolis, and in those migratory waves he destroyed old myths and historical sentimentalism. Bigger, according to Richard Wright, had gone North and he was no longer a peasant, a sharecropper. The scalding experiences that swept him beyond his father's life made him and his generation vibrant with a new psychology. The quarter of a century after World War I, during which his mind and consciousness had become so greatly and violently altered, made Richard Wright realize, when he revisited his father, that "even though ties of blood made us kin, though I could see a shadow of my face in his face, though there was an echo of my voice in his voice, we were forever strangers, speaking a different language, living on vastly different planes of reality."[1]

The Charlie Parkers and Bigger Thomases were part of a continuum of creative struggle, but they had become new men with a language that would transform the North American landscape drastically – as they began to tear down the barricades, and engage in war on all fronts. President Roosevelt knew that this "harmattan" was gathering momentum. Even though the Black vote was solidly in his pocket, it was an angry vote, crying out at the injustices of the society, and ready to explode at any moment. He could not fight a war overseas to make the world safe for democracy and at the same time engage in a war at home to abort democracy. This dilemma could only lead to an inevitable confrontation, despite Eleanor Roosevelt's attempt to negotiate diplomatically and symbolically a temporary peace. But what could be done with the Bigger Thomases and Charlie Parkers? For them, the revolution had been historically determined. They could only execute it and unleash their creative life force in the society, even if it meant their deaths. The war was on. The battleground would be the Harlems of America.

Harlem, in New York City, became the command center for launching this struggle in 1940. It was the focal point of Black political and cultural activity because it had inherited the legacies of Garveyism and the Harlem Renaissance. It had spawned religious leaders like Father Divine, and Adam Clayton Powell, Jr., and labor leaders like A. Philip Randolph and Sufi Abdul Hamid. Furthermore, in the cultural arena, there were people like Langston Hughes, Duke Ellington, Ossie Davis, Pearl Primus, Katherine Dunham and Billie Holiday. Paul and Essie Robeson had returned from London to live in Harlem in October, 1939. According to Claude McKay in his *Harlem Metropolis*:

> Harlem was the queen of black belts, drawing Afro-americans together in a vast humming hive. They had swarmed in from different states, from the islands of the Caribbean and from Africa. And still they kept coming in spite of the grim misery that lurked behind the inviting facades. Overcrowded tenements, the harsh Northern climate, and unemployment did not daunt them. Harlem remained the magnet.[2]

Harlem was both the extended metaphor and the grim reality. What would occur there in this critical juncture in American history would soon impact not only this nation but the world.

When Malcom X first arrived in Harlem, he was mesmerized. For him, it was like some technicolor bazaar. He was seventeen years old. On his first night, he went to Smalls Paradise, to the Apollo Theatre to hear the Jay McShann band with Charlie Parker playing "Hootie Blues" and Walter Brown singing "Confessin' The Blues," and to the Braddock Hotel on 126th Street – where he saw, along the jam-packed bar, Dizzy Gillespie, Billy Eckstine, Dinah Washington, Billie Holiday and Ella Fitzgerald. Then, after walking up and down between Lenox, Seventh and Eighth Avenues, he went to the Savoy Ballroom, where Lionel Hampton was appearing for the traditional Thursday night-off for domestic workers, kitchen workers, defense workers and war wives. Here people were lindy-hopping to Hamp's "Flying Home" and Earl 'Fatha' Hines' "Second Balcony Jump," as well as such greats like Arnett Cobb, Illinois Jacquet, Dexter Gordon, Alvin Hayse, Joe Newman, and George Jenkins played in the Hampton band. It was the people and the music, close to each other in a celebrative, ritualistic experience. Later, after a couple of slow numbers cooled the pace off, they brought on Dinah Washington, and when she did her "Salty Papa Blues," the people just about tore the Savoy's roof off.[3] This was the tremendous impact of Harlem on Malcolm, who had just obtained a job on the railroad from Boston to New York. It had seduced him culturally; later it would shape him politically. But Malcolm, at this time, was no different from Charlie Parker, Dizzy Gillespie, Thelonious Monk, Charlie Christian, Oscar Pettiford, Machito, Joe Guy, etc. – all of whom had come to Harlem to explore and expand their creative sensibilites. Harlem would soon become the incubator for a cultural revolution.

As World War II expanded in the European theatre during 1940 and American involvement became inevitable, President Roosevelt – faced with elections in November – had to monitor separately the anti-war and the pro-fascist sentiments in the country. The Black vote had been important to the New Deal coalition, but the masses of Black people felt they had been minimally rewarded for their support by Workers Progress Administration, Citizens Conservation Corps, and minor legislative reforms which affected labor organizing. Racism was still rampant throughout the country, especially in the South, and it was frightfully embarrassing to ackowledge that Washington, D.C. was still a segregated city. The tragic death of Bessie Smith, who, after an automobile accident in 1937, had been refused admittance to a white hospital in Clarksdale, Mississippi, and the denial of the use of Consititution Hall in Washington, D.C. on Easter Sunday, 1939 by the Daughters of the American Revolution for a Marian Anderson concert, were known all over Black America. Blacks were angered by these events, even though Eleanor Roosevelt and other eminent persons in the Roosevelt Administration sponsored an outdoor concert at Lincoln Memorial Park, which 75,000 persons attended.[4] Ms. Anderson sang brilliantly and movingly.

Of the nearly 13 million Blacks in the United States, more than 5 million were in the labor force in 1940. Yet, a disproportionate number of them, as compared with whites, were unemployed.[5] With the expanding war economy, the demand for workers in defense industries soon absorbed all the available white males in the labor supply, and the industrialists began crying out for more workers.[6] But the color bar remained. The war jettisoned the American economy and saved Roosevelt's New Deal policies, but there were new problems on the immediate horizon.

Blacks, who had migrated North from the oppressive South, began to demand jobs in the expanding industries, but racial discrimination in the corporate structure and in the labor unions, especially the American Federation of Labor, denied them entry. Robert Weaver estimated that the total number of Blacks who migrated North between 1915 and 1940, most of them going into industry, was about 1,750,000. Several hundred thousand more in the decade (1940-1950) can be added to this figure.[7] During this period, some 500,000 Blacks left the land for the cities, about half to the Southern munitions centers and the rest to the North and West. Although employers, for example, in the aircraft industry were begging for workers, Blacks who applied for jobs were informed that "the Negro will be considered only as janitors and in other similar capacities." One senior executive stated quite frankly in 1941, "while we are in complete sympathy with the Negro, it is against company policy to employ them as aircraft workers and mechanics regardless of their training....There will be some jobs as janitors for Negroes."[8]

While building contractors were begging for construction workers in 1941, 75,000 experienced Negro carpenters, painters, plasterers, cement workers, brick layers and electricians, could not get employment. It had been announced in January 1941, that 250,000 workers would be absorbed in supplying defense needs, but there was little place for Negro workers regardless of training.[9] Looking at the situation closer to New York City, one would find that of the more than 400,000 Blacks who were living there, a meager 140 were hired in the ten defense plants in the area, which employed over 29,000 people. Westinghouse Inc., with government contracts worth over $8 million, employed three Blacks out of eight hundred workers in its Baltimore factory. There were only twelve Blacks among 12,000 workers in the aircraft industies of Southern California.[10] Labor shortages were reported in 102 industrial areas in December 1942 and were anticipated in 77 others. Yet, the National Urban League estimated that about one million Blacks were available for employment in those very areas. In the year 1941, some 118,000 Blacks were trained for industrial, professional or clerical work. Of these, more than 56,000 completed trades and industrial courses in technical schools. But only a small fraction of these trained, skilled Black workers had been placed in war employment by the end of 1942.[11]

Blacks were angry with this situation, and, having paid their dues during the Depression years, they were no longer prepared to take it lying down. Furthermore, they had put President Roosevelt back in the White House for the third time and they were not going to put up with this crass discrimination any longer, especially in the North. An analysis of fifteen Black wards in nine Northern cities showed that Roosevelt had captured four in 1932, nine in 1936 and fourteen in 1940.[12] Blacks were conscious of their political posture and pushed their leadership to react militantly against this situation.

Coupled with employment discrimination, there was widespread discrimination in the armed forces. By 1940, there were less than 5,000 Blacks in the American army composed of 230,000 enlisted men and officers. At the beginning of the war emergency, there were less than a dozen Black officers in the regular army.[13] When Blacks began to enlist in the military – comprising 16.1% of all enlistment – they were mainly sent to Jim Crow units in Jim Crow training camps or assigned to the duties of laborers and servants. Thurgood Marshall dispatched a letter immediately to Secretary of War Henry L. Stimson, listing the services that excluded Blacks. He warned that when conscription was enacted, Blacks who were refused the right to serve in all branches of the service would prefer to go to jail.[14]

The tensions mounted throughout the country. The war clouds lengthened. Blacks demanded from the Roosevelt Administration to know precisely what considerations would be given to them in the armed forces and in the manufacture of materials for modern warfare. In September 1940, A. Philip Randolph, Walter White and T. Arnold Hill, among other Black leaders, submitted a seven point program to President Roosevelt outlining minimum essentials for giving Blacks just consideration in defense programs.[15] The Executive response to this statement was the promotion of Colonel Benjamin O. Davis on October 5, 1940 to the rank of Brigadier General and the subsequent appointments of Colonel Campbell Johnson as Executive Assistant to the Director of Selective Service and Attorney William H. Hastie as Civilian Aide to the Secretary of War. However, Blacks recognized that these appointments were too close to the November elections not to have political implications.

However, the policy of the War department with regard to Blacks became much clearer on October 9, 1940, when Stephen Early (Secretary to the President) called a press conference to announce, "The policy of the War Department is not to intermingle colored and white enlisted personnel in the same regiment organizations."[16] He went on to say that Blacks would be received into the army on the general basis of the proportion of their population in the country; they were to be organized into separate units and existing Black units, "which were officered by

Whites and would receive no Negro officers, other than medical officers and chaplains."[17] The Democratic Party had feared the damaging effect Early's announcement might have on President Roosevelt's re-election campaign. This was turned into absolute consternation, when, in late October, Early kicked a Black New York City police officer in the groin. The officer had been assigned to protect the President and did not allow Early to cross a police line.[18]

Blacks were incensed and outraged all over the country and they made known their indignation in the press and on the street corners. Local and national leaders denounced the situation arguing that although Fascism was despised abroad, segregation and discrimination against Blacks persisted in the United States. Moreover, they were not prepared to serve in a Jim Crow army, fighting and dying to make the world safe for democracy – a democracy that had never been realized at home. The strange paradox, however, was that they supported Roosevelt in the November elections. One could safely admit, that this pragmatic decision was weighed against the possibilities of a victory by a conservative Republican Administration, which would have joined forces with Southern Dixiecrats to reverse the New Deal reforms.

In January 1941, at a time of bitterness and frustration among Blacks, A. Philip Randolph decided to organize 10,000 Blacks to march down Pennsylvania Avenue in protest against a Jim Crow army and the denial of jobs for Blacks in defense industries. Even though the regular press carried little news about Randolph's proposal, and the Roosevelt Administration tried to ignore it at first, the "call" struck an immediate response among the Black masses. The response was so great that by the end of May the numbers increased to 100,000 marchers, receiving broad support from national Black leadership. On January 15, 1941, Randolph issued a categorical statement that defined the precepts of the march. It was a bold and daring ploy. He said:

> Power and pressure are at the foundation of the March for social justice
> and reform....Power and pressure do not reside in the few and the
> intelligentsia. They lie in the flow from the masses. Power does not
> even rest with the masses as such. Power is the active principle of

only the organized masses, the masses united for a definite purpose. Hence Negro Americans must bring its power and pressure to bear upon the Agencies and representatives of the Federal Government to exact their rights in National Defense employment and the armed forces of this country.[19]

He went one step further by maintaining that he did not want whites to take part in the March:

> We shall not call upon our white friends to march with us. There are some things Negroes must do alone. This is our fight and we must see it through. If it costs money to finance a march, let Negroes pay for it. If any sacrifices are to be made,....let Negroes make them.[20]

Later in May, when he was calling for 100,000 marchers for the July 1st, 1941 March, he said:

> When 100,000 Negroes march on Washington, it will wake up Negro as well as white America. I will call upon Negroes everywhere... to gird for an epoch making march and demonstration....Let the Negro masses march....Let the Negro masses speak.[21]

This was the fullest expression of Charlie Parker's *Now is the Time*, Dizzy Gillespie's *Things to Come*, and Duke Ellington's *A New World A-Coming*. This Black steam-roller was going to descend on Washington, D.C. and in its ranks would be Kenny Clarke, Max Roach, Philly Jo Jones, Dizzy Gillespie, Charlie Parker, Billie Holiday, Dinah Washington, Duke Ellington, Count Basie, Adam Clayton Powell, Jr., Richard Wright, Rayford Logan, Sterling Brown, W.E.B. DuBois, Ossie Davis, Langston Hughes, Margaret Walker, Paul Robeson, Essie Robeson, Katherine Dunham, Pearl Primus, Charles White, Elizabeth Catlett, Romare Bearden, Lena Horne, Ethel Waters, Ruby Dee and Canada Lee. These folks would be there because the "New Negro" had developed a political and cultural consciousness that would propel Blacks to mass action. It was in the air, creatively and instinctively, ready to explode. The dialectic was in motion. Furthermore, between January and May, A. Philip Randolph – instead of burying himself in strategy conferences and administrative matters in his Harlem office – stayed on the streets.[22] He trekked up Seventh Avenue, down Lenox, and up Eighth. He walked into beauty parlors and said a few words; he invaded pool rooms and spread the message; he rallied inhabitants of bars, shops, and restaurants; he went into Minton's and Clarke Monroe's Uptown, Smalls Paradise, the Braddock and Theresa Hotels; he spoke on street corners and in theatre lobbies.

By June, the Roosevelt Administration wanted the March called off, realizing it would embarrass the United States abroad. A meeting was called at New York's City Hall on June 13, 1941 at the request of the President. Mayor Fiorello LaGuardia, Mrs. Eleanor Roosevelt, A. Philip Randolph, Walter White, Lester Granger, Ms. Anna Rosenberg and Audrey Williams attended. Mayor LaGuardia and Mrs. Roosevelt urged that they cancel the March, but the Black leadership stood firm on their principles. Mrs. Roosevelt reminded them of her sympathy for the cause of racial justice and assured them that she intended to continue pressuring the President to act. She further raised the possibility of violence and other practical problems, such as where all the Blacks would eat and sleep in Washington, D.C. A. Philip Randolph informed her that the demonstrators would simply march into the Jim Crow hotels and restaurants and order food and shelter. Further, he insisted the March would not be called off unless the President issued an excutive order banning discrimination in the defense industry and armed forces. Mrs. Roosevelt argued that this sort of action could lead to violence, while Randolph maintained that there would be no violence unless her husband ordered the police to crack Black heads.[23]

On 18 June 1941, a White House meeting was set up with President Roosevelt, Henry Stimson (Secretary of War), Robert Patterson (Undersecretary of War), Frank Kown (Secretary of the Navy), William Kundsen and Sidney Hillman (of the Office of Production Management), Aubrey Williams, (of the National Youth Administration), Ms. Anna Rosenburg (of the Social Security Board), Mayor Fiorello LaGuardia, Walter White and A. Philip Randolph. The Black leadership held firm for they were confident that the masses were solidly behind them. The President was angry that they would not accept his word at that meeting or even a compromise. However, on June 25th, 1941 – a few days before the scheduled march – he signed and issued Executive Order 8802, declaring it to be the policy of the United States:

> that there shall be no discrimination in the employment of workers in the defense industries or government because of race, creed, color or national origin.... And that, it is the duty of employers and of labor organizations...to provide for the full and equitable participation of all workers in defense industries.[24]

To enforce the order, the President appointed a temporary Fair Employment Practices Committee to "receive and investigate complaints of discrimination, and to take appropriate steps to redress grievances."[25] Mark Ethridge of the *Louisville Courrier Journal* was appointed by the President to chair this committee.

The March was called off. But it was severely criticized by the rank and file because it had compromised on one side of the social equation: nothing was done about segregation in the armed forces. Although prepared to carry on the struggle, Blacks would have to pay a tremendous price in a Jim Crow army. On the positive side, the Executive Order meant that Blacks could not be barred from equal employment opportunity in the Federal government or in any institution fulfilling government contracts. Of course, its fulfillment meant strict monitoring not only by FEPC, but by the March on Washington Movement, which set itself up as a permanent watchdog organization.

In 1941, after the betrayals of Reconstruction, the dis-illusionments of 1919, the privations of the Depression and the unmet expectations of the New Deal, Executive Order 8802 was considered the first major act by the Federal government to remedy abuses suffered by Black citizens. The threat of mass actions, its organization and unified leadership were also significant historically; this represented a new form of protest activity. "Up until then," wrote Lerone Bennett, Jr.,

> the dominant issues in Negro life were poll-tax legislation, separate-but-equal schools, and the white primary. But from 1941 on, Negro strategy would be based on, implicitly and explicitly, the

necessity for decisive intervention by the Federal government. It would be based too, on the need for unrelenting pressure on the government.[26]

It was a new political ball game, and Blacks were galvanized for action. The legal arm of the NAACP had been set in motion to fight major constitutional battles. The Brotherhood of Sleeping Car Porters had already placed the issue of systemic racism on the table in the American labor movement and under the courageous leadership of A. Phillip Randolph they had dug in for an extended struggle. The Council on African Affairs led by Dr. W.E.B. Dubois, Paul Robeson and Dr. Alpheus Hunton had pushed the debate of colonization and independence in foreign policy matters.

The challenge to the federal government for the remainder of the decade centered around the diffusion of this time bomb. But, even more importantly, the Administration's immediate concern focused on the method of implementing the Executive Order. On a short term basis, this would be vital to the stabilization of a potentially explosive situation. The Federal government, the labor unions, the armed forces and the corporations were embroiled in a new social process.

Undergirding this march of Black humanity – both in the migration from the rural South to the urban centers, and the identifiable political consciousness evident among the people – was a creative revolution, which impacted every aspect of Black culture. In the forefront of this motion, one could identify Black music; but dance, poetry, painting, literature, theatre and films all played important parts in this incubatory period. New aesthetic principles, immersed in the concrete realities of Black life, grounded in that continuum of technical excellence and craftsmanship, and imbued with that spirit of creative spontaneity, surfaced in the artistic celebrations of these early war years.

The cultural revolution ushered in new ideas, new titles and new aesthetic formulations, with a sense of daring and individuality, that made the last stanza of Margaret Walker's poem "For My People" seem to reverberate,

Let a new earth rise. Let another world be born. Let a bloody peace be written in the sky. Let a second generation full of courage issue forth, let a people loving freedom come to grow, let a beauty full of healing and strength of final clenching be the pulsing in our spirits and our blood. Let the martial songs be written, let the dirges disappear. Let a race of men now rise and take control.[27]

The age of minstrelry was over. Black artists confident of their creative sensibilities joined the assertiveness of Black people in the lengthening of the urbanization process. Interestingly, however, the art critics and historians who have written about this particular period have emphasized the technical breakthroughs in the so-called "Jazz" arena, which were made by Kenny Clarke, Max Roach, Thelonious Monk, Jimmy Blanton, Charlie Christian, Tadd Dammeron, Bud Powell, Charlie Parker and Dizzy Gillespie as they executed the "changes" from "swing" to "bop." Yet, they have rarely examined the creative and political milieu from which this important music emerged.

Generally, these critics have examined the harmonic, rhythmic and conceptual advances made by the musicians, as though this creative work was simply the logical result of musical experimentations. Actually, this development was part of the maturation process that influenced the creative sensibilities of Black people, in general – who were dealing not only with the migratory process, but the technological advancements of urban society and war economies. Black artists recognized that the "changes" in American society's dominant structures were authoritarian and autocratic in form. More specifically, Black musicians realized that the centralization of power in the music industry, as well as the cultural apparatus, provided them with little room for creative expansion. Even the important seminal music of Count Basie with Lester Young and Herschel Evans, Jo Jones, and Duke Ellington with Ben Webster, Jimmy Blanton and Billy Strayorn found itself contained within the dictates of John Hammond, Joe Glaser and Irving Mills. Irving Mills never wanted Duke Ellington to change the directional focus of his music. Likewise, Joe Glaser and John Hammond kept Louis Armstrong, Count Basie and Billie Holiday in a traditional cast.

Young musicians were yearning for new ways to express themselves that were consistent with the continuum of creative Black music, but reflective of the social forces in motion. Henry Minton, the first Black delegate to Local 802, reconverted the dining room in the Hotel Cecil on West 118th Street, reopened it as Minton's Playhouse in 1941, and eventually brought in Teddy Hill as manager. Teddy Hill hired Kenny Clarke to put together a house band and Kenny Clark encouraged Joe Guy, Thelonious Monk and Nick Fenton to join him. Soon, they instituted after-hours jam sessions, where musicians came to explore and examine new ideas. It was a continuation of a tradition, which evolved in New Orleans, Chicago, Memphis, St. Louis, Kansas City, New York etc., that allowed a musician to demonstrate that he had absorbed complex ideas, as well as developed the ingenuity to bring his individuality and musical personality to the forefront. These "jam" sessions engaged both audience and musicians in a free exchange of creative spontaneity. They became legendary in Black communities across the country.

Soon Dizzy Gillespie, Charlie Christian, Ben Webster, Coleman Hawkins, Jo Jones, Lester Young, Jimmy Blanton, Tadd Dammeron, Charlie Parker and Billie Holiday became regulars at these sessions. *Epistrophy*, *'Round About Midnight*, *Shivers*, *Up On Teddy's Hill*, *Little Benny*, *Bellevue for You*, *Slo Flight*, *Run Down*, and *Nuts to Notes* were already finding their way into the musician's lexicon. Kenny Clarke remembered that he heard Tadd Dammeron playing flatted fifth's at Minton's. "It sounded very odd to me at first. Tadd was also the first person I heard playing an eighth note sequence in the new legato style."[28] Kenny Clarke himself began playing off-rhythms on his bass drum for accents, while shifting time-keeping to the top cymbal and using his left hand to accent on the snare drum – as a compliment to his right foot, which helped to state the beat. He often referred to the techniques of this rhythmic departure as "coordinated independence.[29] He had formulated new rhythmic conceptions beyond that which had preceded him, in establishing the drum as more than a time-keeping instrument, and he expanded on the innovative work of Jo Jones. Max Roach took these rhythmic innovations a step further by the introduction of new time signatures and playing the instrument melodically. Stan Levy, a young drummer from Philadelphia stated,

> The first time I heard Max, I was petrified. He was working at the time with Dizzy's group at the Onyx....Hearing Max was a radically new experience for me. Thing was, he was completely different in his technique and musical approach. He concentrated more on melodic playing; he split time in ways I'd never heard.[30]

At a musicians conclave in Lennox, Massachusetts, during the summer of 1956, Oscar Pettiford stated that Kenny Clarke was the link and the groundbreaker, since he was the first to play in broken rhythm. Yet, Max Roach elaborated the style, bringing more complex rhythms into play.[31] Francisco Chano Pozo, who later joined the Dizzy Gillespie orchestra, contributed an additional dimension to these polyrhythmic innovations.

Charlie Christian, who introduced the amplified guitar, took the instrument out of the rhythm section and highlighted it as a solo instrument. He revolutionized the instrument, as Oscar Pettiford said, "with such clarity — like Bird. Every note fits in place rhythmically and melodically."[32] It was Charlie Christian who first told Oscar Pettiford, "You'd better watch out for a guy named Jimmy Blanton." Both Charlie Christian and Jimmy Blanton had a tremendous influence on the music of this period. Thus, it was tragic when they both died in their early twenties in 1942 from tubercolosis — Charlie in a Staten Island sanitorium and Jimmy in a Pasadena sanitorium. Duke Ellington wrote about Jimmy Blanton:

> He revolutionized bass playing and it has not been the same since. No one had played from the same perspective before. He played melodies that belonged to the bass and always had a foundation quality. Rhythmically, he supported and drove at the same time. He was just too much. We were doing wonderfully with him. He had given us something new, a new beat, and new sounds. We made records of just bass and piano, and altogether it was a great period. Then he got sick, with TB.[33]

Tadd Dameron explained his first meeting with Charlie Parker at Clarke Monroe's Uptown,

> Bird was cleaning up the club. I never knew he played horn until at one jam session he pulled out this raggedy alto saxophone with the pipetone he had then. I couldn't hear anyone but him, because I could hear his message. So we got together and we were playing "Lady Be Good," and there were some changes I played in the middle where he stopped playing and ran over and kissed me on the cheek. He said, "that's what I have been hearing all my life, but nobody plays those changes." So we got to be very good friends. He used to come over to my house everyday and we would practice for hours. This was in 1941. This was during the war. I remember it definitely. And my wife would cook. And the people used to knock on the door and I would say, "Oh! I am sorry we are making so much noise." "No," they would say, "we want you to leave the door open because he was playing so pretty."[34]

Bud Powell, both shy and introspective as a young man, recalled how Theolonious Monk would take him to his home in Harlem and teach him many things. It was through Monk's endorsement that he gained recognition at Minton's while he was still a teenager. Later, Jackie McLean related his experiences with Bud Powell.

> Bud lived on St. Nicolas Avenue between 140th and 141st Streets. On Fridays, after school, I would go over to Bud's home and practice with him whenever he felt like it. When he would go to the piano, I would take out my horn. Lots of times I would just sit and listen – sometimes an hour or two straight of Bud playing. Most of the time the conversation was music — actually Bud sitting down and playing. He would sit and play, and I would just be quiet. He would play through some ballads and ask me if I had heard this or that. Then he would play something by Monk and quite a lot of tunes I had never heard before. He spoke of Monk quite a bit. He really loves Monk. He started to help me to play different tunes.[35]

Charlie Parker referred to his youthful experience at Clarke Monroe's Uptown, when he came to New York with the Jay McShann band in 1941, "At Monroe's I heard sessions with a pianist named Allen

Tinney; I would listen to trumpeters like Oran Lips Page, Roy Eldridge, Dizzy Gillespie [Many musicians have maintained that Dizzy Gillespie's harmonic understanding was far ahead of his times by 1941] and Charlie Shavers out-blowing each other all night long."

> And Don Byas was there, playing everything there was to be played. I heard a trumpeter named Vic Coulsen had the regular band at Monroe's with George Treadwell also on trumpet and a tenor saxophonist named Prichett. That was the kind of music that caused me to quit McShann and stay in New York.[36]

During this period within the fraternity of musicians, everyone was familiar with each other's work and there was a cross-fertilization of ideas. The musicians lived in the Black community and drew their creative sustenance from their daily experiences. This was reflected, for example, in Billy Strayorn's *Take the A Train*, *Things Ain't What They Used to Be*, and Duke's Harlem *Airshaft*. In addition, Duke Ellington wrote the music for a series of annual concerts starting with *Jump for Joy* (1941), *Black, Brown and Beige* (1943), *New World A-Coming* (1943), *Deep South Suite* (1946), *Liberian Suite* (1947), and *The Beautiful Indians* (1946), all of which reflected the mood of the times and were socially relevant. *Jump for Joy* premiered in Los Angeles, while the other concerts were done at Caregie Hall in New York City.

Jump for Joy was an attempt by Duke Ellington and a group of Hollywood writers to make a statement on the comtemporary racial situation. Duke wrote a very controversial piece, in which he attempted to eliminate the stereotype images of Blacks fashioned by Hollywood and Broadway. He included such titles as *Rent Party*, *The Sun Tanned Tenth of the Nation*, *Uncle Tom's Cabin is in a Drive-In Now*, *I've Got a Passport from Georgia (and I am going to the U.S.A.)*, and *Mad Scene from Woolworth's*. The show was a success during its three month run, and Duke described the audiences as "including the most celebrated Hollywoodians, middle-class ofays, the sweet-and-low, scuffling-type Negroes, and dicty Negroes as well (doctors, lawyers, etc.). The Negroes always left proudly with their chests sticking out."[37] In a later interview he was asked, "Is there any achievement, outside the realm of music that you are proud and happy about?" He replied promptly, "the first social significance show, *Jump for Joy* in 1941, and its various successors continually since."[38]

Duke Ellington was particularly proud of his sources of inspiration. He stated emphatically,

> My men and my race are the inspiration of my work. I try to catch the character and mood and feeling of my people. The music of my race is something more than the American idiom. It is the result of our transplantation to American soil from Africa, and it was our reaction in plantation days to the life we lived. What we could not say openly, we expressed in music. The characteristic melancholic music of my race has been forged from the very white heat of our sorrow and from our groping.[39]

Black, Brown and Beige was planned as a tone parallel to the history of the African-Americans. The first section *Black*, delved deeply in this past, drawing the connections between the work songs and the spirituals. The second section, *Brown*, recognized the contributions made by Black people to this country in blood, and the heroic leadership of Toussaint L' Overture. The third section, *Beige*, addressed Black accomplishments in science, art, education and the struggle for freedom and dignity.[40] The proceeds from this benefit concert, at which three thousand people packed Carnegie Hall, were given to the Russian War Relief Fund. *Black, Brown and Beige* created a great deal of controversy, but it led to another major composition later that year, entitled, *A New World A-Coming,* from the title of Roi Otley's book. Roi Otley, in his search for a better world for Blacks after World War II, had projected this optimistic note: "In spite of selfish interest, a new world is a-coming with a sweep and fury of the Resurrection." Duke Ellington visualized this new world as a place in the distant future: "where there would be no war, no greed, no categorization, no non-believers, where love was unconditional and no pronoun was good enough for God."[41] Duke was certainly not talking about the United States and his subsequent composition, *Money Jungle*, became the metaphor for New York City, with its Wall street, Park Avenue and Rockefeller Plaza.

This sense of deep social concern was expressed in many other major compositions during this period, all of which became extremely popular among the masses of Black people. The following, among others, represented this trend: The Golden Gate Quartet (*No Segregation in Heaven*), Sally Martin (*Just a Closer Walk with Thee*), Thomas A. Dorsey (*Precious Lord* – as sung by Mahalia Jackson), Ira Tucker and the Dixie Hummingbirds (*I Don't Know Why and Move Up a Little Higher*), R.H. Harris and the Soul Stirrers (*I Am Gonna Tell God How You Treat Me*), Muddy Waters (*Rolling Stone, I'd Rather Drink Muddy Water*), Huddie Ledbetter (*The Midnight Special and Goodnight Irene*), Billie Holiday (*Lover Man, Travelling Light, Strange Fruit*, and *God Bless the Child* (who has got his own)), Erskine Hawkins (*After Hours*), Jerry Valentine (*Blitzkreig*), Bud Powell (*Echoes of Harlem, Reverse the Charges* and *Do Some War Work Baby*), and Tadd Dammeron (*A Hundred Years From Today*). All of these compositions dealt with the concrete social reality of the Harlems of America. Simultaneously, they expanded our musical palette by introducing new conceptions of rhythm, harmony and melody.

During the early war years, Black culture was essentially national in spirit. It constantly examined the North American socius and often confronted it with challenging statements. Black culture reflected and sought to express the needs, hopes and persecutions that Blacks had endured since they were brought to the Americas from Africa. Harry Haywood maintained in his book, *Negro Liberation*, published in the forties,

> The entire development of Negro music, literature, poetry and painting, of churches, fraternal groups and social societies bears the imprint of this struggle for liberation. The psychological as well as the economic need for continous struggle to gain equal democratic status, to throw off the oppressive chains and assume the upright posture of a free people – this is and has been the dynamic of Negro culture.[42]

In art, there was a new thrust that moved away from naturalism and Biblical commentaries to a realistic appraisal of the conditions of the Black worker. Charles White, Elizabeth Catlett, Romare Bearden, Eldzier Cortour, Charles Alston, Augusta Savage, Aaron Douglas and Hughie Lee-Smith were outstanding during this period. They opened up deeper layers of concern for the contradictions in the urban experience and those oppressive elements that denied Blacks social justice. Eldzier Cortour, for example, used figures as metaphors for depicting a sense of alienation and estrangement. One writer stated that Hughie Lee-Smith's "penetrating but quietly painted statements on urban desolation and tranistion were so true of city life anywhere in the West, that he must be regarded as an artist of world significance."[43] A careful inspection of Lee-Smith's world has revealed that he was deeply concerned with the relationship of urban man to his environment and to other members of society.

Horace Pippin, who was crippled in World War I, spoke out forcefully against war and segregation in this country. In 1941, his critical work "Mr. Prejudice" lashed out against the historical racism experienced not only by the Black worker or soldier but even a Black Statue of Liberty, which he depicted as being brutally ravaged by the Ku Klux Klan and all segments of white America. In the painting, the victory sign of democracy is being destroyed by a sledge hammer.

In 1944, he did "Man on a Bench," in which he is wearing a military hat and contemplating the experiences of another war. In the same work there are themes of crosses and soldiers appearing – as they were in the series of four works around the transitional painting: *The Temptation of St. Anthony.* Pippin emphasized that he included the crosses and soldiers to indicate his concerns over the agonies of another World War, and also, in his words, to protest "What is going on in the South Today." In his final words, "Man on the Bench," the "man" symbolized Horace Pippin himself, who, having completed his journey and his mission, was sitting wistfully in the autumn of the year, all alone on a park bench. Reflecting on the contemporary situation he wrote,

To my dear friend. The world is in a bad way at this time. I mean war. And men have never loved one another. There is trouble every place you go today. Then one thinks of peace, yes there will be peace — peace, so I look at Isaiah Chapter XI, verse 5-6, there I found that there will be peace..... Everytime I read it I got a new thought on it. So I went to work... Now my picture would not be complete of today if the little ghost-like memory did not appear in the left of the picture. As the men are dying today, the little crosses tell us of them in the first world war and what is happening in the South today — all of that we are going through now. But there will be peace.[44]

Horace Pippin was articulating graphically the deepest concerns of Black cultural workers like Paul Robeson, Dr. W.E.B. DuBois, Langston Hughes, Duke Ellington and Richard Wright in their quest for peace and social justice. Consequently, in 1940, Dr. Alaine Locke made the following critical appraisal of Black art.

More and more a sober realism is to be noted which goes beyond the mere superficial picturesqueness of the Negro color, form and feature and a penetrating social vision goes deeper than the surface... Much of our contemporary art is rightly an art of social analysis and criticism, touching the vital problems of religion, labor, housing, lynching, unemployment, social reconstruction and the like. For today's beauty cannot afford to be merely pretty with sentiment and local color; it must be solid and instructive with an enlightening truth.[45]

It was during this period that Richard Wright dealt with the phenomena of migration and urbanization, as they impacted on Black life. He wrote a brilliant collection of short stories, *Uncle Tom's Children* (1938), out of which *Bright and Morning Star* has remained a classic in the history of revolutionary literature. He, subsequently, wrote *Native Son* (1940), *Twelve Million Black Voices* (1941) and *Black Boy* (1945). Richard Wright lived and lectured in Harlem as *Native Son* became one of the most widely discussed books in the Black community. Bigger Thomas exploded on the literary scene with,

They wouldn't let me live and I killed. Maybe it ain't fair to kill and I reckon I really didn't want to kill, but when I think of why all this

killing was, I began to feel what I wanted, what I am... I didn't want
to kill. But what I killed for I am. I didn't know I was really alive in
this world until I felt things hard enough to kill for them.[46]

Bigger, as protagonist, became one of the most controversial characters
of the war years, for he was the new urban Black lumpen proletariat who
anticipated Malcolm X and George Jackson.

At the same time Langston Hughes was writing "Goodbye Christ,"
"Air Raid Over Harlem," "Christ in Alabama," "Roar China" and "Sunset
in Dixie, " which anticipated the Black student revolts and Civil Rights
Struggle of the Sixties:

The sun
Is gonna go down
In Dixie
Some of these days
With such a splash
That everybody whoever knew
What yesterday was
Is gonna forget
When that sun
goes down in Dixie.[47]

And in his address, "To Negro Writer," he maintained,

There are certain practical things American Negro writers can do
through their work. We can reveal to the Negro masses from which
we come, our potential power to transform the new ugly face of the
Southland into a region of peace and plenty. We can reveal to the
white masses those Negro qualities which go beyond the mere ability
to laugh and sing and dance and make music, and which are part of
the useful heritage that we place at the disposal of a future free
America. Negro writers can seek to unite blacks and whites in our
country, not on the nebulous basis of an inter-racial meeting, or the
shifting sands of religious brotherhood, but on the solid ground of the
daily working class struggle to wipe out, now and forever all the old
inequities of the past.[48]

During the early years, the Rose McClendon Players formed a theatre workshop and struggled to give such young men and women as Fred O'Neal, Ossie Davis, Helen Martin, Maxwell Granville, Claire Leyba and Freddie Carter their first opportunity to perform, rehearsing and playing in the evening after they had finished their daily jobs elsewhere (in factories and kitchens). In 1940, Ted Ward formed the Negro Playrights Company. During its first production, *Big White Fog*, the struggling company's difficulties with the white theatrical unions forced it to close. Previously, The Suitcase Theatre, a small group performing only on weekends in a fraternal hall in Harlem, had chalked up the longest run to date for a single play in that community – 135 performances of Langston Hughes' *Do You Want to be Free?*

In 1942, The American Negro Theatre directed by Abram Hill came into being, and its acting group included Sidney Poitier and Harry Belafonte who were developing their burgeoning talents. Abram Hill's comedy, *On Striver's Row*, which parodied the imitative values of the Black middle class, became a Harlem hit in 1944 and was often revived. In 1944, The American Negro Theatre presented Hilda Simms and Canada Lee in *Anna Lucasta*. As a result of being a tremendous success uptown, it was quickly taken downtown to Broadway – where it ran for almost three years, chalking up 957 performances.[49] Its amazingly talented cast included Hilda Simms, Canada Lee, George Burke, Earle Hyman, Frederick O'Neal, Hilda Haynes, and Alice Childress.

Canada Lee became one of the important actors of film and stage during this period. A former boxer, he turned to theatre with no previous training and was sensational as Bigger Thomas in *Native Son*, and in *Anna Lucasta*, as the lead actor in *On Whitman Avenue*, which dealt with problems of segregation in housing and ran for 148 performances on Broadway. He also acted as Caliban in Shakespeare's *The Tempest* on Broadway, as Othello in summer theatre, and as a boxer in the film *Body and Soul*. He was undoubtedly the Bigger Thomas and/or Charlie Parker of stage and film...a brilliant voice who rose up from among the ranks of the people. It was at Canada Lee's Chicken Coop Restaurant in Harlem, where Bud Powell, as a teenager, first met Thelonious Monk, pianist-composer, who recognized Powell's sheer brilliance. Monk subsequently became Bud's mentor, teacher and friend. In 1949 Bud first recorded Monk's "Off Minor," and later he did "A Portrait of Thelonious."[50]

On stage, Katherine Dunham and Pearl Primus blazed a trail in modern dance. Miss Dunham's *Tropical Revue*, which opened at the Martin Beck Theatre in 1943, was an instant success. *The Herald Tribune* states "there is nothing arch about a hot style, that its expression is serious and sometimes angry," while the *New York Post* wrote, "her dance conceptions offer color, variety, as well as an unusual human warmth." However, it was the dance critic of the *Afro-American*, who reported:

> Nothing in *Tropical Revue* makes you ashamed of your people. There is no Uncle Tomming, no vulgar cavorting, nor humorous attention called to racial differences....Every scene is like a painting by Orozco or Rivera or like the Brazilian artist, Portinari. The stage is actually a canvas upon which Miss Dunham painted.[51]

In 1945, her next Broadway performance was *Carib Song*, followed in 1946 by *Bal Negre*. Her troupe included Eartha Kitt, Vanoye Aikens, Lucille Ellis, Lenwood Morris and Jean Leon Destine.

Pearl Primus, a 1940 graduate of Hunter College in New York City, who was preparing to enter medical school, won an unexpected scholarship to the New Dance Group. At its studio, she created a solo sequence entitled "Cermonial," utilizing African motifs. Immediately, this creation brought her to the forefront of the modern dance world. She, then, began to take a deep interest in the use of spirituals and the blues as backgrounds for interpretive movement. After forming her own group in 1944, she performed in concert for seven days at the Belasco Theatre – dancing to spoken poetry and music, with blues guitarist Josh White accompanying her and Gordon Heath as narrator. The *New York Post* wrote: "Vital and always deeply moving, her personality hits you between the eyes."[52]

Both Pearl Primus and Katherine Dunham became important ethnographers and choreographers in the dance world, uniting the creative elements of African music, dance, poetry and sculpture with the essential rhythms of the Caribbean, South America and North America. Their work has been invaluable and it coincided with the rhythmic, harmonic and melodic explorations of Dizzy Gillespie with Chano Pozo, and Charlie Parker with Machito and Max Roach.

At the cultural level during this period, Katherine and Pearl were merely exploring the political dreams of Paul Robeson's Council on African Affairs organized in 1941 and the 1945 Fifth Pan African Congress at Manchester, where Dr. W.E.B. DuBois, Kwame Nkrumah, George Padmore, Paul Robeson and Jomo Kenyatta discussed not only the future independence of Africa from colonial domination, but the unification of African and African-American peoples in the struggle for freedom, justice and equality. Artists like Katherine Dunham, Pearl Primus, Dizzy Gillespie, Max Roach, Chano Pozo, Machito, Charlie Parker, Duke Ellington, Paul Robeson, Richard Wright and Margaret Walker provided the cultural underpinning that helped to spark the revolt towards authenticity, creative integrity and political independence, but in so doing, they returned to their sources and essences. They were the archetypes.

In 1939, Hattie McDaniel was the first Black to win an Academy Award in film. She was chosen as the Best Supporting Actress for "Gone with the Wind." But the struggle of Blacks in film has been a grim and humiliating one. They had to accept stereotyped roles as maids, coons or buffoons. (See Donald Bogle's *Toms, Coons, Mulattoes, Mammies, and Bucks*.) In order to contain or appease Black anger, a few all-Black films were produced during the forties, while there were some outstanding Black performances in controversial films like Leigh Whiper in "The Ox Bow Incident" (1943), Canada Lee in "Body and Soul" (1947), James Edwards in "Home of the Brave" (1949), Ernest Anderson in "In This Our Life" (1942), Ben Carter in "Crash Dive" (1943), Juano Hernandez in "Intruder in the Dust" (1949), and Ethel Waters in "The Member of the Wedding." In terms of all-Black movies, there were the hit musicals, such as "Stormy Weather" (1943) and "Cabin in the Sky" (1940), both starring Lena Horne. Additionally, there were three melodramas that dealt with the color question: "Imitation of Life" (1943), "Pinky" (1949), and "Lost

Boundaries" (1949).[53] Lena Horne and Ethel Waters were the important actresses who flowered during this period.

One of the most difficult tasks for the Black artist, particularly in motion pictures, theatre, radio and television, was to break through the stereotypes, dating back to the turn of the century when they were slanderously depicted as clowns and disreputables. This caricature in popular culture was designed to assuage white supremacist ideals and to exploit a Jim Crow market. But Charlie Parker, Max Roach, Duke Ellington, Dizzy Gillespie, Canada Lee, Katherine Dunham, Charles White, Pearl Primus, Lena Horne and Paul Robeson rejected the premises of these caricatures and attempted to bring dignity and integrity to the Black creative process. Its potency and life force invigorated the human spirit, while its spontaneity accentuated the dynamic changes taking place in the American ethos.

Paul and Essie Robeson returned to Harlem in 1939, and it was their tremendous stature and penetrating interpretations that expanded the cultural milieu. Paul Robeson was in great demand as actor, singer and cultural worker. He became a source of inspiration in the struggle of the C.I.O. to organize workers in North America, Panama, and Hawaii, in the founding of the Council on African Affairs, and in the 1948 campaigns of the Progressive Party with Henry Wallace as its presidential candidate. In 1940, he appeared in the New York stage play, *John Henry* – a folk legend based on the life of a railroad worker. He was the narrator in the documentary film, "Native Land," based on the La Follette Report on Civil Liberties. This film, which supported New Deal reforms, was produced by Frontier Films, an independent film company. Finally, in the winter of 1940, he began a nation-wide concert tour, but he refused any engagements where Blacks and whites were compelled to sit apart. As a result of this decision, Robeson could only sing in the South under the auspices of Black colleges and universities, where the faculty were willing to open their doors to any white people who wanted to come. And they came.[54]

Paul Robeson was confident of his role as an artist. He had elected to fight for freedom and like Langston Hughes, Richard Wright, Essie

Robeson, A. Philip Randolph and Walter White, he fought for "Four Freedoms" on four fronts: (1) with the executive, judicial and legislative arms of government, (2) inside the labor unions, in the corporate structure, and on the streets against segregation and racial discrimination (3) on the cultural front, on the stage, in the churches and in the factories, and (4) in the armed forces – with Bill Hastie, who eventually resigned from the Roosevelt Administration after fighting to eliminate a Jim Crow military apparatus. It was Paul Robeson's rendition of "Ballad for Americans" that became the national patriotic song of the early war years, cutting across all political lines. On June 30, 1940, this rendition was played at the Republican Convention; an irony of history because by the end of the decade he would be haunted and persecuted by these conservative leaders. Into "Ballad for Americans," he poured his deepest feelings, especially in the lines:

> Man in white skin can never be free
> While his black brother is in slavery
> Our country's strong, our country's young
> And her greatest songs are still unsung.[55]

On June 23, 1941, Paul Robeson sang before 15,000 persons at New York's Lewisohn Stadium. His earlier nation-wide concert tour had been a tremendous success. As he earned unprecedented applause in major cities across the country, he began to immerse himself in the forefront of Black cultural leadership by fighting to improve the working conditions of the Black masses. He also spoke out against discrimination in employment and education. Paul Robeson sang and talked wherever working class people invited him, in Harlem, Washington, D.C., Winston-Salem, Oakland, Chicago, Detroit, etc. He remained at the service of those in struggle. Over 54,000 persons attended a labor victory rally at Yankee Stadium, New York on May 2, 1943, where he sang work songs and songs of freedom. He urged the workers, Black and white, to fight to defeat fascism at home, as well as abroad. In his remarks, he said, "we are here because we believe in the dignity of man and the right to freedom of all mankind."[56]

On the last Friday of June, 1943, Robeson was scheduled to sing in Washington, D.C. at the Watergate open-air concert, two blocks from the Lincoln Memorial. The Detroit riots had occured on June 20, 1943, a few days earlier. It had been the most serious race riot of the war years. Paul Robeson was outraged at the news and before a crowd of twenty-thousand persons, who called for several encores, he sang "Ballad for Americans." The audience was silenced because they were fully aware of the Jim Crow conditions in the nation's capital.

But, while Robeson was making this statement in the cultural arena, A. Philip Randolph was warning the 1943 A.F. of L. Convention in Boston, as he proclaimed,

> The race problem is the number one problem of America today. It is also the number one problem of the American Federation of Labor. And brothers, let me warn you that unless a sound, unequivocal and definite position is taken on the question of democracy for Negroes in the A.F. of L. and other agencies, the tides of Fascism are going to rise in this country and wipe out not only the Negroes but organized labor as well.... Fascism will use the Negro as scapegoat, but while they are attacking Negroes today, they will attack Jews tomorrow, and they will attack Catholics the next day.[57]

Randolph was, in fact, predicting McCarthyism and the reign of terror which would end the decade of the forties.

During 1943 and 1944, Paul Robeson was given honorary membership by many labor unions for his tremendous contribution to the cause of labor. In addition, he received honorary degrees from several colleges and universities for his service to humanity, as well as was presented with the Diction Award of the American Academy of Arts and Letters, a citation from the National Federation for Constitutional Liberties for "his outstanding contribution toward building international unity within our country and throughout the world," and the Spingarn Medal by the N.A.A.C.P. in October 1944 – for "his active concern for the rights of the common man of every race, color, religion and nationality." [58]

On October 19, 1943, Shakespeare's *Othello* opened at the Shubert Theatre on Broadway with Paul Robeson as Othello, Jose Ferrer as Iago and Uta Hagen as Desdemona. It was a resounding success and ran for 296 performances, establishing a record beyond any Shakespearean production on Broadway. Robeson had performed the role successfully in London in 1930 and throughout Europe in the succeeding years. One British commentator wrote after the London performance, "from the moment that Robeson appears in the beginning to his last sigh at the end, the man is gigantic in power."[59]

Thirteen years later, *Life Magazine* reported that "Robeson received one of the most prolonged and wildest ovations in the history of the New York Theatre." The magazine further referred to the production staged by Margaret Webster and the Theatre Guild as "magnificent." John Chapman, drama critic, wrote,

> It is an Othello of depth and body and rich sound, and in its title role Paul Robeson has majesty.... a voice whose resonance and deepness almost pass belief.... This new Othello... presents a Black man of dignity and intelligence in the role of a Black man of dignity and intelligence.[60]

The *New York Post* described Paul Robeson as "the most imposing personality on Broadway today."[61]

In the field of classical music, Dean Dixon had become the first Black man to achieve an entire career solely as a conductor of major symphony orchestras, both in Europe and the United States. He was the first Black to conduct the one hundred year old New York Philharmonic Orchestra in the summer of 1943 at the Lewisohn Stadium. At the same time he was invited to be the guest conductor, he was only 28 years old and his performances were highly acclaimed by the critics. However, since the late forties, he has lived in Europe, where he has been the resident conductor of Gothenberg Symphony, Radio-Diffusion Francaise in Paris, and guest conductor to several major orchestras.[62]

This was the quality of cultural life in Harlem during the early part of World War II. The Black artists not only lived and performed there, but provided leadership and vision within the community. A cultural revolution had fermented, moving beyond the creative outpourings of the

Harlem Renaissance, and imbued with a spirit of struggle that challenged the status quo. The dynamic elements of Black culture were closely interlaced with the political struggle for freedom, dignity and the elimination of second-class citizenship; it was the creative expression of cultural workers as artists who had come from working-class origins. As Paul Robeson told the International Longshoremen's and Warehousemen's Union in 1943, upon receiving honorary life membership, "I have labored and I come from a laboring people... I have hooked many a load, taken many a tray... I know what poverty is."[63] Dr. W.E.B. DuBois pointed out these dynamic elements in Black culture in his introduction to an appeal to the United Nations:

> The so-called American Negro group, therefore, while it is in no sense absolutely set off physically from its fellow Americans, has nevertheless a strong, heriditary cultural unity, born of slavery, of common suffering, prolonged proscription and curtailment of political and civil rights; and especially because of economic and social disabilities. Largely from this fact have arisen their cultural gifts to America – their rhythm, music and folk-song; their religious faith and customs; their contributions to American art and literature; their defense of their country in every war, on land, sea and in the air; and especially the hard continuous toil upon which the prosperity and wealth of this continent has largely been built.[64]

The Harlems of America were explosive entities during the early war years for certain social forces were set in motion by the progressive cultural and political tendencies. Obviously, the cataclysmic changes brought on by World War II, heightened the domestic contradictions and pushed the Black community to draw on its creative resources. Professor Archie Shepp, a brilliant tenor saxophonist, composer, and arranger put it rather succinctly in a letter he wrote to the author:

> At a time when the United States of America had barely emerged from a depression and was entering World War II, the American Negro sought a renewed vision of himself and his role in a complex technological urban society. Thus, the Black community was forced to readjust its perspective on all levels, culturally as well as socio-economically. The blues, gospel, spiritual music of the

American Negro wanted refurbishment; even his language would turn from "hot" to "cool." Subsequently, it was left to the Black musician to take stock of these cataclysmic changes and transform his collective experience into an aural language of dialectical dimension, one whose continually expanding reference would accommodate the universal implications of Black culture. This tendency first revealed itself in the Gillespie orchestra of the forties and the inclusion in its repertoire of Cuban rhythms (via Francisco Chano Pozo) as well as other musical styles common to South America and the Caribbean. Later Mr. John Coltrane was to explore the modal and pentatonic scales of African and Eastern music.[65]

In the early forties, the Harlems of America exploded in New York, Detroit, and Los Angeles, for Black people were prepared to stand up and fight back.

In June 1942, in spite of the work of the F.E.P.C., the Federal Security Agency declared,

Over 500,000 Negroes who should be utilized in war production are now idle because of the discriminatory hiring practices of war industries. Several million other Negroes were engaged in unskilled jobs and were prevented from making occupational advances.[66]

When Blacks in Seattle, Washington demanded the elimination of the union color bar at the Boeing Aircraft plant, the district organizer of the International Association of Machinist declared, "Labor has been asked to make many sacrifices in this war and has made them gladly, but this sacrifice is too great." In a Newport, Rhode Island war housing project, where it was required to admit all families of war workers, it was said, "In these critical times, it is more important than ever to preserve the principle of white supremacy." In Shreveport, Louisiana, the Mayor rejected a federal grant because of the provision that skilled Black workers be given a chance to work on its construction. He said, "Of equal importance to winning the war is the necessity to keep Negroes out of skilled jobs."[67]

The first clash, resulting from this type of containment, occured in February 1942, when Detroit exploded as a result of an unsuccessful attempt by whites to prevent Black families from occupying their approved homes in the Sojourner Truth Federal Housing Project. In the ensuing battle, 38 persons were injured and 100 arrested. Still, on June 20, 1943, Detroit became the scene of another rebellion as Blacks and whites clashed; twenty-five Blacks and nine whites were killed, while 500 persons were injured, a million man hours of war effort were lost, property damage was estimated at $2,000,000, and the federal government spent nearly $1,000,000 to maintain an occupation army during the confrontation.

In Mobile, Alabama a murderous clash took place between Blacks and whites in 1943. At the same time, half of the Black section of Beaumont, Texas was burned by a white mob. In the summer of 1943, Watts and Harlem exploded. Malcolm, in discussing the Harlem riots, stated:

All through the war, the Harlem racial picture was never too bright. Tension built to a pretty high pitch. Old timers had told me of the 1935 riots, when millions of dollars worth of damage was done by thousands of Negroes, infuriated chiefly by the white merchants in Harlem who refused to hire Negroes even as their stores raked in Harlem's money....During World War II, Mayor LaGuardia officially closed the Savoy Ballroom. Harlem said the real reason was to stop Negroes from dancing with white women. Harlem said that no one dragged the white women in there. Adam Clayton Powell made it a big fight. He had successfully fought Consolidated Edison and the New York Telephone Company until they had hired Negroes. Then he had helped to battle the U.S. Navy and the U.S. Army about their segregating of uniformed Negroes. But Powell couldn't win this battle. City Hall kept the Savoy closed for a long time. It was just another one of the "liberal North" actions that didn't help Harlem to love the white man any. Finally, rumor flashed that in the Braddock Hotel, white cops had shot a Negro soldier. I was walking down St. Nicolas Avenue; I saw all of these Negroes hollering and running from 125th Street. Some of them were loaded down with armfulls of stuff... I remember it was the bandleader, Fletcher Henderson's nephew "Shorty" Henderson who told me what had happened. Negroes were smashing store windows, and taking everything they could grab and carry – furniture, food, jewelry, clothes, whisky. Within an hour, every New York City cop seemed to be in Harlem. Mayor LaGuardia and the NAACP's Secretary, Walter White, were in a red fire-car, riding around pleading over a loud-speaker to all those shouting, milling angry Negroes to please go home and stay inside. After the riot, things got very tight in Harlem. [68]

The closing down of the Savoy in 1943 marked the beginning of the dismantling of the cultural apparatus in Harlem. Given that there was a fusion of political assertiveness and cultural regeneration in the community, it became necessary to diffuse this situation, so that Harlem could be contained and efficiently controlled by City Hall. In the twenties, during the height of the Garvey movement and the Harlem Renaissance, the downtown "literati" descended on the creative artists and writers – luring them to the Mabel Dodge salon of Greenwich Village and the stage shows of Broadway. Claude McKay writes in his *Harlem Metropolis*:

> The build-up of a fashionable and artistic Harlem became the newest fad on Manhattanites in the middle nineteen-twenties... New Yorkers had discovered the existence of a fashionable clique, and an artistic and literary set in Harlem. The big racket which crepitated from this discovery resulted in an enormously abnormal advertisement of bohemian Harlem. And even solid real estate values were affected by fluid idealistic art values of Harlem.[69]

In the sixties, when Black nationalism and its creative expressions fused into a potent force, the cultural workers were siphoned off into the universities and the college lecture circuit, leaving the Black communities defenseless as their leaders were wiped out. This same "brain-drain" and "Cultural-drain" occured in the forties under the subtle guise of integration in the cultural apparatus. When it became obvious to the Roosevelt Administration that A. Phillip Randolph and his associates were serious about the proposed 1941 March on Washington, the President instructed them to call it off. Mr. Randolph stated clearly "I shall have to stand by the pledge I have made to the people." It was Mayor LaGuardia who broke the impasse and suggested that they all begin "to seek a formula."[70] The formula led to the subsequent shift of Black culture from uptown to downtown.

The administration felt that the mood and tone of the country had not indicated any readiness for integration or for the dismantling of a Jim Crow superstructure. Therefore, Mayor LaGuardia and others traded off jobs with federal protection for a Jim Crow armed forces. In addition, they began to organize a strategy that would redirect the creative energies stored up in Harlem. Harold Cruse has maintained in his *Crisis of the Negro Intellectual*,

American's entry in World War II marked the beginning of the end of Negro ethnic group insularity; an entirely new phase of American Negro life was underway. Until 1940, the word integration had not appeared, even in the language of the NAACP; the war inspired the first articles in *Crisis*, NAACP's official publication demanding the "integration of the armed forces" (Prior to that the organization's theme had been Civil Rights).[71]

Even though the armed forces were not desegregated, "integration" became the key social instrument used to dismantle the cultural apparatus in Harlem. What were the strategies involved? The "war-tax", which had been placed on dancing in clubs, was strictly enforced in New York City, especially uptown. This compelled the bands to play for the listener rather than the dancer. But, at this time, Black instrumental and vocal music was dance music, making popular the Audubon, the Renaissance, the Lido, and the Savoy Ballroom, where there was not only continous dancing, but large revue shows that included a chorus line, comedians, tap dancers, and shake dancers. As a result of this "war-tax," these gala revues folded one by one, and after 1943 things really got tight for "the night people."

When the Savoy Ballroom was closed down by Mayor LaGuardia, he also declared Harlem off-limits for white servicemen. The police also tried to discourage white civilians from going uptown, but there were those who continued to do so. Additionally, city and military police began to stop interracial couples on the streets, using the war as an excuse to harrass them, especially grilling the man about his draft status. These actions began to dry up the entertainment market in Harlem, which had thrived since the mid-twenties. Soon night clubs, restaurants, bars, hotels, guest houses etc. began to close down. These businesses had direct linkages to the entertainment market. The Cotton Club, Connie's Inn, the Lenox Club, Club Barron, the Nest Club, Jimmy's Chicken Shack, Minton's, The Savoy, the Lido, the Renaissance, the Golden Gate, Small's Paradise and Jimmy Daniels – all battled for the crowds when Harlem was jumping. Now, they were struggling to survive. The community began to feel an economic squeeze.

Furthermore, there was a sharp increase of drugs brought into the community. It must be remembered that, during slavery, morphine and other drugs were used in order to make slaves work from sun up to sun down because it temporarily increased their energy output and caused them to eat less food. Yet, the flooding of the community with drugs exposed the young artist to a dangerous situation.

At this time, there was also a sharp increase of young Blacks into the armed services, especially among the artists. Several of them, in order to avoid entering a Jim Crow army, turned to drugs and other extreme types of behavior patterns to beat the draft. Many of them got hooked. Malcolm X has referred to this experience in a rather interesting way:

> In those days only three things in the world scared me: Jail, a job, and the Army. I had about ten days before I was to show up at the induction center. I went right to work.... I started noising around that I was frantic to join... the Japanese Army. When I sensed that I had the ears of the spies, I would talk and act high and crazy. A lot of Harlem hustlers actually had reached that state – as I would later. It was inevitable when one had gone long enough on heavier and heavier narcotics, and under the steadily tightening vise of the hustling life. [72]

This was the great "put-on" by Malcolm – total Black theatre, rooted in a very precise historical experience. Dizzy Gillespie and Kenny Clark explained that many Black musicians acted this way in order to stay out of the army. They maintained that Blacks acted crazy at the induction centers, pretended that they were homosexuals or transvestites and increased their intake of drugs. Drugs kept Charlie Parker out of the military draft: an army psychiatrist took one look at the needle marks on his arm and immediately classified him as 4-F. [73] Of course, it was dangerous to their health, but many of them argued that it was an alternative to the contradictions of dying in a war to make the world safe for democracy, a democracy which they could not enjoy at home. It was the deeper revolt of the subconscious, which Frantz Fanon explored in the *Wretched of the Earth*. A. Philip Randolph pointed out that the results of a survey taken among Blacks in Harlem between the ages of 18 and 25 years indicated that more than 80 percent of them felt they were not prepared to fight and die in a Jim Crow army. The antagonism, which surfaced against the war in Vietnam during the sixties, provoked the same type of reaction among draft resisters, who later became "flower children" in the peace movement.

There had been an organic link between Malcolm, Bird and Dizzy, as they engaged in a struggle for survival. The national conflict seemed to have canalized all their anger and nationalized all their affective movements. Thus, Malcolm wrote,

> Many times since, I have thought about it, and what it really meant. In one sense, we were huddled in there, bonded together in seeking security and comfort from each other and we didn't know it. All of us – who might have probed space, or cured cancer, or built industries – were, instead black victims of the white man's American social system. In the ghettoes, the white man has built for us, he has forced us not to aspire to greater things, but to view everyday living as survival – and in that kind of a community survival is what is respected.[74]

Ross Russell in his book *Bird Lives* attempts to explain Charlie Parker's attitude, when the latter first met Marshall Stearns, as that of a "shyster who was fond of practical jokes." It was unfortunate that Russell didn't grasp the deeper meaning of Bird's revolt. The following is how the story unfolded:

> In April 1948, Charlie Parker met Marshall Stearns and Sidney Finkelstein at the Onyx, where he was playing opposite the Margie Hyams Quartet. In the house that night were Georgie Auld, Milt Jackson, Barry Ullanov, Chubby Jackson, Leonard Feather and Billie

Holiday. Marshall Stearns was then associate professor of English at Cornell, a Chaucer scholar, an authority on English poets Robert Henryson and Dylan Thomas, and America's leading jazz historian. Stearns had founded the first jazz club in American, at Yale, where John Hammond had been a protege. Finkelstein was the principal Marxist jazz critic, and author of the recently published *Jazz: A People's Music*. Both had world wide prestige and contact; both were authorities on Black music; but up to 1948, neither had seen Charlie Parker in a live performance. Finkelstein, something of a recluse, seldom visited night clubs. Both were eager to meet Bird. The authorities would confront the innovator eight years after he had hit the New York scene.

Charlie Parker very shrewdly and quickly sized up both men. These were the "cats who wrote books about jazz." Finkelstein he ignored. He concentrated on the patrician Stearns, born to wealth, educated at Harvard and Yale. Much to Stearns' discomfort, Charlie insisted on calling him "Professor." When Stearns went to the men's room, Bird followed. As Stearns stood at the urinal, Bird stood immediately behind, and said: "Look in the mirror, Professor." When Stearns looked up, there eyes met. "Here we are, Professor. You and me. Two human beings. You started at the top and I started at the bottom..." Then he explained that he was urgently in the need of money and asked for a loan of fifty dollars, a sum that Stearns would never have dreamed of bringing to a night club. As Stearns fumbled to rearrange his clothing, wash his hands and extricate himself from this strange and embarrassing situation, Charlie began to lower the amount of the requested loan. When it reached five dollars, Stearns came across. Later I took Charlie to task for his actions, pointing out that Dr. Stearns was in a position to advance his career, and that his own earnings were probably in excess of an associate English professor's salary at Cornell University. Charlie grinned at me. "Coming on like Billy Shaw now," Bird said. "I only hit him for a nickel note man!" Then he fished out a five-cent piece from his pocket and held it up. "That's my hype," he said. He put the coin back in his pocket and clipped the new saxophone to his neckpiece. Then, with the evening's squares put in their place, he whisked through a brilliant set. After the set he walked past us into Fifty-second Street as if the table was empty.[75]

There was a direct link between Bird and Malcolm in the Theatre of Revolt, and these two vignettes represented more than "practical jokes."

They were the articulations of a deeper confrontation in the social matrix, which one could only grasp at the level of resistance and self-protection. Short of armed struggle and a liberation movement, Bird and Malcolm had to resort to these attempts to undermine the superstructural reality. It was a constant sabotage of the institutional fabric and interpersonal relationships based on falsehoods. Frantz Fanon in writing about the colonial situation stated,

> The period of oppression is painful; but the conflict, by restating the down-trodden, sets on foot a process of reintegration which is fertile and decisive in the extreme. A people's victorious fight not only consecrates the truimph of its rights; it also gives to that people consistence, coherence and homogeneity. For colonialism has not simply depersonalized the individual it has colonized; this depersonalization is equally felt in the collective sphere, on the level of social structures. The colonized people find that they are reduced to a body of individuals who only find cohesion when in the presence of the colonizing nation. The fight carried on by the people for its liberation leads it according to circumstances, either to refuse or else to explode the so-called truths which have been established in its consciousness by the colonial civil administration, by the military occupation, and by economic exploitation. Armed conflict alone can really drive out these falsehoods created in man which force into inferiority the most lively minds among us and which, literally, mutilate us.[76]

Billie Holiday and Teddy Wilson were among the first to be taken downtown to 52nd Street in the early forties. Teddy Wilson played intermission piano at "the Famous Door" and Billie sang. Billie was very critical of this early experience, but it merely paved the way for bringing the Black creative artist downtown, especially to capture the growing market of white servicemen, who had found Harlem off-limits, and the socialites who had been discouraged form going uptown. Billie stated:

> You can be up to your boobies in white satin, with gardenias in your hair, and no sugar cane for miles, but you can still be working on a plantation....Take 52nd Street in the late thirties and early forties. It was supposed to be a big deal. "Swing street," they called it. Joint after joint was jumping. It was this "new" kind of music. They could

get away with calling it new because millions of squares hadn't taken a trip to 131st Street. If they had they could have dug swing for twenty years. By the time the ofays got around to copping "swing" a new style of music was already breaking out all over uptown. Ten years later that became the new thing when the white boys downtown figured out how to cop it... Anyway, white musicians were "swinging" from one end of 52nd Street to the other, but there wasn't a black face in sight on the street except Teddy Wilson and me.... There was no cotton to be picked between Leon and Eddie's and the East River, but man, it was a plantation anyway you looked at it. And we had to not only look at it, we lived in it. The minute we were finished with our intermission stint we had to scoot out back to the alley or go out and sit in the street. Teddy had an old beat-up Ford he used to drive to work in. Sometimes we'd just go out and sit in it parked at the curb.... But 52nd Street couldn't hold the line against Negroes forever. Something had to give. And eventually it was the plantation owners. They found they could make money off Negro artists and they couldn't afford their old prejudices. So the barriers went down, and it gave jobs to a lot of great musicians.[77]

One of the earliest ventures downtown was a concert at the Museum of Modern Art in November 1941. The Benny Carter sextet – featuring Dizzy Gillespie and vocalist, Maxine Sullivan – performed at this concert. In January 1942, the group went into the Famous Door and Kelly's Stables, but it disbanded by late February. In 1942, John Hammond booked the Dixie Hummingbirds at "Cafe Society Downtown," which had become the Greenwich Village showcase for Black talent. The Dixie Hummingbirds triumphed at Cafe Society then, just as they did at Newport twenty-four years later – before they retired in 1966 to the relative obscurity of their respective churches.

By late 1943, 52nd Street had expanded to a group of small clubs which had acted as the dotwown incubator for the new music since it attracted many of the creative giants from uptown. During 1944, it became the center of the modern movement. The block between Fifth and Sixth Avenues was the location of the Three Deuces, the Downbeat, the Famous Door, the Spotlite, Jimmy Ryan's, Samoa, Kelly's Stables, the Yacht Club and the Onyx; between Sixth and Seventh there stood the Hickory House and the Club 18, which later became the Troubador. By the end of the decade, the Street expanded around Broadway to the Royal Roost, the Aquarium, Basin Street, Bop City, and Birdland.[78]

The Dizzy Gillespie-Oscar Pettiford quintet opened at The Onyx early in 1944. They both received $75.00 per week, while the rest of the group got $60.00 per week. Earlier, they had turned down the same offer from Kelly's Stables. They wanted Charlie Parker to come in at this time but he didn't have a union card. Malcolm X described the Onyx Club, when he went with Jean Parks to see Billie Holiday: "We took a taxi on down to 52nd Street.... 'Billie Holiday' and those big photo blow-ups of her were under the lights outside. Inside the tables were jammed against the wall, tables about big enough to get two drinks and four elbows on. The Onyx was one of those little places."[79]

It had been quite a change from the big uptown clubs with dancing and a revue-show. After Billie finished singing "You Don't Know What Love Is," she spoke with Malcolm and Jean, whom she had not seen in quite some time. Malcolm referred to Lady Day movingly: "She sang with the soul of Negroes from the centuries of sorrow and oppression. What a shame that proud, fine, Black woman never lived where the true greatness of the Black race was appreciated." [80] But Billie was working on the 52nd Street plantation. After the set, Malcolm and Jean Parks went back uptown to the La Marr-Cherie bar on the corner of 147th Street and St. Nicolas Avenue. Ross Russell gave this description of 52nd Street:

> By day the street was dingier than most, a dispiriting block that lay between chic Fifth Avenue and the flitter of Broadway two blocks west. The clubs that sprang up there during the war years occupied unused basements or abandoned ground floors of the brownstone buildings... In front of each club the inevitable badge of the period cabaret, a marquee – its green canvas bleached by sun, stained by rain, supported by two iron poles – extended from the brownstone to the curbstone. Some of the clubs were nothing more than damp converted basements, thirty feet wide and not much deeper, low of ceiling, with tiny check rooms and miniature bars, furnished with a clutter of tables and chairs most likely picked up at an auction sale. "The Famous Door" was described by band leader Woody Herman as a "ratty, overcrowded little basement joint." Prices ran high for those days [Black working class patronage was almost priced out]: seventy-five

cents for a bottle of beer or a dilute, insipid whisky high-ball. Customers sat at tables large enough to cover with a pocket handkerchief, and paid a cover charge of three dollars. The Street was a hustler's operation, geared to a high level of turnover. After every thirty minute set, the clubs were cleared and the customers prodded along to the next place of entertainment. Each club displayed on its wall a printed card saying "Maximum Occupancy Permitted On These Premises Is 60," or whatever total assigned by the New York Fire Department. The limits were flagrantly violated on busy nights when the bar stood four or five deep with stags or bluffs. Most of the operators were New York editions of the Black Hand, the same breed that had flourished in Kansas City under boss Tom Perdergast.[81]

The musicians were brought from uptown to the "slave-catches" of 52nd Street and locked into another kind of ambience. Within a few years, they would be destroyed by narcotics, police beatings, alcohol, insane asylums or prisons, for they were wide open without any protection from their natural environment. In 1944, the Coleman Hawkins quintet with Max Roach and Howard McGhee was at "the Onyx." At "the Famous Door" was the Art Tatum Trio with Tiny Grimes and Slam Stewart. At "the Club Downbeat" was Mildred Bailey, accompanied by her husband Red Norvo and a mellow gathering of white musicians. The Fats Waller quintet was at "the Spotlight." Advertised as "Fifty-Thousand Killer Watts of Jive," Leo Watson and his Spirits of Rhythm led the show at "The Samoa." There were also other groups performing, like the Don Byas quintet at "the Onyx," the John Kirby Sextet and the Ben Webster Quartet at "the Famous Door" and the Stuff Smith Trio at "the Downbeat."[82] On the street, there was continuous music from 9:00 p.m. on the hour until 3:30 p.m.. Dizzy Gillespie and Oscar Pettiford were hired for $75.00 per week, while Charlie Parker and Erroll Garner were platooned at the Three Deuces for $65.00 per week. Because a ten percent cabaret war-tax had been imposed on these clubs and there was a constant change in ownership, the musicians really had to hustle. Since the bandstands in these clubs were very small, big bands were not brought in, but the whole point of the street was to supercede the big entertainment package, which had developed successfully in the Harlem ambience – with the budget package under the guise of integration.

Soon the Black creative giants, who had been nurtured by their communal experiences in Harlem, found themselves cut off from their moorings and adrift in a stormy sea of narcotics, alcoholism and crass exploitation. They were defenseless, and Billie Holiday wrote that even though she was earning $175.00 per week on 52nd Street as top billing, she was one of the biggest slaves around.

> I spent the rest of the war on 52nd Street, and a few other streets. I had the white gowns and the white shoes. And every night they'd bring me the white gardenias and the white junk. When I was on, I was on and nobody gave me any trouble. No cops, no treasury agents, nobody. I got into trouble when I tried to get off.[83]

Malcolm referred to the experience of this period in the following way: "I stayed so high that I was in a dream world. Now, sometimes, I would smoke opium with some white friends who lived downtown."[84] Malcolm even went further as he dealt with the sensation of timelessness, while shuttling back and forth from uptown to downtown, and being heavily under the influence of drugs. After he had gone to see Billie Holiday at the Onyx, he had a confrontation with another hustler at the La Marr-Cheri bar in Harlem. He went back downtown immediately.

> It must have been five in the morning when I went downtown. I woke up a white actor I knew who lived in the Howard Hotel on 45th Street off Sixth Avenue. I knew I had to stay high. The amount of dope I put into myself within the next several hours sounds inconceivable. I got some opium from that fellow. I took a cap back up to my apartment and I smoked it. My gun was ready if I heard a mosquito cough. My telephone rang. It was the white lesbian who lived downtown. She wanted me to bring her and her girlfriend fifty dollars worth of reefers. Opium made me drowsy. I had a bottle of benzedrine tablets in my bathroom; I swallowed some of them to perk up. The two drugs working in me had my head going in opposite directions at the same time. I knocked at the apartment right behind me. The dealer let me have loose marijuana on credit. He saw I was so high that he even helped me roll it - a hundred sticks. And while we were rolling it, we both smoked some. Now opium, beneeezedrine, reefers. I stopped by Sammy's on the way downtown. He motioned me to sniff some cocaine crystals. I didn't refuse. Going downtown to deliver the

reefers, I felt sensations I cannot describe, in all those grooves at the same time. The only word to describe it was a timelessness. I can't imagine how I looked when I got to the hotel. When the lesbian and her girlfriend saw me, they helped me to bed; I fell across it and passed out.[85]

The experiences of Malcolm and Bird were inextricably linked to the type of ambience in which this creative music had been exploited as the musicians were brought downtown to the Money Jungle of 52nd Street, where they were locked into the basement clubs with all of the destructive possibilities. In addition, the musicians were surrounded by a new clientele, who exploited their rootlessness, their alienation. This experience represented another migration away from their sources.

As mentioned previously, Duke Ellington had begun a series of annual concerts at Carnegie Hall, beginning with *Black, Brown and Beige* in 1943. Paul Robeson appeared in *Othello* in 1943 with record breaking performances. The American Negro Theatre's *Anna Lucasta* with Hilda Simms and Canada Lee, which opened in Harlem in 1944, was quickly brought downtown to Broadway the same year; it ran for almost three years. As a result of the success of *Anna Lucasta*, the American Negro Theatre consciously began to aim its uptown productions at the downtown consumer market, thereby losing its ethnic touch as well as its community audience. It soon fell apart.[86] Since then, there has been nothing like it in Harlem for the development of either actors or playwrights until the sixties. All of the American Negro Theatre's creative talent was absorbed on Broadway, off-Broadway, in touring companies, or in Hollywood. This was integration into the cultural apparatus 1944-style.

During this period the big musicals with all-Black casts hit Broadway: *Cabin in the Sky*, *Carmen Jones* and *St. Louis Woman*. The cast of *Cabin in the Sky* included Ethel Waters, Katherine Dunham, Rex Ingraham, Todd Duncan and Dooley Wilson, while "St. Louis Woman" included Pearl Bailey, Ruby Hill and the Nicholas Brothers. Another musical production of this era was *Swingin' the Dream*, the jazz adaptation of Shakespeare's *Midsummer Night's Dream*, with Louis Armstrong as Puck and Maxine Sullivan as Titania. On the theatrical stage, Lillian

Smith's 1945 drama of miscegenation, *Strange Fruit* (inspired by Billie Holiday's musical composition), introduced to the theatre the talented Jane White. And *Deep are the Roots* found the young Gordon Heath (a soldier back from the war) playing opposite Barbara Bel Geddes.

This brain drain was taking place right before the eyes of the Black political and cultural leadership, and they did not understand that it would lead to the physical and cultural disintegration of the community. What had been happening in Harlem, New York by 1944 was strategically taking place in the Harlems of North America. Integration into the cultural matrix meant integration into another set of values that the creative artist would have to deal with in order to continue what had taken place in Harlem during the early war years.

Unlike Malcolm when he arrived in Harlem in 1942, Ray Brown spoke of his first arrival in 1944.

> The very night I arrived at my aunt's place in New York, I asked my nephew to take me down to see where 52nd Street was. That night I saw Erroll Garner, Art Tatum, Billie Holiday, Billie Daniels, Coleman Hawkins and Hank Jones. I had known Hank before. While we were talking, Hank said, "Dizzy Gillespie just came in." I said, "Where? Introduce me to him." So Hank introduced us. Hank said to Dizzy, "This is Ray Brown, a friend of mine and a very good bass player." Dizzy said, "You want a gig?" I almost had a heart attack. Dizzy said, "Be at my house for rehearsal at seven o'clock tomorrow." I went up there the next night and got the fright of my life. The band consisted of Dizzy Gillespie, Bud Powell, Max Roach, Charlie Parker and me! Two weeks later we picked up Milt Jackson who was my room-mate for two years.[87]

Ray Brown was eighteen years old at the time; Max Roach and Bud Powell were nineteen and twenty respectively. Dizzy Gillespie was twenty-seven years old and Charlie Parker was twenty-four. The ball game had changed. The arena had changed. It was a new battleground for the cultural struggle. The risks were higher downtown and the casualties were greater, but the messages of these innovators soon subverted the American cultural matrix in spite of all opposition. It also reverberated around the world, creating new definitions in an authentic language of struggle. These cultural workers would become victims of the integrative process in the subsequent years, but they would explore universal truths, challenge old assumptions of time and space, while negating the plasticity of computerized falsehoods.

Paul Robeson understood this when he said at his 46th birthday party on April 9, 1944, at the 17th Regiment Armory of New York (sponsored by W.C. Handy, Duke Ellington, Count Basie, Hope Stevens, Olin Downes, Joe Louis, Lilian Helman, Lena Horne, Ben Davis, and Mary McLeod Bethune), "The mainspring of my life as an artist and as a person is a responsibility to the democratic forces for which I fight."[88] And, in an interview on April 12, 1944, published in *the New York Times*, he further stated, "the problem of the Negro in this country is a very serious one. The American Negro has changed his temper. Now he wants his freedom. Whether he is smiling at you or not, he wants his freedom. The old exploitation of people is definitely past."[89]

Robeson then called a conference on April 15, 1944 entitled AFRICA-NEW PERSPECTIVES, sponsored by the Council on African Affairs, which he had organized in 1941. At the conference, he highlighted the future of Africa in the post World War II period. Paul Robeson knew that Max Roach, Duke Ellington, Lena Horne, Charlie Parker, Katherine Dunham, Charles White, Canada Lee, Dizzy Gillespie, Bud Powell, Billie Holiday and Malcolm all wanted their freedom whether they were smiling or not, and that their creative energies would lead them to this freedom because they had made their choices. They were prepared to join Langston Hughes and Paul Robeson on the Freedom Train, even if they had gone downtown into the slave-catches of 52nd Street, or the glitter of Hollywood and the Broadway stage. But Robeson also knew that Africa would be critical to their future work as well as the liberation struggle in North America. Like Dizzy, Max, Katherine Dunham and Pearl Primus, Robeson had heard the drumming and chanting of Machito and Chano Pozo. He had seen that the drum that had been taken away for four hundred years, found its way back into the spiritual life of our creative work through the genius of the Afro-Cuban drummers, who were also Yoruba Santeria priests.

Paul Robeson had known that the Army had destroyed Lester Young, "Prez.", who had been sentenced to five years in dentention barracks at Camp Gordon, Georgia, because a white major from Louisiana cracked on him for having photographs of his wife, Mary, in his locker. His wife was white. Later, the sentence was reduced to one year. It has also been argued that Prez. was somewhat of a conscientious objector. The spirits of this gentle innovator had been bruised, battered and mutilated by this army experience. He was never the same person after he got out of the army. Robeson knew that Kenny Clark, Mercer Ellington, Jimmy Jones, who wrote *Lover Man* and took it to Billie Holiday to record, had all been drafted in the Armed forces. He knew that Billie would be put in prison and that Charlie Parker, Theolonious Monk, Bud Powell and Charles Mingus would all be put in the insane asylums like Scott Joplin and Buddy Bolden before them. He understood that Charlie Christian, Jimmy Blanton, Clyde Hart, Fats Navarro and many more beautiful ones would die young from tuberculosis, narcotics addiction and over-exploitation. He realized that there would be many casualties among these cultural freedom fighters. He suspected that Adam Clayton Powell, Jr. would be elected in November 1944 as the first Black Congressman from Harlem and that many Black men would go to prison before they were 21 years old – as Malcolm X did in February 1946.

Paul Robeson knew these things because he understood the forces of history that had been set in motion. He understood the dialectical processes of revolt, which no cosmetic cultural integration based on false premises could permanently stop. Integration might deflect it, but it could not curtail the advancement of progressive forces inside the U.S.A. Moreover, he recognized in *Dexterity, Epistrophy, Red Cross, A Night in Tunisia, Hot House, 52nd Street Theme, Max is Making Wax, Overtime, Victory Ball, Anthropology, Round About Midnight, Visa, Passport, Disorder at the Border, Wooky'n You, Crazeology, Drifting on a Reed, Orinthology, Street Beat, Congo Blues, Ko-Ko, Groovin' High, Emanon, Quasimodo, Klactoveesedstene, Confirmation, Cosmic Rays, Dynamo, Afro-Cuban Suite, Manteca, Algo Bueno, Ah-Leu-Cha,* that there were hidden messages which were like an addenda to *Things to Come, A New*

World A-Coming, and *Now's the Time*. He saw the mask and irony in these titles that reminded him of *Steal Away, Singing with a Sword in my Hand, How I Got Over, Joshua Fit de Battle ob Jericho*. He even reversed Bird's title and used the slogan "The Time is Now" in his appeal to Black leadership in his book *Here I Stand*.

But Paul Robeson even went further, recognizing that Africa would become critical to the African-American creative process, and that Charlie Parker's composition, *Ah-Leu-Cha* would soon become *A Luta Continua:* the slogan of the struggle for independence in Angola, Mozambique and Guinea Bissau. Likewise, he realized that Bird's composition, *Chi-Chi* dealt with the cosmological underpinning of the Igbo people of Nigeria and not the simplistic explanation of Bill Simon, Associate Music Editor of *Billboard Magazine*, who wrote in his liner notes to the Verve recording of the album, *Now is the Time*: "Side two starts with three versions of another blues-based Parker original, this one with a set theme and an exuberant tempo, and altogether unfittingly entitled *Chi-Chi*. If there's anything Bird wasn't it was Chi-Chi."[90] This critic not only knew very little about Bird's work technically, but also philosophically. However, he has spoken with great authority inside the cultural apparatus, and his "ignorance" has been widely circulated.

Chinua Achebe in his essay, *Chi in Igbo Cosmology* has brought us closer to the significance of Bird's title:

> There are two clearly distinct meanings of the word, Chi, in Igbo. The first is often translated as god, guardian angel, personal spirit, soul, spirit double etc. The second meaning is day, or daylight, but is most commonly used for those transitional periods between day and night or night and day....In a general way, we may visualize a person's Chi as his other identity in spirit land – his spirit being complementing his terrestrial human being; for nothing can stand alone, there must always be another thing standing beside it. The central place in Igbo thought is the notion of duality. Where ever something stands, something else will stand beside it. Nothing is absolute. The world in which we live has its double and counterpart in the realm of spirits. A man lives here and his Chi there. Indeed the human being is only one half (and the weaker at that) of a person....There is a complimentary spirit being, Chi.[91]

Chinua Achebe further explains two stories in Igbo folklore that illuminates the notion of Chi:

> There is a story of how a proud wrestler, having thrown every challenger in the world, decides to go and wrestle in the world of spirits. There he also throws challenger after challenger, including many multiple headed ones – so great was his prowess. At last there is no one left to fight. But the wrestler refuses to leave. The spirits beg him to go; his companion praise – singer on the flute pleads with him. But it is all in vain. There must be somebody left; surely the famed land of spirits can do better than this, he said. Again everyone begs him to collect his laurels and go, but again he refuses. Finally his own Chi appears, reluctant, thin as a rope. The wrestler laughs at this miserable looking contender and moves forward contemptuously to knock him down, whereupon the other lifts him clear off the ground with his little finger and smashes him to death.[92]

This cautionary tale, Achebe observed, is concerned mainly with setting a limit to man's aspirations. The limit is not the sky; it is somewhere much closer to earth. A sensible man will turn round at the frontiers of absolutism and head for home again. The second story was even more intriguing:

> There is another cautionary tale about Chi, this time involving the little bird, NZA, who ate and drank somewhat more than was good for him and in a fit of recklessness, which inebriation alone would explain, taunted his Chi to come down and get him if he could. Whereupon a hawk swooped down from the clear sky and carried him away. Which shows the foolishness of counting on Chi's remoteness, for Chi need not come in or act directly, but may use one's enemy who is close by. This special power that Chi has over its man (or the man's special vulnerability to his Chi) is further exemplified in a proverb: No matter how many divinities sit together to plot a man's ruin, it will come to nothing unless his Chi has unprecedented veto over a man's destiny.[93]

Interestingly on the *Now's the Time* album, Bird did *Cosmic Rays* and *Confirmation*. Bill Simon had the following to say about *Cosmic Rays*:

Cosmic Rays, a medium blues, is just as vague as the theme and is also represented by two identically routine takes. But only the routines are identical. Bird takes the first three choruses, and this is Bird, the Preacher. With all his modernisms, Bird is a folk artist. He's steeped in the sounds, the inflections of the sharecropper's blues and the backwoods preacher. He sputters and exclaims, he exhorts. He raises his eyes to heaven and rolls them around, pleading, and when he finishes his sermon, there's nothing to add but "Amen."[94]

Chinua Achebe discussed this cosmic force in the Igbo world in a penetrating way.

But one day I stumbled on the very important information that among the Igbo of Awka a man who arrived at the point in his life when he needs to set up a shrine to his Chi will invite a priest to perform a ritual of bringing down the spirit from the face of the sun at daybreak. Thereafter, it is represented physically in the man's compound until the day of his death when the shrine must be destroyed. The implication of this is that a person's Chi normally resides with the sun, bringer of daylight, or at least passes through it to visit the world, which itself may have an even profounder implication, for it is well known in Igbo cosmology that the Supreme Deity, Chukwa himself, is in close communion with the sun. Every act of creation is the work of a separate and individual agent, Chi, a personified and unique manifestation of the creative essence. Still farther west, the Akan of Ghana believe in a moon goddess whom they call Ngame, Mother of the World, who gives a "soul" to every human being at birth by shooting lunar rays into him. The Igbo, seemingly more reticent about such profound events, may yet be hinting at a comparable cosmic relationship between their Chi and solar rays. This would explain the invocation of Chi form face of the sun at the consecration of its shrine and account also for the second meaning of the word: daylight. [95]

In essence, we are dealing with Bird's *Dance of Death* as he challenged the outer limits of this warped time capsule. Charlie Parker, symbolizing the contradictions of the forties as well as the tragic motion from uptown to downtown...from swing to bop...from plasticity to hard core defiance and revolt, genuinely believed that he was an iron in a changing world. He was Bird....in flight. He once told Max Roach in a hotel suite, "you see this body....I'll blow it out to the last breath...to the last note....to the last sound of laughter in this cell of insanity. My real mission on this planet is not about music....but rather to show others what they should not do with their health, their bodies, their lives." Max was stunned as Bird stood stripped naked in the doorway. He has never forgotten this scene. It was obvious that Bird was dealing with his Chi. 'Nuff said. Professor Ed Love, a brilliant and daring Black sculptor saw Bird as,

> ...one of the conductors who attempt to deal with the in-between; that space of Middle Passage that his people seem to occupy; that place between two points; that chord between mother and child; between wall and appliance, between earth and sky, between freedom and liberation....These conductors represent the elegance of struggle and the will of being undefeated.[96]

The conductors emerged from Charlie Parker's *A-Leu-Cha* to their political connections and converges with Max Roach's *Sweet Mao* and *Suid Afrika '76*, with John Coltrane's *Giant Steps*, *Africa Brass* and *Alabama*, with Archie Shepp's *Attica Blues* and *Song for Mozambique*, with Miles Davis' *Tutu* and *Amandla*, for the struggle continues.

The decade of the forties provided an anchor as well as a point of reference for resolving the contradictions and discontinuities which erupted in American culture. The bankruptcy of racism and labor exploitation had been defiantly exposed by its victims, who changed the terms of the discourse as well as the mode of the discourse. Post World War II America would never be the same again — uptown or downtown — as the voices of resistance grew stronger and more assertive. *Now is the Time*, *Things To Come* and *A New World's A-Coming* boldly led us to *Freedom Now Suite* and *A Love Supreme*.

NOTES

1. Richard Wright, *Black Boy* (New York: Harper and Row Publishers, 1944) p. 42.

2. Claude McKay, *Harlem: Negro Metropolis* (New York: A Harvest Book, Harcourt Brace Jovanovich, Inc., 1940) p. 16.

3. *The Autobiography of Malcolm X* (New York: Grove Press, Inc., 1964) p. 74.

4. Julius Mattfeld, *Variety Music Cavalcade* (Englewood Cliffs, N.J.: Prentice-Hall Inc., 1971) p. 529.

5. Philip S. Foner, *Organized Labor and the Black Worker 1619-1973* (New York: Praeger Publishers, 1974) p. 238.

6. Ibid., p. 238

7. William Foster, *The Negro People in American Society* (New York: International Publishers, 1954) p. 512.

8. Foner, Op. Cit., p. 238.

9. Jervis Anderson, *A. Philip Randolph: A Biographical Portrait* (New York: A Harvest Book, Harcourt Brace Jovanovich, Inc., 1972) p. 241.

10. Ibid., p. 242.

11. Foner, Op. Cit., p. 242.

12. Anderson, Op. Cit., p. 246.

13. John Hope Franklin, *From Slavery To Freedom* (New York: Vintage Books Editions, Alfred A. Knopf Inc., 1969) p. 576.

14. Anderson, Op. Cit., p. 243.

15. Franklin, Op. Cit., p. 576. The seven-point program urged that all available reserve officers be used to train recruits; that Negro recruits be given the same training as whites; that existing units in the army accept officers and men on the basis of ability and not race; that specialized personnel, such as physicians, dentists and nurses be integrated; that responsible Negroes be appointed to draft boards; that discrimination be abolished in the Navy and Air Forces; and that competent Negroes be appointed as civilian assistants to the Secretaries of War and Navy.

16. Anderson, Op. Cit., p. 244.

17. Franklin, Op. Cit., p. 577.

18. Anderson, Op. Cit., p. 245.

19. Ibid., p. 249.

20. Ibid., p. 253.

21. Ibid., p. 251.

22. Ibid., p. 251.

23. Ibid., p. 255.

24. Ibid., p. 259.

25. Ibid., p. 259.

26. Lerone Bennett, Jr., *Confrontation Black and White* (d-Baltimore, Penguin Books Inc., 1965) p. 152.

27. Margaret Walker, *For My People* (New Haven: Yale University Press, 1942) p. 14.

28. Ira Gitler, *Jazz Masters of the Forties* (London: Collier Macmillan Publishers, 1966) p. 177.

29. Ibid., p. 176.

30. Ibid., p. 188.

31. Ibid., p. 183.

32. Ibid., p. 152.

33. Duke Ellington, *Music is my Mistress* (New York: Da Capo Press, Inc., 1973) p. 164.

34. Gitler, Op. Cit., p. 20.

35. Ibid., p. 123.

36. Ibid., p. 22.

37. Ellington, Op. Cit., p. 175.

38. Ibid., p. 460.

39. Rob Backus, *Fire Music* (Detroit: Vanguard Books, 1976) p. 30.

40. Ellington, Op. Cit., p. 182.

41. Ibid., p. 183.

42. Harry Haywood, *Negro Liberation* (Chicago: Liberator Press, 1948) p. 147.

43. David C. Driskell, *Two Centuries of Black American Art* (New York: Alfred A. Knopf Inc. and the Los Angeles County Museum of Art, 1976) p. 76.

44. Horace Pippin, *Introduction to Catalogue, Phillips Art Gallery Retrospective Exhibition,* 1977.

45. Driskell, Op. Cit., p. 76.

46. Richard Wright, *Native Son* (New York, signet Classics, the New American Library of World Literature, Inc., 1940) p. 392. '

47. Faith Berry, Ed., *Good Morning Revolution,* Uncollected Social Protest Writings by Langston Hughes (New York: Lawrence Hill and Company, 1973) p. 15.

48. Ibid., p. 125.

49. Langston Hughes and Milton Meltzer, *Black Magic* (New York: Bonanza Books, 1967) p. 125.

50. Gitler, Op. Cit., p. 113.

51. Hughes and Meltzer, Op. Cit., p. 267.

52. Ibid., p. 266.

53. Ibid., *p.* 302.

54. Marie Seaton, *Paul Robeson (*London: Dennis Dobson, 1958) p. 135

55. Ibid., p. 129

56. Charles H. Wright, Robeson: *Labor's Forgotten Champion* (Detroit: Balamp Publishing, 1975) p. 37.

57. Anderson, Op. Cit., p. 291.

58. Seaton, Op. Cit., p. 159.

59. Hughes and Meltzer, Op. Cit., p. 202.

60. Ibid., p. 202.

61. Ibid., p. 202.

62. Ibid., p. 134.

63. Wright, Op. Cit., p. 45.

64 Haywood, Op. Cit., p. 147.

65. Archie Shepp, Personal Correspondence to Acklyn Lynch.

66. Anderson, Op. Cit., p. 252.

67. Ibid., p. 252.

68. Malcolm X, Op. Cit., p. 113-114.

69. McKay, Op. Cit., p. 26.

70. Anderson, Op. Cit., p. 258.

71. Harold Cruse, *The Crisis of the Negro Intellectual* (New York: William Morrow & Company Inc., 1967) p. 208.

72. Malcolm X. Op. Cit., p. 105-107.

73. Ross Russell, *Bird Lives* (New York: Charterhouse, 1973) p. 141.

74. Malcolm X, Op. Cit., p. 105-107.

75. Russell, Op. Cit., p. 261-262.

76. Frantz Fanon, *The Wretched of the Earth,* (New York: Grove Press Inc., 1963) p. 238.

77. Billie Holiday, *Lady Sings the Blues* (New York: Lancer Books, 1956) p. 95.

78. Russell, Op. Cit., p. 163.

79. Malcolm X, Op. Cit., p. 128.

80. Ibid., p. 129.

81. Russell, Op. Cit., p. 163.

82. Ibid., p. 164.

83. Holiday, Op. Cit., p. 114.

84. Malcolm X, Op. Cit., p. 123.

85. Ibid., p. 130.

86. Hughes and Meltzer, Op. Cit., p. 199.

87. Gitler, Op. Cit., p. 170.

88. Seaton, Op. Cit., p. 162.

89. Paul Robeson, *Here I Stand,* (Boston: Beacon Press, 1958) p. 88-89.

90. *The Genius of Charlie Parker #3, Now's the Time,* Verve V6-8005, Notes by Bill Simon.

91. Chinua Achebe, *Morning Yet on Creation Day* (New York: Anchor Books, 1975) p. 131.

92. Ibid., p. 134.

93. Ibid., p. 135.

94. Simon, Liner Notes - *Now's the Time.*

95. Achebe, Op. Cit., p. 140.

96. Ed Love, *Introduction to Catalogue for an Exhibition at the Washington Project for the Arts.*

REMEMBERING MALCOLM

"My whole life has been a chronology of changes."
— *Autobiography of Malcolm X*

The journey from Malcolm Little — born in Omaha, Nebraska on May 19, 1925 — to Detroit Red to Malcolm X to El-Hajj Malik El-Shabazz (assassinated in New York City on February 21, 1965) will remain one of the more exciting historical experiences of the twentieth century. In a few years, this shining star blazed across the American firmament disrupting the Great Milky White Way and ushering in a new social, cultural and political dynamic that changed the character of American life. It set in motion new rhythms, a strident rhetorical stance and creative possibilities that inspired writers, artists, poets and dancers to celebrate the emergence of a new life force. Malcolm has, therefore, remained one of this century's dominant political figures, whose reputation, ideas, and critical incisiveness expanded even beyond his death. He has been both a national and international patriot, who – in the struggle for freedom, justice and human dignity – left us with a legacy of courage and manhood. Together with Dr. Martin Luther King, he spearheaded one of the phalanxes of the Black resistance movement challenging and confronting the dominant social ethos with intense conviction. His presence on the world stage has not been forgotten.

Malcolm was the seventh child of Reverend Earl Little who was born in Reynolds, Georgia. Reverend Little left Georgia as a young man at the turn of the century first moving to the North, and then to the Midwest. He was part of that migratory wave of Black peasantry who attempted to find new hope from the terror of the Ku Klux Klan and the harsh exploitative conditions of sharecropping. In the North, he became a Baptist minister and a dedicated organizer for Marcus Garvey's Universal Negro Improvement Association. Ms. Louise Little was born in Grenada, West Indies, a small island in the Caribbean. She, too, had been part of that migratory process of Caribbean peoples who came to the metropolis in search of new opportunities.

During Ms. Little's pregnancy with Malcolm, she witnessed an attack on her home by hooded Ku Klux Klan night-riders. They surrounded the house, brandishing their rifles, and warned her to encourage her husband to leave town because he (as a Garvey organizer) had been a "trouble maker." One can imagine the traumatic experience of this young, pregnant woman with her three children huddled next to her in front of the door listening to threats on her husband's life. George Jackson dramatized this historical predicament of the Black woman from slavery to the present, as she fears for her yet unborn son as follows:

> It always started with Mama. Mine loved me. As testimony of her love and fear for the fate of her manchild, all slave mothers hold, she attempted to press, hide, push, capture me in the womb. The conflicts and contradictions that will follow me to the tomb started right there in the womb. The feeling of being captured....this slave can never adjust to it. [1]

Malcolm recognized the impact of this prenatal experience and he dealt with it stoically, "It has always been my belief that I, too, will die by violence. I have done all that I can to be prepared." Malcolm arrived at this position as a result of the experiences of his uncles, as well as his father — who decided to risk and dedicate his life to help disseminate Garveyism among Black people:

> He had seen four of his six brothers die by violence, three of them killed by white men, including one by lynching. What my father could not know then was that of the remaining three, including himself, only one, my Uncle Jim would die in bed of natural causes. Northern white police were later to shoot my Uncle Oscar. And my father was finally himself to die by the white man's hands. [2]

After Malcolm's birth, his father moved the family to Lansing, Michigan, where his house was burned down by the white Black Legionnaires in 1929, shortly after his sister Yvonne was born. It was a nightmarish experience for the four year old Malcolm, and the family then moved to the outskirts of East Lansing. However, when Malcolm was six years old, his father was brutally murdered by the same Legionnaires who, after killing him, laid his body across the railroad tracks where it was almost cut in half. These were the earliest experiences of a manchild who traveled with his father, while he preached in small storefront churches in Nebraska, Michigan, Wisconsin and Illinois. In 1929, Reverend Little predicted,

> It would not be much longer before Africa would be completely run by Negroes—by Black men was the phrase he always used. No one knows when the hour of Africa's redemption cometh. It is in the wind. It is coming. One day like a storm it will be here. [3]

This was his vision of the world and it must have had some impact on young Malcolm because he lived to share this dream when he visited Africa and the Middle East in 1959, 1964, and 1965. Malcolm not only met with several heads of state including Dr. Kwame Nkrumah, Julius Nyerere, Jomo Kenyatta, Dr. Milton Obote, Nnamdi Azikiwe, Gamal Abdel Nasser and Prince Faisal, but he also presented the Afro-American's case before the Organization of African Unity's First Assembly of Heads of State in Cairo, Egypt on July 17, 1964.

When Malcolm's father died, the insurance company tried to reject his mother's claim on his small insurance policy, arguing that Reverend. Little had committed suicide. However, she finally got the money. After their savings dwindled, she began to work as a maid in Lansing and to buy on credit. Reverend Little had always been against "credit." He argued that "credit is the first step into debt and back into slavery." (It is the harsh reality of the sharecropper's experience in Georgia But today, as Black people we are deeper in debt than we have ever been and we owe almost everything to the commissary. It is the painful price of progress in a consumer-oriented world.) Malcolm, in his speech before the O.A.U. Summit Conference in 1964, warned, "Don't escape from European colonialism only to become even more enslaved by 'friendly' American dollarism." [4] Very few leaders have listened closely to this warning, and

Ngugi Wa' Thiongo's *Petals of Blood* is a graphic example of this betrayal and corruption.

By 1934, the depression had hit the Little family very hard. They began to suffer. They depended on charity and, like many other poor Blacks, they often went hungry. Destitution set in and the family's pride, which Reverend Little had nurtured, began to slip away. The older boys went out to work in an effort to supplement the token welfare relief check. But, after Malcolm was caught stealing, the State welfare authorities began to put pressure on Ms. Little to split up the family. In 1937, she was put in a State Mental Hospital (in Kalamazoo, Michigan), where she remained for the next 26 years. Her children were made wards of the state and Malcolm was sent to a reform school. As a result of the painful experience in 1952 when he visited his mother and she failed to recognize him, he wrote,

> my mother in there was a statistic that didn't have to be, that existed because of a society's failure, hypocrisy, greed and lack of mercy and compassion. Hence I have no mercy or compassion in me for a society that crushes people, and then penalizes them for not being able to stand up under the weight. [5]

He was pained at the disintegration and desolation of his mother, and when he tried to talk to her, she simply replied "all the people have gone."[6] This was part of her racial memory going back to the rape of the African continent, the Middle Passage and the systematic dispersion of our people in the plantation model. It was also the loss of her husband and her children who had been farmed out to different foster homes.

Malcolm was sent to reform school in Mason, Michigan, where he was enrolled in Mason Junior High School, an all white school about twelve miles from Lansing. He performed quite well academically and in the seventh grade he was not only at the top of his class but he was also elected class President. In a discussion with his English teacher, who was his advisor, Malcolm expressed some desire to become a lawyer. The advisor deterred him, suggesting that he might consider carpentry. The episode discouraged Malcolm. At the end of the eight grade he left Mason and went to live with his older sister Ella in Boston. He reflected later, "I have thought about that time a lot since. No physical move in my life has been more pivotal or profound in its repercussions." [7]

Malcolm went to Boston in 1939, where he lived with his sister in Roxbury. It was here that he first got in touch with Black popular culture through music and dance. He rejected the imitative lifestyle of the "dicty Hill folks" and turned to the glitter of the street life while he worked as a shoe-shine boy at the Roseland State Ballroom. It was the swing era and the big bands of Duke Ellington, Erskine Hawkins, Count Basie and Cootie Williams played one night for Blacks, while Benny Goodman, Artie Shaw and Woody Herman played the following night for whites. This was the period in which the one night stands were popular and everybody was "lindy-hopping," as Duke played "It don't mean a thing, if it ain't got that swing."

Malcolm was somewhat big for his age, so he soon became a "hipster," hustling, drinking, gambling, smoking reefer and cigarettes, and dancing. He processed his hair, bought his "zoot" suits on credit and, at the Roseland, he was doing the "kangaroo," the "flapping eagle" and the "split." He had come a long way from Omaha, Lansing, Mason and his father's dream. The "hip" world had started young Malcolm along the path of self-destruction. During one of the big dances at the Roseland Ballroom, he humiliated a quiet, young Black woman (Laura), whom he had taken to the dance, when he chose to leave with Sophia (a white woman), whom he had seen for the first time. Later, he reflected on this experience:

> One of the shames that I have carried for years is that I blame myself for Laura's wreckage. To have treated her as I did for a white woman made the blow doubly heavy....She was a smart girl, a good girl. She tried her best to make something out of me and look what I started her into—dope and prostitution. I wrecked that girl. [8]

Malcolm saw himself as so many of his Black brothers today, just deaf, dumb and blind.

Frantz Fanon in *Black Skin White Masks* analyzed the labyrinth of emotional responses in black/white relations and suggested that the compulsive motion away from insularity is a reflection of powerlessness. He saw it as an expression of the devaluation of self and a desire to be authenticated by the legitimizing claims of the dominant culture. Inside this matrix, Fanon referred to Jean Veneuse, a Black, who wished to marry Andree Marielle, a white poetess, claiming that "her love takes me onto the noble road that leads to total realization." In his examination of this historical dilemma, Fanon argued,

> It is this tripod—the *anguish* created by every abandonment, the *aggression* to which it gives rise, and the *devaluation* of self that flows out of it—that supports the whole symptomatology of this neurosis.[9]

Malcolm observed later in life as he dealt with Black musicians in New York in the forties,

> all you had to do was put a white girl anywhere close to the average Blackman and he would respond. The Black woman also made the white man's eyes light up—but he was slick enough to hide it. In those days, there were no Negroes more white-woman crazy than most of the musicians. People in show business, of course, won't tell you that, but it also works in reverse.[10]

As a result of his relationship with Sophia, Ella, treated him like a viper. He had betrayed her trust and confidence. He left her home to share an apartment with his musician friend, Shorty, but he soon got a job on the railroads working between Boston, New York and Washington, D.C. on the Yankee Clipper.

When Malcolm first arrived in New York, barely 17 years old, it seduced him culturally; later it would shape him politically. Taking Duke Ellington's famous "A-Train," the quickest way to get up to Harlem, he was mesmerized when he hit the scene. It was like some technicolor bazaar. On his first night, he went to Small's Paradise, to the Apollo Theatre where he heard the Jay McShann Band with Charlie Parker playing *Hootie Blues* and Walter Brown singing *Confessin' the Blues*, to the Braddock Hotel on 126th Street, where he saw along the jam packed bar Billie Holiday, Dinah Washington, Ella Fitzgerald, Dizzy Gillespie and Billy Eckstine. Then, after walking up and down between Lennox, Seventh and Eighth Avenues, he went to the Savoy Ballroom where Lionel Hampton was playing *Flying Home* and *Second Balcony Jump* with such greats as Arnette Cobb, Illinois Jacquet, Dexter Gordon and Joe Newman. The dancing fascinated Malcolm, "I had never seen such fever heat dancing. After a couple of slow numbers cooled the place off, they brought on Dinah Washington. When she did her 'Salty Papa Blues,' the people just about tore the Savoy's roof off."[11] It was the people and the music, close to each other in a celebrative, ritualistic experience. This was the tremendous impact of Harlem on Malcolm. Harlem, in 1942, was both the extended metaphor and the grim reality, but what would occur there at this critical juncture in American history, would soon influence not only this nation, but the world. Harlem would soon become the incubator for a cultural revolution.

Malcolm lost his job on the railroads, but he quickly got a job at Small's Paradise as a waiter. He had settled permanently in Harlem during a period of enormous transition. A new musical language was beginning to enrich the creative continuum as Charlie Parker, Dizzy Gillespie, Thelonious Monk, Kenny Clark, Machito, Max Roach, Tadd Dammeron, Bud Powell, Charlie Christian, Jimmy Blanton, Oscar Pettiford and others stepped on the scene. The new music was incubating at Clark Monroe's Uptown, Minton's, Barron's, Connie's Inn, The Lido, Jimmie's Chicken Shack, The Lennox Club etc., while folks were dancing at the Savoy, Renaissance, the Golden Gate and the Audubon Ballrooms. It was at Small's Paradise that he began to learn about the cultural and social history of Harlem from old timers. They taught him not only the tricks to hustling, but also the dynamics of Black popular culture. He developed lasting personal relationships with many Black artists, and this knowledge base became useful to him later in life.

On reflecting on the Harlem he knew as a young man, Malcolm said:

Many times since, I have thought about it, and what it really meant. In one sense, we were huddled in there bonded together in seeking

> security and warmth and comfort from each other, and we didn't know
> it. All of us—who might have probed space or cured cancer, or built
> industries—were, instead, black victims of the whiteman's American
> social system.... In the ghettoes the white man has built for us, he has
> forced us not to aspire to greater things, but to view everyday living
> as survival — and in that kind of a community, survival is what is
> respected. [12]

Today, the notion of survival has become the password for Blacks at every
level in the social matrix. We have been consumed with the urgency and
immediacy of survival as politicians, professionals, preachers, educators,
factory workers, students, ball players, pimps, prostitutes, prisoners and
welfare recipients. We have had very little time to plan for the future and
we have given minimum thought to it. Our signals "freedom now" have
been replaced by "survival here and now," "looking out for number one,"
and "freak of the week." We have accommodated ourselves to a prag-
matism that has made us "situationists," "realists" and "crass opportunists." Corruption has limited our possibilities to the status quo. That
courage necessary to take hold of the circumstances surrounding our lives
and transform this reality has remained in the subterranean channels of
revolt.

Malcolm was fired from Small's Paradise for "impairing the morals
of a soldier." He turned to the street once again and began to hustle so
that he could eat, pay rent and stay high. After the rebellions of Summer
1943, conditions became more difficult and Malcolm began hustling
uptown and downtown; selling drugs, pimping and steering. His life
deteriorated as he entered that world of timelessness on heroin, cocaine,
reefer, Benzedrine and whiskey. He was courting death. It was a dance
of death that so many young Black men have played out on the streets of
Harlem. He stated that, in those days, only three things in the world scared
him: jail, a job and the Army. He had beaten the Army with a "crazy"
theatrical performance; he was out of a job; the police were closing in on
him; and death was at his doorstep. The police advised him to leave town
and in 1946 he returned to Boston.

Malcolm had become part of an environment that brutalized his
sensibilities and stultified his vision of tomorrow. He was living for that

instant "high" under a canopy of suspended tension and terror. In Boston, he organized a small burglary gang, but they were caught. In February 1946 (not yet twenty-one years old), Malcolm was sent to prison and received eight to ten years on three counts to run concurrently. George Jackson, in reference to his own, similar experiences, stated,

> Black men born in the U.S. and fortunate enough to live past the age of eighteen are conditioned to accept the inevitability of prison. For most of us it simply looms as the next phase in a sequence of humiliations. Being born a slave in a captive society and never experiencing any objective basis for expectation had the effect of preparing me for the progressively traumatic misfortunes that lead so many black men to the prison gate. I was prepared for prison. It only required minor psychic adjustments. [13]

It was in prison that Malcolm entered another decisive phase in his life. His first response was an utter dislike for being caged and soon he was nicknamed "Satan." He maintained,

> Any person who claims to have a deep feeling for other human beings should think a long, long time before he votes to have other men kept behind bars—caged—not saying that there shouldn't be prisons, but there shouldn't be bars. Behind bars a man never reforms. He will never forget. [14]

It was in the Charleston State Prison in Massachusetts that Malcolm first met Bimbi, a jail-house philosopher. Bimbi recruited Malcolm by encouraging him to study. He suggested that he should take advantage of the prison correspondence courses and the library. Malcolm began by taking courses in English and Latin. In 1948, Malcolm was transferred to Concord Prison facility, where his brother Philbert first wrote him about the Nation of Islam and the Honorable Elijah Muhammad. He encouraged Malcolm to stop smoking and eating pork. Malcolm complied with great discipline. Philbert referred him to Islamic teachings, "If you take one step towards Allah, Allah will take two steps towards you."[15] In an attempt to correspond with his brother, Malcolm realized that his writing skills and penmanship were poor. He attacked it systematically by studying the dictionary and writing in a ledger daily.

Malcolm became a hermit in Norfolk Prison Colony, as he organized a program of study and began debating with other inmates. He recognized that knowledge increases freedom.

> I was either reading in the library or on my bunk. You wouldn't have gotten me out of books with a wedge....months passed without even thinking of prison....in fact, up to then, I had never been so truly free in my life. I took special pains to hunt in the library for books that would inform me on the details of black history. [16]

Malcolm read Dr. W.E.B. DuBois, Dr. Carter Woodson, J.A. Rogers, Gregor Mendel, H.G. Wells, Frederick Olmstead, Arnold Tonybee, Herodotus, Schopenhauer, Kant, Hegel, Neitzche, Spinoza, Dr. Leakey, Mahatma Ghandi, Pierre Van Passen, Homer, Shakespeare, Francis Bacon, Milton etc. He studied history, philosophy, religion, linguistics, and literature. He said later,

> I have often reflected upon the new vistas that reading opened to me. I knew right there in prison that reading had changed forever the course of my life. As I see it today, the ability to read awoke inside me some long dormant craving to be mentally alive. I certainly wasn't seeking any degree, the way a college confers a status symbol upon its students. My homemade education gave me with every additional book that I read, a little bit more sensitivity to the deafness, dumbness and blindness that was afflicting the Black race in America....When I discovered philosophy, I tried to touch both occidental and oriental. The oriental philosophers were the ones I came to prefer. [17]

Malcolm was on the road to developing a critical consciousness which would not only provide him with new insights into reality but would urge him to organize and educate the masses. After reading Pierre Van Passen's *Days of Our Years,* Malcolm said "it was right there in prison that I made up my mind to devote the rest of my life to telling the white man about himself—or die."[18] Malcolm had gone a long way from Detroit Red, drawing ever closer to his new mission. Similarly, George

Jackson reflects on the nature of developing critical consciousness in the prison situation:

> Believe me my friend, with the time and incentive that these brothers have to read, study and think, you will find no class or category more aware, more embittered, desperate, or dedicated to the ultimate remedy —revolution. The most dedicated, the best of our kind—you'll find them in the Folsoms, the San Quentins and Soledads. They lived like there was no tomorrow. And for most of them there isn't. Somewhere along the line they have sensed this. Life on the installment plan, three years of prison, three months of parole; then back to start all over again, sometimes in the same cell....The holds are being fast broken. Men who read Marx, Lenin, Fanon, Mao, Giap and Che don't riot, they mass, they rage, they dig graves.[19]

In 1951, Malcolm was sent back to the Charleston State Prison because the officials at Norfolk Prison Colony had become upset with his correspondence, his position on Islam and his intellectual development. In Charleston prison, he attended Bible classes taught by a seminary student from Harvard University. Malcolm used this class to challenge the teachings of Christianity and to pull the brothers' coats to the Honorable Elijah Muhammad.

In August 1952, Malcolm was (at twenty seven years old) paroled from prison. On returning briefly to Boston his sister, Hilda, gave him some money with which he bought a new pair of eyeglasses, a suitcase and a watch. These three items would become important to his future life. The eyeglasses would help to correct the astigmatism that he had developed from reading extensively in prison under poor lighting conditions; the suitcase would be used in his extensive travels; and the watch would be important to his busy appointment schedule because he had become "very time conscious and very punctual." Malcolm left Boston for Detroit, where he was welcomed in his brother Wilfred's home. The orderliness, organization, warmth and spirituality of this home allowed Malcolm to make an easy transition into the Muslim world.

Malcolm got a job at a furniture store, where his brother Wilfred worked, and then later at Ford Motor Company's Lincoln-Mercury

Division. He attended meetings at the relatively small Detroit Temple Number One, under Minister Lemuel Hassan. On the Sunday before Labor Day in 1952, Malcolm went to Chicago with a small car caravan of Detroit Muslims to hear and see the Honorable Elijah Muhammad for the first time. It was a mementous occasion and quite inspiring for Malcolm when Mr. Muhammad asked him to stand and tell the small gathering "how strong I had been while in prison."

Later, in a discussion with the Messenger about the expansion of the Nation of Islam, Mr. Muhammad advised Malcolm "to go after young people. Once you get them the older people will follow through shame."[20] Malcolm followed this advice, and he began "fishing" in the streets of Detroit with the Temple's Minister, Lemuel Hassan. Within a few months of plugging away, Temple Number One tripled its membership. Malcolm was deeply impressed when Mr. Muhammad paid the Temple a personal visit. During this time, Malcolm received his "X," which replaced the white slave master's name of "Little" and he now entered another phase of his life. In summer 1953, he was named Assistant Minister to Detroit's Temple Number One.

Malcolm studied very hard under the guidance of Mr. Muhammad, and on one occasion he lived at the Messenger's home in Chicago, where he was trained to be a Minister. Later, he was sent to Boston and Philadelphia to assist in the organization of temples in those cities. He was a disciplined organizer and he preached with a fierce intensity. After measuring up to his responsibilities, Malcolm X was appointed by the Honorable Elijah Muhammad to be the Minister of Temple Number Seven (in New York City) in June 1954. Malcolm humbly reflected "I can't describe for you my welter of emotions." He was returning to Harlem a new man with a mission that would transform him, the Nation of Islam, the Black world and the American nation state.

On arriving in New York, Minister Malcolm X took to the streets to check the scene and look for familiar faces. The structures of decay were still there: drugs, alcohol, prostitution, pimping, hustling, dilapidated housing and severe unemployment were very evident. The national economy was entering a recession and Harlem was hit hard. It was the post Korean war blues. Malcolm knew the turf and he had faith in the people. He was confident that he could take the message to them, even if it took some time for them to wake up. He had understood earlier the social history of Harlem and he was determined to work hard at organizing a new Temple, which he opened as a storefront. Very few people had heard of the Muslims in 1954. Yet ten years later, only would the Nation of Islam grow immensely, but Minister Malcolm X would become a household name throughout the Harlems of America.

Malcolm began "fishing" on the streets of Harlem, on the fringes of nationalist meetings and around the small storefront Christian churches. He tailored his teachings for those whom he attracted. He stated "I had learned early one important thing, and that was to always teach in terms that people would understand." He would pass out leaflets among the people informing them about meetings at Temple Number Seven. He would pull their coats saying "Come to hear us brother, sister... you haven't heard anything until you have heard the teachings of the Honorable Elijah Muhammad."[21] He helped to organize new temples in Springfield and Hartford. He visited Philadelphia and Boston regularly. He was back on his old railroad run, except this time he had a different sense of purpose, a different mission. He was actively helping the Messenger to build the Nation of Islam.

By 1956, the Nation of Islam had grown sizeably. Malcolm worked hard, for he was dedicated to the cause and teachings of Mr. Muhammad. Every night at Temple Number Seven, there were special classes for the Fruit of Islam, Unity Night, Muslim Girls Training Night and on Friday nights General Civilization Study sessions. On Sundays, services were held in the early afternoons.

On January 14, 1958, Malcolm married sister Betty Shabazz, a teacher and nurse at Temple Number Seven and who lectured to the women's classes on health affairs. In 1959, Malcolm started the newspaper *Muhammad Speaks* – which, subsequently, moved to Chicago, where it became one of the most influential newspapers in the Black community during the sixties. New temples were being built all around the country and it was obvious that the Muslims had developed a strong base in urban America. Mr. Muhammad sent Minister Malcolm X on his first trip to Africa and the Middle East, where he visited Ghana, Nigeria, Sudan, Egypt and Saudi Arabia.

> Anyway, national publicity was in the offing for the Nation of Islam, when Mr. Muhammad sent me on a three week trip to Africa. Even as small as we then were, some of the African and Asian personages had sent Mr. Muhammad private word that they liked his efforts to awaken and lift up American Black people. Sometimes the message had been sent through me. As Mr. Muhammad's emissary in 1959, I went to Egypt, Arabia, to the Sudan, Nigeria and Ghana.

Malcolm had become a national and international spokesman for the Honorable Elijah Muhammad. This was the period of Africa's surge for independence with Nkrumah, Nasser, Kenyatta, Lumumba, Ben Bella and others at the forefront of the anti-colonial struggle. Dr. Martin Luther King Jr., Congressman Adam Clayton Powell, Jr., Dr. W.E.B. Dubois, George Padmore and others were in Ghana in 1959 attending the All African People's Congress at the invitation of President Kwame Nkrumah.

During late 1959, Mike Wallace produced a television show entitled "The Hate That Hate Produced." It was a documentary on the Nation of Islam, and when it was aired, it shocked the entire country. By 1960, C. Eric Lincoln had completed his book *Black Muslims in America*, which he started in 1957. Soon newspaper articles began to respond to this sleeping giant in urban America and journalists labelled them "Black segregationists," "Black supremacists," "Black racists" and "Black fascists," who were preaching hatred of white people.

Mainstream Black leaders responded immediately with their outrage, calling the Nation of Islam an "irresponsible cult... and unfortunate image, just when the racial picture has been improving."[22] However, no sooner had they attacked the Muslims and referred to progress in race relations, when, on February 2, 1960, North Carolina A&T students "sat in" at the Woolworth lunch counter in Greensboro demanding to be served and signalling a new level of resistance against racial segregation. The Black student movement ushered in a new decade with sit-ins, wade-ins, freedom rides, freedom marches, and voter registration drives. The South was a battlefield of confrontation as young and old people challenged the morality of the existing order, demanding their democratic rights and insisting that the federal government offer optimum protection for the dispensation of those rights. Dr. Martin Luther King Jr. provided one dimension of leadership of this mass movement in the South. Malcolm X, as a national spokesman for Mr. Muhammad, attacked the problem head on from another wing of the movement — especially in the urban North and Midwest, where he had built a strong base. Malcolm challenged the ethical principles on which the country had been founded and denounced its historic compromises. He tore at its social fabric, criticizing sharply its leadership, its hypocrisy, and its unjust social order. He asserted the rights of all citizens to freedom, justice and equality and he championed the call for independence against colonial domination in Africa, Asia and the Caribbean.

Later, the *New York Times* reported that a meeting of Negro intellectuals had agreed that Dr. Martin Luther King Jr. could secure the allegiance of the middle and upper classes of Blacks, but Malcolm X alone could secure the allegiances of the Blacks at the bottom. The *Times* reporter stated:

> The Negroes respect Dr. King and Malcolm because they sense in these men absolute integrity and know they will never sell them out. Malcolm X cannot be corrupted and the Negroes know this and therefore respect him. They also know that he comes from the lower depths as they do and regard him as one of their own. Malcolm X is going to play a formidable role because the racial struggle has now shifted to the urban North.... If Dr. King is convinced that he has sacrificed ten years of brilliant leadership, he will be forced to revise his concepts. There is only one direction which he can move, and that is in the direction of Malcolm X. [23]

As Malcolm became more prominent on the lecture circuit, he demonstrated that he was not only extremely articulate, but also that he was a lively debater who mixed humor and sarcasm with historical analysis. His violent attacks on the white press, as well as the establishment Black leadership, unnerved many debaters but endeared him to the Black urban masses who felt that Malcolm was "their man." As his stature and prestige increased among the Harlemites, Malcolm continued "fishing" among the drug addicts, the unemployed, the miseducated—in short, the lumpen class. He encouraged many addicts to kick the habit and clean themselves up. He attacked their bad health and eating habits by suggesting Mr. Muhammad's *How To Eat To Live,* which condemned eating pork, drinking alcohol, and smoking cigarettes. His scathing denunciations of the American system of justice brought cheering crowds to their feet at Muslim rallies. Malcolm's confrontation with Harlem police, when Mr. Johnson Hinton was brutally beaten by two white policemen in front of Temple Number Seven, compelled the Deputy Chief Inspector of the 28th Precinct to say "No one man should have that much power."[24] The discipline and combativeness of the Fruit of Islam endeared the Muslims to the Harlem masses.

By 1961, *Life, Look, Newsweek, Time, Playboy, Reader's Digest* and several national newspapers were writing articles on the Nation of Islam. Malcolm would generally introduce himself on radio and television shows with the statement, "I represent The Honorable Elijah Muhammad, the spiritual head of the fastest growing group of Muslims in the Western Hemisphere."[25] With his charismatic personality and articulate posture, he would criticize integration as a smoke screen and a false agenda. He argued:

> Human rights. Respect as human beings. That's what America's Black masses want. That's the problem—social and economic injustice. Give the Black man everything he deserves. They want to live in an open, free society, where they can walk with their heads up, like men and women. Not to be walled up in slums, in the ghettoes like animals.[26]

He would then move on to demonstrate that racism was systematic to the character of American life and to repudiate the intellectual, moral and political leadership of the country. He argued that Western society had become bankrupt, overrun with immorality and was deteriorating from its internal contradictions. He maintained,

> The Western world's most learned diplomats have failed to solve this grave race problem. Her learned legal experts have failed. Her sociologists have failed. Her civil leaders have failed. Her fraternal leaders have failed. Since all of them have failed to solve this race problem, it is time for us to sit down and reason. I am certain that we will be forced to agree it takes God Himself to solve this grave racial problem.[27]

Between 1960 and 1964, Minister Malcolm X had become an anathema to America's conscience. He rejected the non-violence of Dr. Martin Luther King Jr., the hypocrisy of integration and the vision of the 1954 Supreme Court decision. He attacked the March on Washington, the leadership of Presidents Kennedy and Johnson, American intervention in Vietnam and neocolonialism in Africa. He predicted the urban rebellions of the sixties, the alienation of Black urban youth, and the revitalization of Black pride through cultural nationalism. He saw culture "as one indispensable weapon in the freedom struggle. We must take hold of it and forge the future with the past." His speeches, "Message to the Grass Roots" (November, 1963) and "The Ballot or the Bullet" (April, 1964), challenged the national political agenda.

Malcolm argued for a program of self-reliance and self-development in the Black community. He felt that Black people should build an internal economic base, take the question of education of our youth seriously, demand political accountability from Black elected officials, and embark on a program of moral revitalization. He stated,

> The American black man should be focusing his every effort toward building his own business, and decent homes for himself. One thing the white man can never give the black man is self-respect! The black man never can become independent and recognized as a human being who is truly equal with other human beings until he has what they have, and until he is doing for himself what others are doing for themselves. The black man in the ghettoes, for instance, has to start

self-correcting his own material, moral and spiritual defects and evils. The black man needs to start his own program to get rid of drunkenness, drug addiction and prostitution. The black man in America has to lift up his own sense of values.[28]

Malcolm believed that the Black man had the political strength and power to change his destiny overnight. However, there was a need for daring leadership, community strength and disciplined political organizing. He argued for an independent political leadership not tied to any of the major political parties, not wedded to the myth of integration, and having an economic base in the Black community, rather than being dependent on white philanthropic sources. He suggested, for example, that an independent Black lobby be built in Washington, D.C. in order to accrue political power. (Instead, there has developed a Black Congressional Caucus, which is tied by its navel string to the Democratic party and its token patronage. It has had minimal impact on governmental processes and appropriations.)

In the Johnson-Goldwater campaign of 1964, Malcolm stated clearly,

> I wouldn't have put myself in the position of voting for either candidate for the Presidency or of recommending to any Black man to do.... Don't register and vote. Register. That's intelligent. Don't register and vote for a dummy, you can vote for a crook, you can vote for another who'd want to exploit you. "Register" means being in a position to take political action anytime, anyplace, and in any manner that would be beneficial to you and me; being in a position to take advantage of our position. But as soon as you get registered and you want to be a Republican or Democrat, you are aligning. And once you are aligned, you have no bargaining power—none whatsoever. [29]

Where would Malcolm have stood on the Presidential elections of the 1980's and 1990's? Would he have supported any of the major presidential candidates? Would he have offered us "the lesser of two evils" argument?

When President John F. Kennedy was assassinated on November 22, 1963, Mr. Muhammad issued an order to all of his ministers that they should make no remarks on this tragedy. He instructed that if pressed for comments, they should say, "No Comment."[30] Shortly after these events, Malcolm spoke at the Manhattan Center in New York, and when asked for his opinion on President Kennedy's assassination, he said, "It was a case of the chickens coming home to roost." Mr. Muhammad summoned Malcolm immediately and questioned both his poor judgment and lack of discipline.

> That was a very bad statement. The country loved this man. The whole country is in mourning. That was very ill-timed. A statement like that can make it very hard on the Muslims in general. I'll have to silence you for the next ninety days so that the Muslims everywhere can be disassociated from the blunder.[31]

Malcolm agreed with the decision of Mr. Muhammad and recognized later that it meant not only was he banned from speaking in public or to the press, but that he couldn't teach in Temple Number Seven.

Soon rumors began to spread throughout the Black community and the Nation of Islam that the problems between Mr. Muhammad and Malcolm had deepened. Malcolm felt pressured and turned to Betty,

> The only person who knew was my wife. I never would have dreamed that I would ever depend so much upon any woman for strength as I now leaned upon Betty. There was no exchange between us; Betty said nothing, being the caliber of wife that she is, with the depth of understanding that she has—but I could feel the envelopment of her comfort. I knew that she was as faithful a servant of Allah as I was, and I knew that whatever happened, she was with me. [32]

Events precipitated the rift and it soon became obvious that Malcolm had to function outside the Nation of Islam and to rely on his international image. Malcolm called a press conference in New York on March 2, 1964 and announced,

> I am going to organize and head a new mosque in New York City known as the Muslim Mosque, Inc. This will give us a religious base and the spiritual force necessary to rid our people of the vices that

destroy the moral fiber of our community. Muslim Mosque Inc. will
have its temporary headquarters in the Hotel Theresa in Harlem. It
will be the working base for an action program designed to eliminate
the political oppression, the economic exploitation and the social
degradation suffered daily by twenty-two million Afro-Americans.[33]

Malcolm once again turned to his sister Ella and asked her to finance his
pilgrimage to Mecca. She agreed. Malcolm wrote of his sister,

> I couldn't get over what she had done.... She deals in real estate, and
> she was saving up to make the pilgrimage. She told me there was no
> question about it; it was more important that I go.... She had played
> a significant role in my life.... I had brought Ella into Islam, and now
> she was financing me to Mecca.[34]

Malcolm began to study orthodox Islamic teachings seriously and,
with the approval of Dr. Youssef Shawarbi, he was given letter of
introduction — which would clear the way for him to make the Hajj, a
religious obligation. This pilgrimage in April 1964 would bring Malcolm
to the final chapter in his brief life because in Mecca he would genuinely
feel the spiritual force of "The Oneness of Man under One God." The trip
to Cairo and Jedda prepared him for the illuminating experiences in
Mecca. Malcolm wrote,

> Never have I witnessed such sincere hospitality and the overwhelming
> spirit of true brotherhood as is practiced by peoples of all colors and
> races here in this Ancient Holy Land, the home of Abraham,
> Muhammad and all the other prophets of the Holy Scriptures. For the
> past week, I have been utterly speechless and spellbound by the
> graciousness I see displayed all around me by people of all colors.

> I have been blessed to visit the Holy City of Mecca. I have made my
> seven circuits around the Ka'ba led by a young Mutawaf named
> Muhammad. I drank water from the well of Zem Zem. I ran seven
> times back and forth between the hills of Mt. Al-Safa and Al-Marwah.
> I have prayed in the ancient city of Nina, and I have prayed on Mt.
> Arafat.[35]

The spiritual transformation was now pushing Malcolm to new conclusions on the brotherhood of man, in the search for truth and definition. It forced him to rethink many of his ideas and earlier conclusions. However, he maintained,

> This was not too difficult for me. Despite my firm convictions, I have always been a man who tries to face facts, and to accept the reality of life as new experience and knowledge unfolds it. I have always kept an open mind, which is necessary to the flexibility that must go hand in hand with every form of intelligent search for truth.[36]

After his pilgrimage to Mecca, Malcolm became an official guest of the state and he was invited to meet with His Excellency Prince Faisal of Saudi Arabia. He was deeply honored and moved: "never have I been made to feel more humble and unworthy." Malcolm also met with the grand Mufti of Jerusalem, Hussein Amini, who expressed a great interest in his work. From Jedda, he went to Beirut, Lebanon, where he spoke at the University, then back to Cairo and Alexandria in Egypt and then on to Lagos, Nigeria and Accra, Ghana.

It was in Nigeria and Ghana that Malcolm was warmly received by young students, Pan-African nationalists, American expatriots, ambassadors of Third World countries, and national politicians. At Ibadan University in Nigeria, they gave him a Yoruba name, Omowale, meaning the "one who has come home."[37] In Ghana, he addressed the members of Parliament and had a personal audience with Dr. Kwame Nkrumah. Malcolm stated "we agreed that Pan-Africanism was the key also to the problems of those of African heritage."[38] The African-American expatriots in Ghana had organized an impressive schedule for Malcolm, which included lectures at the University of Ghana and the Kwame Nkrumah Ideological Institute at Winneba, meetings and luncheons with the Ambassadors from Algeria, Cuba, China and the Nigerian High Commissioner, and an unforgettable luncheon at the home of Ms. Shirley Graham DuBois.[39]

Everywhere Malcolm went on this trip, the response to his presence was electrifying. It was obvious that he had gained world stature, but more important that he had been highly respected both in the Middle East and Africa. The United States Information Agency attempted to discredit his prestige and diffuse the impact of his visit. From Ghana, Malcolm went to Liberia then to Senegal and on to Algeria before he finally returned to New York on May 20, 1964. Immediately upon his return, Malcolm began to argue that Blacks should take their case "before the United Nations on a formal accusation of denial of human rights." He also brought messages of brotherhood and support from Africa stating,

> My pilgrimage broadened my scope. It blessed me with new insight. In two weeks in the Holy Land, I saw what I had never seen in thirty-nine years in America. I saw all races, all colors—in true brotherhood! in Unity! Living as one! Worshipping as one!

> In my thirty-nine years on this earth, the Holy City of Meca had been the first time that I had ever stood before the Creator of All and felt like a complete human being. [40]

Malcolm X – who had now become El-Hajj Malik El-Shabazz – had radically altered his whole outlook on brotherhood and he was compelled to fuse his spiritual ideal with his political activism. How do you fuse orthodox Islam and Pan-Africanism in an organizational reality without profound complexities and contradictions? Dr. Martin Luther King Jr. was never faced with this dilemma and, therefore, he could continue to challenge the moral fabric of the American society under the Southern Christian leadership Conference banner and the Civil Rights movement. El-Hajj Malik, on the other hand, had to find a place in the sun on the national political scene, while building an oganizational format to sustain his ideas. His task for the next nine months would be enormous. The Arab world would be looking closely at this orthodoxy in order to see if he would be useful to their design in the West (through Nasser's plan of five concentric circles and Prince Faisal's vision of the future). The U.S. government would be monitering his influence on the explosive situation in Northern urban centers and, more importantly, the impact of his linkages with Africa and the Caribbean. The Nation of Islam, which had seen him as a traitor to Mr. Muhammad's ideas and work, would be checking his every move to understand its impact on their growth and development. (Any war between these rival groups could be detrimental to the future.) The Communists, Trotskyites and Socialists were searching for any wedges in his concept of international brotherhood that might push him (the orthodox Muslim preacher and Pan-African Nationalist) closer to proletarian struggle, thereby, providing them with a mass leader whose charisma could project their ideas. And finally, Blacks —artists, intellectuals and nationalists—who had grown disenchanted with the hypocrisy of bourgeois liberals were hoping that he would become the moral center for a new leadership that would not only articulate their deepest aspirations but would give them a sense of being and purpose.

El-Hajj Malik El Shabazz standing alone on 125th Street and Lennox Avenue in Harlem, was both beloved and feared because in his person there were many possibilities. He was dangerous to the respective constituencies because each one had a stake in his present and his future. Moreover, the contradictions were so immense that wherever he turned he would undoubtedly alienate one or more of these interests. He was trapped by the logic of events. He did not have much space. He began a dance of death, certain of his uncertainty. He was clear that he had not only come full circle, but that he had been to the mountaintop. He launched into this new phase with a sense of urgency because he knew that he had to build an organization, deepen the links which he had already forged internationally and provide the world with a document of his journey.

He established the Organization of Afro-American Unity, which was independent from Muslim Mosque Inc. It would become the political instrument through which he had hoped to function in the Civil Rights struggle and on the international scene. He stated,

> My new organization is a non-religious and non-sectarian group organized to unite Afro-Americans for a constuctive program toward the attainment of human rights. I am going to join the fight, whenever Negroes ask for my help. Anyone who wants to follow me and my movement has got to be ready to go to jail, to the hospital and to the cemetary before he can be truly free. Brother, do you realize that some

of history's greatest leaders never were recognized until they were safely in the ground.[41]

He outlined the OAAU's charter and program, which he presented before a Harlem audience in June 1964; he drew up the petition to the United Nations charging genocide against twenty-two million Black Americans; he made a major speech on July 17, 1964, and he presented a press statement to the Second African Summit Conference on behalf of the Organization of Afro-American Unity. On his second trip abroad in 1964, he spent eighteen weeks in the Middle East and Africa. He wrote,

> The world leaders with whom I had private audiences this time included President Gamal Abdel Nasser of Egypt, President Julius K. Nyerere of Tanzania, President Nnamdi Azikiwe of Nigeria, Osagyefo Dr. Kwame Nkrumah of Ghana, President Sekou Toure of Guinea, President Jomo Kenyatta of Kenya and Prime Minister Dr. Milton Obote of Uganda. I also met with religious leaders African, Arab, Asian and non-Muslim. And in all of these countries, I talked with Afro-Americans and whites of many professions and backgrounds.[42]

Toward the end of 1964, El-Hajj Malik El-Shabazz began to work with a great deal of frenzy, sensing that he knew he was living on borrowed time. He worked very closely with Alex Haley to finish his autobiography, reading the galleys and making minor changes. He stated,

> I have given to this book so much of whatever time I have because I feel and I hope that if I honestly and fully tell my life's acount, read objectively it might prove to be a testimony of some social value.[43]

He knew that time was running out and he never expected to live long enough to read the book in its finished form. In January and February 1965, he was moving around the country trying to fulfill speaking engagements and project his organization. In January, he flew to Canada for a television interview, and in February he went to England to speak at the Oxford Union, the London School of Economics and he was interviewed for the British Broadcasting Corporation. On this trip, he was also invited by the Congress of African Students to speak in Paris, but he was stopped at the airport and President De Gaulle barred him from entering France. He returned to New York on Saturday, February 13, 1965 and early that Sunday morning at about 3:00 a.m, his house in Elmhurst, Queens, was fire bombed. He rescued his four daughters and pregnant wife. Half the house was destroyed. He had no fire insurance. Betty and the children stayed with friends, while he caught a plane to Detroit where he had a speaking engagement. Later that day he told a friend, "I have been marked for death in the next five days." The doors were closing in on El-Hajj Malik. On February 19, 1965, he telephoned Alex Haley and admitted "my nerves are shot, my brain is tired."[44]

On Sunday, February 21, 1965 El-Hajj Malik El-Shabazz went to the Audubon Ballroom in Harlem for an Organization of Afro-American Unity rally. He called his wife Betty Shabazz earlier that morning and asked her to bring the children to the two o'clock meeting. He was tense, sensing that his time had come. He was introduced by Brother Benjamin X, one of his closest followers. "Asalaikum, brothers and sisters." There was a disturbance in the back of the hall. Everyone was distracted momentarily. El Hajj Malik said "Hold it! hold it! Don't get excited. Let's cool it, brothers,"[45] then, suddenly, three gunmen stood up and shot him at point blank range. He was shot in his chest and face. As his hands flew up, the middle finger of his left hand was shattered by a bullet and blood gushed from his goatee. His wife, Betty Shabazz, who had thrown her body over her children when the shooting first started, cried out "My husband! They are killing my husband!" One woman who was seated near the front said,

> The commotion back there diverted me just for an instant, then I turned back to look at Malcolm X just in time to see at least three men in the front row stand and take aim and start firing simultaneously. It looked like a firing squad.[46]

The drama had ended. El-Hajj Malik El-Shabazz had been assassinated before his pregnant wife and four daughters, among Black people in Harlem. The journey to El-Hajj Malik El-Shabazz from Malcolm X from Detroit Red from Malcolm Little reached its end. The news flashed throughout Harlem, the nation and the world. Time froze for an instant on that cold winter afternoon.

After Malcolm died, President Nasser and Prince Faisal died suddenly and mysteriously also; Dr. Kwame Nkrumah and Dr. Milton Obote were overthrown in their respective governments; Dr. Martin Luther King and George Jackson were assassinated; Mr. Whitney Young died in Nigeria and Ms. Shirley Graham DuBois in China. The list of fallen warriors has grown even longer as the African world lost Eduardo Mondlane, Amilcar Cabral, Steven Biko, David Sibeko, Walter Rodney, Maurice Bishop, Jonathan Jackson, L.D. Barclay, Jesse Lang, Ralph Featherstone, Fred Hampton, Bunchy Carter and Lil' Bobby Hutton.

Malcolm's death represented the silencing of one of the most important critics of American society in modern times. He came from among the ranks of the dispossessed. He was one of those men whom George Jackson referred to as "having crawled back from the grave." He was a heroic fighter who dared to live. Ossie Davis in his eulogy said

> Malcolm was our manhood, our living Black manhood. This was his meaning to his people. And in honoring him, we honor the best in ourselves.... And we will know him then for what he was and is—a Prince....our own Black Prince—who didn't hesitate to die because he loved us so. [47]

NOTES

1. George Jackson, *Soledad Brother: The Prison Letters of George Jackson*, pp. 9-10.

2. *Autobiography of Malcolm X* (New York: Grove Press, Inc., 1964) p. 2.

3. Ibid., p. 6.

4. *Malcolm X Speaks*, 2nd ed. (New York: Path Press, 1989) p. 75.

5. *Autobiography of Malcolm X*, p. 22.

6. Ibid., p. 21.

7. Ibid., p. 38.

8. Ibid., p. 68.

9. Frantz Fanon, *Black Skin White Mask*, translated by Charles Markmann (New York: Grove Weidenfeld, 1989) p. 73.

10. *Autobiography of Malcolm X*, p. 93.

11. Ibid., pp. 73-74.

12. Ibid., p. 70.

13. Jackson, Op. Cit. p. 9.

14. *The Autobiography of Malcolm X*, p. 152.

15. Ibid., p.156.

16. Ibid., p.173.

17. Ibid., p. 179.

18. Ibid., p. 184.

19. Jackson, Op. Cit, p.31.

20. *Autobiography of Malcolm X*, p. 198.

21. Ibid., p.125.

22. Ibid., p. 240.

23. Ibid., pp. 417-418.

24. Ibid., p. 309.

25. Ibid., p. 282.

26. Ibid., p.272.

27. Ibid., p. 273.

28. Ibid., p. 275.

29. *Malcolm X Speaks*, p. 43.

30. *Autobiography of Malcolm X*, p. 300.
31. Ibid., p. 301.
32. Ibid., p. 305.
33. Ibid., p. 305.
34. Ibid., p. 319.
35. Ibid., p.339.
36. Ibid., p. 340.
37. Ibid., p.351.
38. Ibid., p. 357.
39. Ibid., p. 359.
40. Ibid., p. 362.
41. Ibid., p. 368.
42. Ibid., p. 370.
43. Ibid., p. 378.
44. Ibid., p. 418.
45. Ibid., p. 434.
46. Ibid., p. 435.
47. Ibid., p. 454.

PART TWO

ART AND RESISTANCE

II. ART AND RESISTANCE

INTRODUCTION

I have always been close to the work of the National Conference of Artists as a result of my on-going interest in the Black creative process. I am a collector and a cultural worker. I have mounted exhibitions of Black artists in the United States, the Caribbean, and Latin America. For a long time, I have believed it is essential that we address issues critical to Black culture in the Carribean and North and South America.

The African influence on visual art in the Western Hemisphere has been very significant since the pre-Columbian period. Archeologist, anthropologists and art historians have documented these influences in terms of images, mathematical coefficients and astrological similarities. Dr. Ivan Van Sertima, in his book, *They Came Before Columbus*, discussed icons, mythical images, religious totems, discursive references and mathematical formulations of ancient Africa which have correspondent references in pre-Columbian culture.

Since the Middle Passage, Africans in the New World have preserved their gods and their orishas, which have influenced cultural modalities in music, dance and the visual arts. One must always remember that the slave ships carried on board not only Black women, men and children, but also their gods, beliefs and folklore. It was this baggage, unlisted in the slave ships' logs, that was to constitute the radical difference of the Black presence in the New World. From the horrors of the Middle Passage to the spiritual joy of sharing their creative sensibilities, Black artists have had the courage and the tenacity to relay their objective reality in many aesthetic languages. The language of the visual artist is but one dimension of that rich mosaic of communication. The music, poetry, dance, humor, religion, rhetoric and revolt have made richer the panorama of the Americas by constantly refurbishing its ethos. On the contemporary scene, the works of Jeff Donaldson, Nelson Stevens, Wilfredo Lam, Emanuel Araujo, Pedro Alcantara, Simon Gouverneur and Le Roi Clarke have been enriched by their serious research on African retentions in the Americas and a careful study of African cosmology.

However, I would like to isolate a specific work I observed at the NCA in Brazil, which I found to be very interesting. It was a huge figure, about 15 feet tall and 8 feet wide of a nude Black Christ, with the symbol of Shango in his right hand and in a capoeira fighting stance. When I was in Colombia about fifteen years ago, there was a great deal of controversy in Bogota over the work of a Black Panamanian artist. It was a daring and stunning peace of sculpture. This Panamanian artist created a nude Black Jesus of nearly the same dimensions as the Brazilians', except the Black Christ was hanging from an imaginary cross in a posture of absolute defiance. It was not only a rejection of slavery and lynching, but it was a refusal to die. The artist gave the work to a radical Colombian Roman Catholic priest, who had been closely associated with Camillo Torres, and who was working in the poor barrios. The priest placed this work of art directly over the altar. Art critics, historians and artists themselves praised the work from an aesthetic point of view, arguing that it was a new expression in Latin American art. Thousands of people came from all over the country to see this nude Black Jesus and in the church, the rich and the poor, the educated and the illiterate, rubbed shoulders as the work sent shock waves throughout the culture. Lively debates ensued, so the Church's hierarchy met and declared the work to be blasphemous. The priest was compelled to take it out of the church. He complied with the Cardinal and archbishop and put the work in the streets where the ordinary people live. The Black Christ was now "at home" and over the years, millions of people have visited the work for one reason or another.

When I saw the piece by the Bahian artist at the museum, it struck an important chord. It is obvious that the connections and convergences are vital to our creative work. Ed Love's totemic sculptors also created the same type of controversy in Washington D.C. It is like Steel Pulse's line "Give I back I witch doctor." That is very difficult in a Christian world, and these retentions challenge the very ground of our being. It is Billie Holiday's *Strange Fruit.*

Art for us is a dimension of life. Art is realistic rather than formalistic; art is not simply an intellectual or egotistical exercise. In 1940, Dr. Alaine Locke made the following critical appraisal of Black art,

> More and more a sober realism is to be noted which goes beyond the mere superficial picturesqueness of the Negro color, form and feature and a penetrating social vision goes deeper than the surface....Much of our contemporary art is rightly an art of social analysis and criticism, touching the vital problems of religion, labor, housing, lynching, unemployment, social reconstruction and the like, for today's beauty cannot afford to be surely pretty with sentiment and local color; it must be solid and instructive with an enlightening truth.

Duke Ellington was also particularly proud of his sources of inspiration. His work is grounded in realism. He stated emphatically,

> My men and my race are the inspiration of my work. I try to catch the character and mood and feeling of my people. The music of my race is something more than an American idiom. It is the result of our transplantation to American soil from Africa, and it was our reaction in plantation days to the life we live. What we could not say openly, we expressed in music. The characteristic melancholic music of my race have been forged from the very white heat of our sorrow and from our gropings.

Whatever we are talking about as a people will be reflected in the work of the artist. If we are about resistance, it will show up in the work of Ed Love, Elizabeth Catlett or Pedro Alcantara. If we are about research and cultural investigation, it will show up in Lois Mallou Jones, Jeff Donaldson and Simon Gouverneur. If we are about the examination of popular expressions of the sixties and seventies, it will show up in the work of Africoba. Our art depicts our strength and will to survive as a people in the New World. It reflects our determination to be dignified and to give definition to the American cultural ethos consistent with our finest sensibilities and warmth. It is a statement of the complexities of the Black experience with all its nuances and qualitative uneveness. Art highlights the magic, mystery and mysticism of the spiritual universe. It is the embodiment of our laughter and our tears, prayer, pain, pride, beauty, heroism, love and violence. It is an expression of the seriousness with which Black women and men have laid bare their souls. It is that voice within the veil speaking to those who are listening outside the veil. Yes, art is a reflection of our life. It is our statement to our gods and our ancestors as we celebrate the essence of our experience. Art, therefore, is immersed in the present, with linkages, to the past and a projection into the future about the tasks which lay ahead of us.

However, if this is understood, it cannot be forgotten that Black people in the Western Hemisphere are very weak in terms of our cultural infrastructure. We do not control our creative work, and we allow others to determine how it is packaged, marketed and critiqued. We must begin to inspire young Blacks to prepare themselves professionally and technically to manage our art work. Successful Black artists must go into high schools and universities and offer scholarships to young Blacks who would work in the entertainment industry as technocrats. Everyone cannot be an artist on the front stage or before the camera. There are many, many more who must tackle the managerial matters. Black atheletes and entertainers are controlled and cordoned off by Jews and Italians. We must confront that problem head on by encouraging young people to pursue careers and develop skills in these industries. They should learn the technical skills to manage the artists, to present their work globally and to be able to write critically about it, so that we have the professional capacity to define or explain what Max Roach, Emmanuel Araujo, Alvin Ailey or Milton Nascimento are really saying. We must become the people who will articulate the historical significance of Bob Marley or Stevie Wonder because we have studied their work seriously. All of this is very important and we must encourage young people to move in that direction, *ie.*, to be cultural historians and archivists. Black creativity continues to be ripped off by people who become millionaires like George Wein and Norman Grantz. If we could only grasp this fundamental need, and challenge our children with their future responsibilites, we would make an enormous leap into the 21st Century.

ART AND RESISTANCE

fragments of roots, scorned in the night of
self contempt....spring to rebirth... the
seed of renewal....exile paid its premium
... in self awareness...we begin to know a
message of hope and contradiction.[1]

I am concerned with our exile and our contradictions. As people of
African descent in the Western Hemisphere, we have suffered exile and
alienation, exile and hope. We have worshiped our gods in exile, while,
at the same time, we have roamed this American continent as people
without gods. My concern is to invoke gods and resistance.

We are at war. We are at war with every dimension of our cultural
experience in the Western Hemisphere and our artists have been at the
frontline of that war. There is nothing imaginary about our historical
suffering. For centuries, the dominant event of modern history has been
the slave trade. Its repercussions, racism and colonization, have been
decisive elements in the tragic destiny of African people. Colonization
and economic exploitation have remained the driving force of imperial
domination, threatening the colonized with the gravest danger to life and
health, to their culture and their faith and even to their bio-physical
equilibrium. Black people, on the African continent and in the diaspora,
have faced the challenges of economic development, cultural impotence
and spiritual perplexity. Yet, we have continued to survive with strength,
resiliency and hope, by our determined efforts to preserve our cultural
patrimony and our will to be free. Therefore, the Black artist must appear
both as witness and combatant in this historic struggle for freedom and
dignity. The artist must take sides like Pedro Alcantara (Colombia), Max
Roach (U.S.A.), Le Roi Clarke (Trinidad and Tobago), Bob Marley
(Jamaica) and Paul Robeson (U.S.A.) who wrote,

Every artist, every scientist must decide
NOW where he stands. He has no alternative.
There is no standing above the conflict on
Olympian heights. There are no impartial observers....
The challenge must be taken up. The artists
must take sides. He must elect to fight for freedom or slavery. I have
made my choice. I had no alternative. [2]

Let us be under no illusion, we live in an age in which artists must testify and articulate their commitment through work. We are bound by the dictates of history. Cultural liberation is an essential condition of political liberation. Today, every major work by a Black writer or artist must bear witness against Western racism and imperialism. And this will go on unabated until the tensions, which have thrown the world out of balance for centuries, have given place to a new order, installed by the free action of peoples of all races and cultures. Exploitation and peace can neither be coexistent nor co-terminous.

As artists and intellectuals, we continue to meet 100 years after the abolition of slavery in Brazil and 125 years after the Emancipation Proclamation. We meet to express our confusion with our gods, with our fellow man, and to pass on the reality of our present and anticipation of the future. We have not been able to end the suffering and misery of our times.

We must seriously ask whether art is relative to the ending of that condition.

The opening of the National Conference of Artists in 1988 was held at the Museum of Modern Art in Salvador, Bahia with the mounting of a joint exhibition of Afro-Brazilian and African American artists. The museum is refurbished and housed in a former sugar factory owned by a rich 19th Century white landowner and built on the backs of Black slave labor. It is located next door to some of the most depressingly painful favelas, which indicate in a microcosm the continued displacement and impoverishment of our people. Why did we gather there? There is an obvious social distance between those who come to the opening of an art exhibition as part of their cultural diet, and the lives of the people in the favelas, as they gaze at the other world in awe and despair. However, as

African Americans, we, too, recognize reciprocal contradictions. If we were to mount a joint exhibition of Brazilian and American artists at the Studio Museum in Harlem, then we would have to explain to our Brazilian friends the sordid realities of drugs, violence and social dislocation on 125th Street and 8th Avenue.

Intellectuals in our time feel themselves, more or less, confusedly at one with God, man and self. Yet, they have failed to solve the calculus of impoverishment for the masses of our people, whether on the right or the left of the ideological debate. However, even though ideas cross frontiers without a passport and art has become an instrument of cultural exchange, the Black artist still feels pressured and threatened by the manipulation of his freedom, and by the fire of criticism focused on the aesthetic. Thus, Black artists constantly shift gears, studios, locations, plantation sites and museums for a public understanding of the significance of their work. They organize gatherings and international conferences that glimpse at the similarities and differences of their creative impulses. Thus, on the cobble-stoned courtyard of the Museum of Modern Art, wealth and poverty, genius and mediocrity can mingle, shake hands, and rub shoulders with democratic self-assuredness and enigmatic smiles, which mask the dialogue among the artistic work after the HUMANOIDS have left. In the silence of the night, the works of art question their presence in that building and whether they represented our suffering, our loneliness, our historical journey, our need to revolt, and even our need to burn the building down and rise up from the ashes to create a new and just social order. The art objects raise the question, "Do those curators, who mounted the show, realize that we are in a state of permanent war, with our condition, with our benefactors, or do they simply prefer us to be objects which adorn their lives as collectors as well as being museum pieces for tourism and cultural manifestations."

The dialogue rages during the night as the works of art summon the ancestors and their gods in order to express their anger and fury. The latter refuse to evoke their anger and politeness, which exists in the courtyard and merely commandeers the spirit of resistance to a distinct historical past. Ganga Zumbi, Toussaint L'Overture, Nat Turner, David Walker,

Cudjoe The Mountain Lion, and even Martin Luther King, Malcolm X and George Jackson have become mere relics of the past. It is as if they have not been invited. Their bones are rattling in the closet, as governors, mayors, ambassadors and other political and business representatives share pleasantries and anecdotes.

As we approach the end of the 20th Century, poverty, injustice and exploitation have not be eradicated. Dr. W.E.B. DuBois' statement reigns across the globe:

> The problem of the 20th Century is the problem of the color bar. But today, I see more clearly than yesterday, that back of the problem of race and color, lies a greater problem which both observes and implements it; and that is the fact that so many civilized persons are willing to live in comfort even if the price of this is poverty, ignorance and disease of the majority of their fellowmen; that to maintain this privilege men have waged war until today war tends to become universal and continuous, and the excuse for this war continues largely to be color and race.[3]

The Black artist must accept the challenge of articulating the historical pain of that color bar. He must strive through his images to confront the widening gap between those persons who live in the favelas and those who frequent the museums. Carolina Maria de Jesus in her brilliant book, *Child of the Dark*, describes life in the favelas:

> Hard is the bread that we eat. Hard is the bed on which we sleep. Hard is the life of the favelado. I wonder if God knows the favelas exist and that the favelados are hungry? Here in the favelas almost everyone has a difficult fight to live. But, I am the only one who writes of what suffering is. I do this for the good of the others.[4]

It is true that the artist has been a witness to the life of the nation and has reproduced its essential types and senses, its manners, customs, beliefs and morals. The artist has sung its beauties, its struggles and its dramas. In essence, the artist has been a professor of the ideal, of courage. He/she is an educator of the public, a singer of hopes and dreams, in antithesis to the hardships and ugliness of the moment. One could, therefore, say that the artist vibrates the beauty of the ideal or bears witness to it by expressing it. However, the Black artist must move beyond mere description. It is now a question of transforming the world and with a real sense of urgency — each one of us working naturally within the sphere, which is proper to himself/herself. It is a question of aiding in the birth of a new order and allowing the creative continuum to be regenerated by the infusion of new ideas. It is in this sense that the artist must expand and revolutionize his palette. The artist must consciously decide to challenge, confront and destroy old social relationships of exploitation and oppression and move towards defining a new order. The maroons of Palmares, Cartagena, Jamaica, and Santiago de Cuba articulated their reason for being. Do we now consider them ancient relics of the past? Which painters are highlighting centers of resistance that are applicable to the present? Pablo Amando Fernandez writes, "it is here ...hungry and in the dark ...that I make everything new."[5]

We are the SURVIVORS according to Max Roach, and our concern as survivors must not be a stylized manifestation of historical reality. However, we must be profoundly clear about the ethic of racial integration and the vision of the assimilados – who continue to have a dependency relationship on Eurocentric ideas and values, while still representing Black people. When we glimpse at the grim drama of racial integration, are we now faced with a kind of betrayal, the most terrible form from which Negro assimilation has assumed? Frantz Fanon argues that "as slaves, we lost identity, assimilating our master's values, overwhelming us to become integrated shadows, undefined and dependent."[6] Derek Walcott extends the historical reality even further in his poem, "Laventville:"

> We left, somewhere a life we never found
> customs and gods that are not born against
> some crib, some grill of light clanged shut on
> us in bondage, and withheld us from the
> world below us and beyond and in its swaddling
> cerements we're still bound.[7]

As we look around us, we find that the assimilados, the Black middle class and the Black intelligentsia are *still bound* to a consumer ethic, to debt crisis, to ambivalence and to a decadent social order as they cling desperately to its CAPITAL, its COMEDY and its CHRIST. It is this assimilated middle class which has dominated the cultural and political leadership in Brazil, the Caribbean and North America. They have become the brokers since the struggle for independence and human rights in the sixties. They have written extensively on the culture of despair and impoverishment, referring to the Black masses as "The Truly Disadvantaged" and "The Black Underclass," and their condition as one of "Persistent Poverty." In addition, they refer to the authentic creative spirit of the favelas as "folkloric" or "primitive art." As the middle classes moved closer to their patrons and away from the Black community, they argue that "to go downhill from here was to ascend," and the only purpose of the dispossessed in the favelas on the hill was to sell their surplus labor cheaply as maids and gardeners to the blancos, triguenos, mulattos and morenos. The favelados could sing of their gods and ancestors as they cleaned the master's home. Derek Walcott continuing to write about "the Hill"... the favelas of Laventville Hill in Trinidad, Salvador and Rio de Janeiro in Brazil, poignantly states: "The Middle Passage never guessed its end. This is the height of poverty for the desperate and the Black."[8]

We cannot afford to lose our names. Call me by my rightful name. We cannot afford to lose the links. The connections must never disappear, rather they must be refurbished as part of an on-going stream. If each generation neither learns, claims, nor nutures the images, stories and customs, the vitality of our African traditions will end. Ayi Kwei Armah writes in *2000 Seasons*, "We are not a people of stagnant waters. We are the moving stream, rememberers of the way."[9] In this age of cultural pollution and synthetic products, we must guard closely the grammar of our continuum, the logic of the archetype. *Steel Pulse* confronts the colonizer with "give I back I witchdoctor."

It is time for us to have a cultural stock-taking. We must understand the crisis of the present, what the future implies, and the tasks before us. The people of the Caribbean and Brazil, especially Salvador, Bahia, have preserved the gods, the orishas, the music, the food, the painting and the sculpture, which was born of sugar cane and slavery. In North America, they understood that the experience of the cotton plantations would produce another type of creative statement, ie., the blues. Ralph Ellison writes in *Shadow and Act,* that,

> the blues is an impulse to keep the painful details and episodes of a brutal experience alive in ones' aching consciousness, to finger its jagged grain, and to transcend it, not by the consolation of philosophy but by squeezing from it near-tragic, near-comic lyricism, As a form, the blues is an autobiographical chronicle of personal catastrophe expressed lyrically. [10]

Therefore, there has been a dynamic linkage between the icons preserved in the Caribbean, the authentic voice of the drum from Brazil to Cuba and the melodic blues line that expresses the depth of suffering in North America. One hears this cross-fertilization clearly in the rebel reggae music of Bob Marley and Peter Tosh. But this creative force is under-girded by the spirit of resistance, which linked Toussaint L'Ouverture, Henri Christophe and Dessalines in their search for freedom, to Gabriel Prosser and Denmark Vessey in South Carolina, U.S.A. In addition, it was Chano Pozo and Machito, Nanguismo High Priests and Santeria drummers who would collaborate with Charlie Parker and Dizzy Gillespie in the reintroduction of the ancient voice of Africa (The DRUM) into our musical lexicon. The result of this collaboration led to a new aesthetic, as music, poetry, dance, painting, language and lifestyles changed dramatically. The synthesis revolutionized concepts of time and space, and new rhythmic possibilities were expanded. Max Roach refined these structures and grounded them in an ethos of resistance.

Also, it is for us to inform our friends in Latin America, that it was the infusion of the spirit of the Haitian Revolution and the material support offered by a liberated people that provided the financial, moral and philosophical underpinning for Simon Bolivar's quest for freedom and the struggle of General Mina of Mexico for national independence. It was Fidel Castro, who, in the seventies, declared Cuba to be an Afro-Latin nation, and grounded its earliest quest for freedom in the examples set by run-away slaves, the mambistas, who fought in the Sierras. He argued that these maroons together with 19th Century independistas were his sources of inspiration. It remains important for us to insist on their historical precedents because it is a result of the knowledge of this immense contribution of Haitian blood to Miranda and to Bolivar in the struggle for independence that we will create a brotherhood favorable to cultural confluence. Racism and imperialism have wiped out all of that history. This must be projected since Latin America artists, intelligentsia and middle class rarely join the Black struggle when they live and work in North America. They continue to have a Eurocentric focus on reality and dismiss the racial stratification which exists in Salvador, Cartagena, Puerto Limon, Panama City and Bluefields. The cycle of pain and poverty for Blacks in Latin America has endured the mirage of social integration argued by blancos, mulattos, morenos and triguenos. Therefore, it will be important for us to have a meaningful dialogue when we attempt to understand the difference between Carybe, Jorge Amado, Sergio Mendes, Flora Purim and Airto and Emmanuel Araujo and Valdeloir Rego. We must understand this carefully because in North America we often hear of our people's soul and creative expressions through the filtered lenses of an assimilationist's eye and through the "ripping off" of the spirit of Ogun, Yemanja and Oshumare. Even capoeira in New York is an art form that informs break dancing, and that is linked up with certain elements of Black dance in the forties, should be of great interest to us. It should accentuate how an African fighting form could be strained of its potency and transformed into a passive non-violent folkloric art form, while the combatants and Black people remain permanently exploited by poverty and violence.

It is important for us to recognize that due to the abandonment of the spirit of resistance in the image and content of contemporary Black art that our youth on the streets of New York, Salvador and Kingston (Jamaica) have had to create their own statement of resistance with graffiti art — the lyrics of Boogie Down Productions in *By All Means Necessary*, Public Enemy's *Welcome to the Terrordome* and Steel Pulse's *Hand-*

sworth Revolution. The work of these desperate young people, living in a cell of insanity on an urban frontier reservation has had no guidance from the intelligentsia or artist. Inside the capsule of violence, they have exploded with rapping, break dancing, hip-hop, and D.C. go-go. They are influenced by Bob Marley and the "yard music" of Jamaica. They see Babylon for what it represents, and they "crack open" the psychic drama of our times. It is exile and alienation in an urban frontier existence. "What can you get for sixty-three cents." "Stop the violence" and "ganga business controls America, illegal business controls America," KRS-1 of Boogie Down Productions raps. The reality is DREAD.

Rap music, scat singing, yard music, all attempt to expand the cracks in the surface and to destroy the pretensions in the so-called civilized language. The young artists try to scratch their way out of their obvious contradictory lives in the 'hood. A will of resistance resides inside the language. Slaves spoke as much or as little as they chose to speak. There was an economy of language, just as in Miles Davis's, Max Roach's or Thelonious Monk's work. In this sense, silence is the logical extreme of play, deadly serious play, signifying that we ain't playing no more. All pretense is ended. There is nothing more to say. The distance between your version of reality and mine admits no possibility of mutual intelligibility.

It is important to remember that the President of Texas Southern University in 1988 was prepared to deface the walls (white wash them) on which John Biggers and his students had painted several murals. The president argued that these images of the sixties were not proper for the aesthetic considerations of the eighties at a Black university. He said "Let us turn to more civilized art." It exemplifies the role of the Black intelligentsia in these dissenting times. I wonder if the President of Mexico or the rector of the University would consider defacing the murals of Diego Rivera, Jose Clementa Orosco and David Siquieros at the University of Mexico. John Biggers' statement represents a painful reality, since it removes, by official fiat, from Texas Southern University a vital part of the continuum of resistance.

At the same time, a young white artist, David Nelson, at the Art Institute of Chicago could present a work for an exhibition, which prostitutes and disrespects the city's late Mayor Harold Washington less than six months after his tragic death, and in the year of Jesse Jackson's Presidential bid for the Democratic Party's nomination. The art work showed Harold Washington dressed in drag, in women's underwear, and there has been no serious effort, not only to destroy the work or art, but to even tear the building down which housed that piece. One can imagine a scenario in which a young Palestinian artist displays in an exhibition on the West Bank a work or art which showed Menachen Begin as a transvestite. The Israeli army would not only destroy the museum or gallery where the work was mounted, but they would arrest and deport all the Palestinian artists in that area. The same response would hold true in Crossroads or Soweto, if a Black artist did a work on Botha or DeKlerk in drag. However, if a Black artist in the U.S.A. submitted a work to the Studio Museum in Harlem depicting Mayor Ed Koch in drag, the curator, director and members of the board would quickly reject the work and be afraid to acknowledge it as a painting, since they know that their funds would be removed immediately and the museum would be permanently closed down.

The need for a radical reclamation of the spirit is endemic in the Western Hemisphere. Wyane Brown states the region's abject loss, and its insistent PRIMEVAL CRY for the new man, when he writes, "I am bored... with stares....What I want now... are all those truths the prophets told."[11]

In the sixties, there was the discovery of new light throughout the region. The promise was one of spiritual and social redefinition. In John Coltrane's *A Love Supreme*, there was hope; in Amilcar Cabral's *Claim No Victories, Tell No Lies,* there were revolutionary possibilities. But then we stepped into the void of the seventies and a period of reaction and darkness set in during the eighties.

For a moment in time, our spiritually fragmented people made a motion toward wholeness. Artists, poets, musicians, dancers, painters, sculptors, cultural workers tried to push us towards identification and awareness, but we let the moment slip through our fingers. Opportunism, corruption and consumerism set in. The O'Jays sang *For The Love of Money*, and The Mighty Sparrow echoed *Capitalism gone mad*. We drowned in our tears, apathy, estrangement, and the historic continuum of resistance was blurred by a new cultural ethos.

It is at this level that we are searching for answers. We continue to meet as artists who have a profound respect for Picasso's Guernica, but we have not done a major work on Jonestown in Guyana, or on the Atlanta children murders and the Wyane Williams "flim-flam," or on the Chorillo District in Panama City or on the Grenada invasion, or on Crossroads and Soweto. Are the artists not inspired by the late James Baldwin's *The Evidence of Things Not Seen*, or maybe they have never read it, or listened to the plaintive lament of Hannibal Marvin Peterson's recording *The Angels of Atlanta*?

My memory stammers, but my soul is a witness. We are challenged by the forces of history. There is a need for explosions in the world, so that time will become free. Hope hangs eternal in the dreams of those who feel weighted by the force of history. Le Roi Clarke, a Trinidadian painter writes:

> People must fight back...come out with poem...music...songs... paintings of resistance. Come out of your bat's sleep in the noon hour and smash the glass of this deaf city...grown more deaf than its Dry River. [12]

We are still functioning in the plantation model. Many artists and curators argue that art must be divorced from politics, but the mounting of major exhibitions become political acts, at which the governors and mayors must speak on "tourism and art," or the creative contributions of Africa to Western folklore and popular culture. In the same manner, Mikhail Gorbachev invited nearly one hundred artists and intellectuals to a special gathering at the Russian embassy in 1987 and there was not a single Black or Hispanic on the guest list. There is no turning back for Black artists but they must clearly understand the exigencies of this precise moment in history and the discontinuities which will emerge in the 21st Century.

No, we cannot make a separate peace as artists and intellectuals – even though I am not certain that we are able to deal with racial treason – but, then, freedom knows no apology. Our struggle is internal as well as external because our people have known cruelty, the kind that makes us cry without tears. Yes, I have known cruelty to pinch the loud cries of pain, leaving my body limp and numb. "Take away your smiles / Give me back your snarls / Give me back my humanity / At the dawn of another day."[13]

> Because, I will settle the account and
> Yes, their bill will be steep... very steep
> When it is handed to them
> So don't worry my friends in the favelas
> Next to the Museum of Modern Art in Salvador, Bahia
> Don't worry
> Don't worry if the champagne
> bubbles when you have no bread
> If noon is striking in your empty belly
> And midnights in your naked hovel
> Don't worry brother... don't worry sister
> Don't worry
> Or if like me you find it tough
> Do like me
> Add up the bill
> Add hunger onto nakedness
> Poverty onto exploitation
> Add up the total coefficients of your life
> Of these classic and tragic everydays
> Yes, their bill will be steep
> Very steep
> When we hand it to them.[14]

Now, Paint that! Brothers and Sisters. It's the challenge of the future.

NOTES

1. John La Rose, "Prose Poem For A Conference," in *Breaklight: The Poetry of the Caribbean*, ed Andrew Salkey, pp. 74-75.

2. Paul Robeson, "The Artist Must Take Sides,"in *Robeson Speaks*, ed. Philip Foner, pp. 118-119.

3. W.E.B. DuBois, "Fifty Years After," in *Souls of Black Folk*, p. xiii.

4. Carolina Maria de Jesus, *Child of The Dark*, pp. 43-49.

5. Pablo Amando Fernandez, "De Nombre A Muerte," in Breaklight, ed. Andrew Salkey, p. viii.

6. Frantz Fanon, "Racism and Culture," in *Presence Africaine: Special Issue*: The First International Conference of Negro Writers and Artists, Paris, (1956) p. 125.

7. Derek Walcott, "Laventville", in *Breaklight*, pp. 24-27.

8. Ibid., pp. 24-27.

9. Ayi Kwei Armah, *Two Thousand Seasons*, p. 299.

10. Ralph Ellison, "Richard Wright's Blues," *Shadow and Act*, p. 90.

11. Wyane Brown, "Soul on Ice," in *Breaklight*, p. 129.

12. Le Roi Clarke, *Douens*, "See How All Passes," p. 50.

13. Serapho Sempala, "At The Dawn Of Another Day," in *The Soweto I Love*, p. 9.

14. Frantz Le Roy, "Settling The Account," *Negritude:The Black Poetry From Africa And The Caribbean*, ed., Norman Shapiro, p. 127.

AN INTERVIEW
WITH
ARCHIE SHEPP

(This interview was conducted in November 1976, by Niany Kilkenney, Fanta Hall, Bill Bower, Skip Bailey and Acklyn Lynch.)

Interviewer: What is music to you? What is this energy form that you create when you blow your saxophone?

Archie Shepp: It is an expression of many things, including personal, cultural, and social expressions. If you look at it in terms of personal expression, it is a "voice." I feel I am a DRUM. I try to become a drum. Then in terms of the social manifestation, I try to achieve the cosmic aspect which would be relevant to a community.

Interviewer: Is there any particular reason why you chose the saxophone as your vehicle for expression as opposed to any other instrument?

Archie Shepp: I started out wanting to play the piano after I heard Reggie Workman play the *William Tell Overture*. He did it so well I told my mother that I was interested in the piano. I had previously taken piano lessons, but at that time I changed my teacher. Later on, I went back to my previous teacher. Then, I must have heard someone play the clarinet, and I wanted to learn to play the clarinet. I got a clarinet when I was about 12 years old. Then I heard Jimmy McGriff, who could play anything, and he was particularly adroit at playing "boogie-woogie." As a child, he performed at the school assemblies. He played everything by ear, but did extraodinarily well. In this case, I heard him play a solo that we all had to know how to sing at that time. It was the "Flying Home" solo of Illinois Jacquet. Jimmy McGriff had picked up this alto saxophone and he was playing this solo. I heard him playing it on the street one day. I was raised in Philadelphia but born in Fort Lauderdale, Florida. But one of the things about the Philadelphia environment at that time, and I suppose even now, was that the family structure still existed and to some extent it acted as a support to the proliferation of all kinds of cultural activities, particularly music, where we had a number of "jam sessions" in people's apartments. So in this case, I heard Jimmy playing outside somebody's house, not his own, but it was quite normal for musicians to take their horns out and play. He had never taken any music lessons, but as I heard him playing I was so moved that I went home and asked my mother to buy me a saxophone. So my grandmother and my aunt contributed to helping me get my first saxophone, but I was really deeply influenced by what I had heard Jimmy McGriff play. Also, there was a thing about music, in general, that had affected me from the very first time I heard it and which led me to the essence of music: it is a magical quality. It was a kind of attraction whenever I heard music, or that sound which moved me. I remember when I was a little boy in Florida, my parents took me to the minstrel show — at that time, Black people sat on one side of the theatre and white people sat on the other — and we saw a group called Silas Green from New Orleans. In those days the minstrel show constituted a kind of ritual in the South because it was the theatre. It was TV and people were much more participative. I will always remember it. The charisma of the performers always stayed with me, the sound of the music, the dancing and the spectacle. I was caught up in it and I have tried to become that type of artist.

Interviewer: You cited Reggie Workman. Can you talk about some of the other musicians who were your contemporaries in Philadelphia?

Archie Shepp: One person who was a big influence on me and taught me a lot of music was Edward Lee Morgan. Then there were Bobby Timmons, James de Priest, Spanky de Priest and Kenny Rodgers. These were the people my age; and there were older musicians like Clarence Sharpe, who was a tremendous influence around Philadelphia as a teacher to everyone. When I was young, John Coltrane's name was a legend in Philadelphia. I knew of him in Philadelphia, but I never actually met him until I went to New York. There was also Jimmy Oliver and Jimmy Heath, who had a tremendous influence on me as a young saxophone player. Even today, I still follow his work. These were a few of the people who were in Philly at that time.

Interviewer: What elements contribute to Archie Shepp's style? When you hit the new music scene, you had a lot of old elements in your music, as opposed to many other new musicians in the Sixties whose work doesn't present as many identifiable streams feeding into their style. Yet, we hear such streams in your approach to playing the tenor saxophone. Are there particular musicians that influenced you, that you feel are identifiable elements that you have incorporated into your style?

Archie Shepp: Well, yes, not only that, but I feel there are forms and images that I identify with. On a musical level, of course there are certain models that musicians look to, and mine goes back as far as my grandmother when she used to take me to the great battles of song; the gospel singers used to come to the churches in Philly, and my grandmother, who had come to stay with us in the North for a while, would take me to these performances. When I was in the South, I used to spend all day Sunday in church. Perhaps the greatest cultural event for me was the choir and the singing and the rendering of verse because there is a whole ritual and cultural life surrounding the church. For example, when I was a child I heard a young preacher who was the type of metaphoric example James Baldwin gives you in *Go Tell It On The Mountain.* In him, there was sheer precocity. I witnessed the genius of the culture at all levels, both in the South and in the North; it was a constantly re-enrichening experience in terms of models. So in my saxophone playing, I first identified the work call, the field holler. In John Coltrane or Louis Armstrong's work, the work song survives as a formal model which the so-called jazz musician deals with on many levels. But not only the so-called jazz musician, but your popular musicians, the James Browns, who utilize techniques that are exactly out of the work song. The spiritual song has given much of the substance to the music; it has given the tonal element to the blues; it has added the soul quality to jazz music. And then, there are other song forms, including children's songs, that can serve as models in our communities. So these have been my inspiration. When you talk about models, just aside from what I might have gleaned from the saxophone, there are people like Wardell Coleman Hawkins, John Coltrane, and Charlie Parker, whom I will never forget.

Interviewer: When we are talking about Black music, what is new music and old music? Is there a difference or definition of each area?

Archie Shepp: Well, I don't know. I think that is a kind of Western way to approach music — to even think about it in that way. If for a minute, we would try to get outside of that frame of reference and look at it from another perspective, if we just dealt with it not in a time thing at all, not new or old, but relevant (whatever is relevant), I think traditional forms remain essentially traditional. They don't essentially change in a span of time from new to old, but they constantly feed on elements within the organism to evolve other organisms. It is a dialectical process within traditionalism.

Interviewer: Do you think Black musicians have a duty or responsibility to Black people or themselves; and if so, what do you think that responsibility is?

Archie Shepp: Well, obviously they have a responsibility because they come out of that experience. As to what that responsibility is, first of all, I think that the question should be asked in the African sense i.e., the "asker" should participate in the question, "What can he/she do in regards to the whole proliferation of his/her own music." We are caught up in the whole specialization thing that whites have imposed on us; we become doctor, lawyer or whatever, and very seldom musician, because the musician is a kind of griot in the hierarchy of this whole thing. Then, it should be asked, "How do Black people look at their own music?" You hear people rave about Stevie Wonder's album, *Songs in the Key of Life*, but ask the average Black person who Tadd Dammeron is. Some people are walking around today bragging that Beethoven was a Black man. Well, maybe so! But at the same time you ask him who Fats Waller was — who was definitely Black — and he knows nothing about him. I think there are fundamental contradictions.

Interviewer: It is a contradiction, I agree. But why is that communication blocked up? Why is it that many of us not only do not know, but really don't even care if an Archie Shepp is in town or Max Roach just left? We are all concerned about the Earth , Wind and Fires and the Stevie Wonders — and I am not saying that they are invalid. I am merely saying that there is a gap in our appreciation and I want to know what is causing it.

Archie Shepp: On the one hand, I would ascribe it to the fact of the assimilation that is at work in the United States. Whether Blacks are progressing or not is not the question. The fundamental reality is that they are being assimilated. On the other hand, I think that we are dealing with language that we do not fully understand, i.e., historical language. For example, we have developed a vocal language, which is very close to our whole treatment of music. Well, it comes from the drum — the tonal language of Africa. On the other hand, we have developed a highly sophisticated para-language in the form of instrumental language. The African has a peculiar facility for speaking a musical sound. Ben Sidran, a young British student, did his doctoral dissertation on this subject — "Communication Among Black People." He describes how the oral tradition functions on another level, particularly in music, and how we are able to communicate, even political ideas. As Professor Acklyn Lynch has indicated, music, culture and ritual worked to ferment the Haitian revolution, which, incidentally, was the only successful Black revolution in the Western Hemisphere; Haiti, being the second oldest republic in this hemisphere. What important implications did Voodoo have to the people who participated in this revolution? Certainly, music has been important. Why would Nat Turner turn to a spiritual like *Steal Away*? That is on one level how our vocal music speaks to us, but there is a close connection between vocal music and dance also. Additionally, we have developed an instrumental language.

Interviewer: To a certain extent, Archie Shepp has been viewed as a contemporary analogue of that aspect of Black music that was conveying politically and socially significant messages.

Archie Shepp: I think, of course, that wherever Black people have posed truthful arguments and have directly challenged the status-quo with regards to our people in this country, we have met with a certain resistance that we can only expect as natural to a system that first enslaved us physically and, later on, economically. And so, if they don't play my records on the radio, I think that that is consistent with the norms and aims of this essentially bourgeois society.

Interviewer: But, going beyond your own experiences, what do you think is happening to the music itself? What is happening to the other musicians who were on the same track that you were on? For example, there were records like "Fire Music" or "Cry," which were obviously moving in that direction. There are not those kinds of programmatic records available now; even in your own work. The last three records which I have heard, i.e., the Montreaux I and II records and your latest Arista record, do not seem to have that political edge on them.

Archie Shepp: Well, I wouldn't say that. It depends. Now, people talk about revolution or guerilla warfare. What do they mean by that? To some extent, I feel as though I am a guerilla warrior; I must live among the people. It is no longer valid for me to exist on the fringes while my people are jumping up and shouting to Stevie Wonder's *Fingertips* and to James Brown's *Popcorn* and I am still hung up with a few revolutionary cadre elite on it. So, I make a recording like *Attica Blues*; it doesn't tell the people about *Popcorn*, but I do try to convey a message to the people about the massacre of our revolutionary brothers at Attica. I must put it in their language. I must live among the people.

Interviewer: I would like to reflect on the music that you produced in the late Fifties and early Sixties, like with the New York Contemporary Five — the stuff that you did with Bill Dixon, some of the early Impulse stuff. Are you saying that that music was on the fringe of the culture?

Archie Shepp: I am saying that it has never penetrated to the masses of our people and it is folly to think that it has. That doesn't question its validity because we do have very fundamental recordings like Mr. Coltrane's *A Love Supreme*, which was a gold record. And when I am saying that it hasn't reached the masses of our people, I don't mean that to construe by any means the kind of thing that Herbie Hancock has indicated when he said that the music of the Sixties was a confused period, because incidentally, *A Love Supreme* was a gold record and it was not one of your top ten or top forty type recordings. But then, why don't you hear that much of Mr. Coltrane's work, particularly his later work, being played today on the radio? I think to a great extent it has to do with what you are saying. Young musicians are not brought into the studio and encouraged to continue to play in the tradition of *A Love Supreme* or *Ascension*. They are told, quite the contrary, that music is confused and it doesn't sell. It gets back to a question raised earlier when I was asked how I feel my music can help the community. What can the community do to make sure that we don't lose sight of the values projected in a work like *A Love Supreme*, of the whole style or way of playing which that represents? I think this style was systematically cut short, or at least the people who are playing that music are starved out. They don't work much. I feel like a good guerilla fighter has to stay around.

Interviewer: There seems to be a pattern where these creative Black musicians are scorned. Who gives the scorners the authority? Who are they? There seems to be no place for creative Black musicans to go to in

America. With this in mind, where then do our creative Black musicans go?

Archie Shepp: Once again, that's a question that the community has to answer for itself in terms of what's worth preserving, in terms of its own cultural product. It gets into some of the questions that Harold Cruse raises in *The Crisis of the Negro Intellectual* — the fact that Black folk have always seemed reluctant to recognize the socio-political and economic implications of the communications industry *viz* radio, television, film, etc.. Therefore in our own music, we see contradictions in the enormous figures of the television, recording and movie industry. We never organize our musical product on a national level or on a collective level. So you get a person like Barry Gordy, who owns Motown, which is a multimillion dollar project. It could have all kinds of potential in the community and yet you see the contradiction between these millionaire "rock and roll" stars and youngsters running out on the highway sticking up people. And that's the metaphor of our Black society. It is the silver coke spoon and stick-ups on the highway; it's the player and the pimp society; it's a music which drives us to dance and which evokes the primordial rhythms without the primordial reasons.

Interviewer: So is that the primary reason, why there is no place for the Black creative musican in America?

Archie Shepp: It's because we are in danger of losing our identity. I think we have one foot in White America and another foot in Black America everyday. Our whole struggle in this country — if you look at us vis-a-vis Puerto Ricans, Cubans, or many people of Third World identity — is that we, unlike the people who speak Spanish, cannot call ourselves Spanish; we cannot call ourselves Arab because we speak Arabic. We speak English, but we don't call ourselves English. We're the only ones that — as the Honorable Elijah Muhammad has pointed out — have no "Negro" land. But it has kept before us the question of our identity. Thus, even with whatever contradictions that exist, you can have an Adam Clayton Powell who declares himself solidly Black, and this be plausible in a land like the United States, even though it would not necessarily be plausible in the West Indies, South America, or in some places in Africa. It would not be plausible. It would be unthinkable that a man that fair (light-skinned) would call himself Black. But we (African-Americans) can believe it, largely because our struggle has kept before us the question of our identity, and our music, the so-called jazz music, mostly reflects that identity, largely because, to my way of thinking, it comes to us completely uninformed by white considerations.

Interviewer: This raises two related issues. Earlier, you talked about the question of Philadelphia and the fact that there was a family structure that promoted the culture. I found that this is the historical process of a certain generation. But it occurs to me that the assimilation of which you speak is really the assimilation of a certain class. It is not the masses of Black people. All of Black America may be assimilated ideologically; some of Black America may be assimilated ideologically; some of Black America is being assimilated materially. There is still a furrow home, if it could be cultivated. Understand the process by which culture is transferred, as well as the complexity of assimilation, how does the music industry act as an obstacle in the transference of culture? For example, we don't have any big bands for the cats to learn anymore; and jam sessions don't happen anymore — the clubs are dying out.

Archie Shepp: Let me give you an example. I had a very interesting conversation with Mr. Coltrane ten or eleven years ago. It was after he had achieved some degree of success financially as a musician. One of his dreams was to build a recording studio in mid-town Manhattan, which would be opened night and day; a place that would be opened to musicians to perform and record in constantly, one which would become a clearing house for tapes, archives, and that would reflect a self-producing mechanism, which would be autonomous, and would eventually extricate the musicians from the entrepreneurial chains, the standard record companies and so on. In other words, he was proposing a cooperative musican's owned establishment. I have never heard anyone speak like this since then, with the possible exception of Max Roach or Charles Mingus — people who have given consideration to matters like this for a long time. Still, what we (the collective) need now is not to simply castigate white folks for what they have not done for our music or even to castigate ourselves for what we have not done, but to answer some of the challenges that Harold Cruse raises — to really begin to define or to set for ourselves some critical awareness of just what our culture is. How do we define it? We see today, for example, Black Studies departments all over the country — I am part of one — but to me the paramount difficulty with all of them, just as in the Black colleges, are their own cultural ineptitude, unawareness or ignorance. You go to places like Fisk University where they produce the Fisk Jubilee Singers, and yet their emphasis today is on Puccinni. Well, that's absurd. They had Donald Byrd at Howard University, and he has to leave Howard to show them what beautiful voices they had because it cannot flourish at Howard. It has to flourish outside these institutions.

Interviewer: What role do you see for the writers, critics, and scholars? What would be your recommendations if you were laying down an agenda for them to participate in the maintenance and further flowering of our culture and the musical aspect of it?

Archie Shepp: I would tell them to start drawing comic books, get close to the people because I think that we are at war with popular culture. We are at war with comic books; so we have to begin to use the language of the people. In the words of Mao Tse Tung, we have to utilize their symbology. If they are listening to blues music, then our revolutionaries have to become blues poets. We have to assume the train of thought that Amiri Baraka takes in *Blues People*. We have to analyze our roots from a cultural point of view, and we have to build our revolutionary perspective, based on a firm knowledge of what that culture is.

Interviewer: Do you think that one reason why the masses have not grasped Black music is because they do not consider our music functional?

Archie Shepp: But the masses have grasped Black music. In fact, that is where our music comes from. When I hear things from Black people in college like Black music has progressed beyond the blues, why, that's absurd. The blues is the very essence of our music. I think that it is the essence of Mr. Ellington's most complex arrangements. It is the very thing that we try to get deeper into, because the blues is that original African sound. It is that quality that whites did not assimilate, which they could not take away from us. The white boys want it. The English boys want it. They want to be able to play the blues. The whole world loves it. The Japanese are in love with that sound. But it is our thing; it is the thing that they couldn't take away from us.

Interviewer: Many of the musicians are teaching in the university. Ed Blackwell is at Wesleyan, Jackie McClean is at Hartford, Brother Ah is at Brown, Max Roach is at Amherst. During the Sixties, all of these people were in New York. Now there is a new group of people in New York, blowing their brains out on the Lower East Side. They seem to be going through the same East Side/Greenwich Village syndrome, while other musicians are in the university teaching. Sort this out for me.

Archie Shepp: Well, Brother Lynch helped to put together a very strong package at the University of Massachusetts in the form of a Pan African Institute of Culture that included Max Roach, Nelson Stevens, Diana Ramos, and Paul Carter Harrison — potentially this included Ed Love and Eleo Pomare, even though that aspect did not work out. But what we had projected with the Institute was to try to effect real changes, both at the academic level (in terms of its awareness of Black cultural institutions) and at the community level (where we had hoped to bring this Institute to the service and to utilize this expertise, to put it at the service of the community). We were not able to get off the ground. We are still struggling with it. But I think that this is the kind of thing which has some potential and viability.

Interviewer: If the old masters whom you used to look up to and were available in Philadelphia and New York are no longer there and that breaks off a link, do the musicians now have to go to these various institutions to get lessons, or to sit at the bell of some great player's horn?

Archie Shepp: Well, I don't think that it is about that so much as a systematic way of scientizing a product. If you want to sell Klennex, you know that there is a certain way of manufacturing paper and so on. If you want to turn out more Stevie Wonders, Aretha Franklins, Max Roaches, and Mahalia Jacksons, how do you do that scientifically? There must be a scientific way. They have people at North Texas State, white boys who are playing just like Count Basie. They can play the Basie band from the period of the Thirties, Forties, Fifties and Sixties; whatever you want. It means that just as they give you a Telefunker or a Sony, they can turn out a Black product. But Blacks can't do it. Ours is the painful, laborious process of birth; but it is always original. There is the question of how long this originality will go on, if we don't begin to nurture it. Somewhat in the way that whites have tended to systematize their product. Because once again, we are at war with technology, and if we don't, as Harold Cruse says, take advantage and begin to own our own product, someone else will.

Interviewer: Going to universities may provide some time to work on it, but I fail to see that as controlling our own product. You see the dispersion of brilliant musicians into places where the amount of contact that they have with Blacks is at best nil.

Archie Shepp: That's what I was saying about controlling your own product. Those musicians would probably be dispersing into places like Howard and Fisk, if Howard and Fisk were calling on them. But, in fact, they are not, and there are no Black institutions which can house our archives, that can hire our people. So the point I am getting at is very fundamental. It is not exactly how a young student learns how to play a saxophone, but how do we create saxophone players? How do we create musicians, painters and writers? How do we even lend a certain dignity to those professions equivalent to such professions, as an economists, lawyers and doctors? Professor Lynch is a very rare man to be as sensitive as he is to the role of culture. Many Blacks who have achieved a certain status think that musicians, writers, painters are beneath them because they are not part of a certain kind of quasi-professional ambience, caste or class. But all of this is white, for once again it points deeply at the whole process of assimilation.

Interviewer: Do you think also that it comes from the fact that we, as a people, have factored out culture from living. In other words, on Sunday afternoon we live culture instead of it being a life process? We separate the two, and therefore, we cannot identify that culture is a part of our life as opposed to something which we do on a Sunday afternoon.

Archie Shepp: Not exactly, but I think that what you are saying may be true. Actually, it points out something else — that we have essentially two cultures among Black people simultaneously, an urban and a rural one. Earlier, we were talking about the difference between the implications of a Blind Lemon Jefferson and a Stevie Wonder and we agreed that a Blind Lemon Jefferson had much more community implication — his song spoke much more to the community, whereas Stevie's songs reflect much more the cult of the individual (the love song as a type of song) — *My Cherie Amor* vis-a-vis the so-called song of allusion — *See that Gal with the Red Dress On.* Everybody sees her. She belongs to the community. Whereas the composer today signs his own work. Stephen Foster signed his name to the spirituals, which makes the spiritual a minstrel song. You see its ritual significance is exorcised. He knew that he was dealing with ritual material but he erased its rituality; by destroying its anonymity he made it personal. It was his, and this is a society in which individuality counts much more than communality.

Interviewer: That goes to a point which I would like to make about these different musicians. I could understand controlling your product, but they make their individual efforts — i.e. Brother Ah trying to do his individual album, Keino Duke trying to do his, brother Mtume trying to do his. Everybody trying to do his/her own little thing. Why can't we do a collective, cooperative thing? Why can't that be successful? Why can't a Strata East survive? I can understand controlling the product as the key, but all these little, individual efforts is the part that I cannot understand.

Archie Shepp: In large, we are handicapped by the fact that we came out of a slave experience in which we owned nothing. Our music, at the time of the minstrel period, was essentially coopted by whites; when the minstrel show became successful, it was white people who made it successful and then later it turned into vaudeville and musical theatre — "Guys" and "Dolls," and these sorts of things which were all based on Black dancing, singing, and music. It was always whites who got credit for it and controlled it. Therefore, it is not surprising at all today that Black folks have very little actual economic hold over the entertainment industry. I think this has done untold economic damage to us psychologically in the sense that we are always coming from behind; we have no money. Most of these self-help efforts that you have mentioned are essentially individual ones, where people put their own money into a project. These people are up against huge corporate entities — ABC, CBS, RCA, Columbia, Capitol. Of course, you have raised a very essential and real question, but, on the other hand, you seem to absent yourself from the solution since you say "these people," when you should be thinking about "us." How do we do it? Everyone, as a student, should not see himself/herself as apart from the problem, but, rather, each must ask, how does he/she as a good guerilla fighter play his/her part.

Interviewer: What we tried in the Institute has not really been understood in educational circles. You don't control your product solely by the creator's satement, but rather by building an infrastructure for control. You have other people who can be creative in the administrative, legal, management, marketing, engineering, research, writing and design areas, that will undergird the work of the musician. This technician's responsibility will be the projection of a product useful to the sustenance of the culture. Black academicians and educational administrators do not have any understanding of this necessity in program design. Nowhere is there built into the educational system the notion that these are essentially creative and important careers. The Institute was therefore established not only for Archie Shepp to perform, but to develop the archives, the researchers, writers, technicians, businessmen — a community of people who would have that professional responsibility. This was the significance of trying to establish the Institute in the university community. Because if the best minds come to the university, they could be attracted to these areas of work, and not merely to be a doctor or lawyer, but, rather, to be developed as trained cadres who would form the infrastructure to sustain our cultural patrimony. In this situation, we are talking about a different ballgame. But it is precisely at that level that we are undermined. We don't have an adequate infrastructure. In an army of ants, it is not just the leader, it is the entire contingent that builds the ant-hill. But time and time again we get defeated in our weak infrastructural capacity. And then, Duke Ellington, Charlie Mingus, Max Roach and others are told, "Why don't you all get together." Yet, they essentially have no apparatus.

Interviewer: It's just like the student who comes to the university with the idea of involving himself or herself in something creative or exciting, but can't find any direction.

Interviewer: That's part of the living culture, I was trying to deal with. When we talk about culture, we have a tendency to think that culture is Sunday afternoon. I was at a workshop yesterday afternoon with Black public school teachers who were trying to deal with the question of culture and education. We came to a unanimous conclusion that we have to live it — if we want our children to appreciate music, we have to sing, play and create a musical environment which would nurture their sensibilities. We have a task as a people to understand our responsibility.

Archie Shepp: I agree with all of you fully. You are talking about approaching culture on the level of the home, a personal approach, in the family, which is in the oral tradition; but I think that the institutional level is fundamental. The institution's approach to culture not only affects our community, but it shapes the minds of the larger community.

Interviewer: I find a marriage between some of the things you have been saying, but I think that we have to get away from the notion inferred by Acklyn's statement that the best minds go to the university. I think that there is a social process that is happening that we have to go to, step back and take a look at how we really want to intervene on it. A lot of cats going to the universities will certainly come into contact with some of the best minds, but part of the richness of our music is that it has taken a long time to be put up in the university — being closer to the community was part of its richness and part of its power (that it could relate to and draw on). There was a dialectical relationship there. Now we have a new situation. As Acklyn and I spoke of before, the industry is so big now that it has just wiped out all of that community/musician interface. Thus, there is North Texas State, the Berkley School of Music, and the New England Conservatory of music and all these Black Studies programs with these musicians in them. And the situations that used to obtain in a Philadelphia, Detroit, Pittsburgh, Chicago or Harlem, New York, where there was a community situation which, through some process, the musicians developed, seems to be less and less the case. The models in that situation are the top forty bands and less and less the bands that created the significant instrumental music which we have. And as we think through the problems we face, that has to be somewhere on the agenda. When we look at at the university, it is not where the best minds go; it is a place, whereby a social process, certain people arrive and most of these people are white and those Blacks who arrive, don't really do so for reasons of intelligence or innate abilities; they end up there for other reasons, including that they may have some intellectual or artistic or some other kind of ability that could be harnessed.

Archie Shepp: Including the fact that they *may* be in the process of becoming white.

Interviewer: But they *are* in the process of becoming white.

Archie Shepp: That is the social process you are addressing. But I think that Acklyn is suggesting a black process, a blackening process, and I am not talking here about the best minds going to the university, because I don't necessarily think that they are in the university that is neither here nor there. It is the social process that you are talking about; how to reorient it — so that it becomes our process.

Interviewer: Right. And useful for us in general.

Archie Shepp: And useful to us. That is what I meant in part about being a good guerilla incidentally, precisely what Brother Lynch was saying about creating a structure, which would be able to help the artist to carry out his work, in the sense of archives, research, technical expertise–things which are quite foreign to us. What happens to the music of a Fletcher Henderson or a Fats Waller or a Duke Ellington? Are these archives made available to any young music student, the way that you could go into any university today and use the works of a Bach or Beethoven. Certainly not. They usually fall into the hands of white folks. In the case of Mr. Ellington, I don't believe so. I think that his sister and his son have held on to a good deal of his work. But in the case of Dr. W.E.B. Dubois, much of his work was sold to the University of Massachusetts. I can't comment on that negatively or positively, but I certainly can say that it didn't go to the Black community.

Interviewer: Your works — *Things Have Got to Change, Message from Mozambique, Poem for Malcolm* — I want to reflect on that thrust in your work, national in form but international in context. Where is that approach headed in you music?

Archie Shepp: Basically, it is probably due to the fact that we have many new African nations pitted against capitalism and imperialism and we see our brothers breaking free from the chains of oppression in these songs. Hopefully, on the cultural level, my music will establish some identity between our struggle and their struggle.

Interviewer: You are probably one of the most ideologically directed of contemporary musicians. How significant do you think ideology is to most musicians?

Archie Shepp: I would question that. Not because I am the most, but because I think that kind of reasoning tends to take us away from the fact that we have many, many Black people from all walks of life, who are thinking about the problems that affect us.

Interviewer: Well, do you think that the musicians themselves are ideologically clear enough about what they do, the relationship between their work and their community, and the problems both international and domestic we face?

Archie Shepp: I wouldn't put it that way. I think that the average Black "cat" is hip. Hip means something. The average brother is hip. You don't have to school the average sister or brother. You really don't. They all have the potential, but it is a question of how you organize that potential. In one sense, we have always looked to charismatic leaders like Dr. Martin Luther King, Jr., El Hajj Malik El Shabazz or the Honorable Elijah Muhammad for our salvation — or Mr. Marcus Garvey. But on the other hand, we are faced with a modern problem: we each have to become responsible. So it is not so much a question of how conscious we are as musicians — we are all conscious and aware — but how do we organize? Organization is a day to day problem of struggle.

Interviewer: The reason why I say that you are the most political, because in terms of programmatic musical statements, in terms of statements on liner notes, in terms of public positions taken, you have been one of the most vocal cats, one of the most articulate cats (in ways in which we are not overburdened with words), getting to the core of certain issues, and making it very clear where you stand. There have been many cats, who may have your stature musically, who have created music that is worth listening to. But how many have been as articulate or as politically conscious as you have been? What is your judgement as to the status of that in the musicians' community? Is it good, or is it bad?

Archie Shepp: Well, we have had, for example, a conference of Black musicians at the University of Massachusetts. It was a very successful conference. It could have led to a number of things. But, once again, the conference was very poorly attended by Black students. We didn't have the maximum effort by the Black students. We had no follow-up after the conference — people who would put the recorded material together, do secretarial work, write up the final draft and so on. These kinds of services were not forthcoming. The faculty was not particularly interested after the first day or so; even though the concerts were packed every night. Only a few Black faculty members played any significant part and they were part of the Institute. So you see, there again, the general level of awareness among the musicians seem to be very high, but we are functioning in a vacuum.

Interviewer: As I was listening to you perform last night, I kept thinking about the Black musician, and the people that are controlling the music. They care about the music and they care about the clubs, but they don't care about the musician, the person. What is the lifestyle of a musician like? What are the ups and downs? What are the negatives and positives?

Archie Shepp: That's hard to answer in a word. It is not what people think it is. It can really be rough and grueling. I think to some extent, we fulfill the journey of the Taureg and the nomads and we are a kind of people who go out and we come back with the stories in a way. In a people where the oral tradition is still alive, as it is in our communities, that is very important. Growing up, I remember that very often it was the musicians who had the stories to tell about far away places. But on the other hand, I think that musicians tend to become very political people, because they have so many international experiences. Perhaps, among all Black people, they are able to be constantly in touch with the shifting tides in various parts of the world. So that we should begin to pay much more attention to them as harbingers of oral tradition and as people who have a certain type of political sensitivity and knowledge, based on their lifestyle.

Interviewer: Would you call it a rough life-style? Does it drain on you? The club atmosphere, the cigarettes, the alcohol, the drugs, the rip-off artists, the "getting your money" problems, the playing, the train, the taxi-cabs, the life pace.

Archie Shepp: Well, it's all summed up in the blues...

Interviewer: What do you think of the influx of the Chicago and St. Louis musicians (In New York)?

Archie Shepp: I think that it represents the further lengthening out of the urbanization process. I think that the musicians from Chicago and St. Louis, like the earlier musicians who came in from Philly and Detroit, will begin to exert another kind of influence, particularly since they have a tradition of collective work and communal style of living, and they have worked together in the meaningful sense of the word for quite a while on a coooperative basis. They bring that lifestyle to New York. It is interesting because, perhaps, it will provide a model to other musicians.

Interviewer: Are there any particular musical voices that strike you out of that group?

Archie Shepp: Well, all of them. I have known Richard Muhall Abrams, Steve McCall, and Joseph Jarman for many years. I just met Henry

Threadgill and I am very impressed with him. Of course, some of them have recorded with me. Some of the St. Louis musicians, like Lester Bowie and Anthony Braxton, recorded with me some years ago. I am very happy that they are living and working in New York for they will bring another dimension to the musical pantheon.

Interviewer: Where do you see our music in world culture? If there is a hierarchy to be talked about in terms of world culture, where is the creative African American music in the panoply?

Archie Shepp: I think that it is not much in the hierarchical sense that you could discuss music or culture, but rather it is perhaps the most relevant music of our times. There was a professor at Amherst college who I asked to lend me some records from the school's library to teach my class. He refused, saying that they had been ripped off too many times. Now, apparently, he was alluding to the fact that students had stolen all of his Charlie Parker, all of his John Coltrane — not only Black students, but white students as well. So I asked him, "why aren't they ripping off Beethoven and Bach?" Because they are not relevant. Nobody even bothers to steal their music.

Interviewer: What is relevant? Is it the improvisational process by which there is a simultaneous interrelationship of different musical things or intelligence or is it the social significance of the music?

Archie Shepp: Black people made the connection between rhythm and dance; so all of our music, on the one hand, overlaps a need in white Western society. Our cultures have fed on each other that way. The fact that we have created a music that is physical — which has physical implications — and the fact that whites are at a crucial juncture where the spirit has been sapped out of the society and the only way to resolve it is through the physical. For example, take the image of the whole resurrection of certain sexual attitudes. The blatant homosexuality is a part of a need to find the spirit through the flesh. The fact that the movies have even become so graphic about physical matters further supports this point. This whole emphasis is fed and Black music becomes a natural adjunct to its drive. One of the first homosexual films I saw, and the only one, which was a very graphic shocking film, had rock and roll music and heavy blues all the way through. Boogying baby. So Boogying has been taken out of Voodoo and has been absorbed in this plastic culture. So the boogie doesn't even have any meaning anymore. The symbols contain themselves.

Interviewer: You talked about the problem on one level, but what about on the level of the music itself — the sound aspect — the investigating of cultures to instruments, the constant evolution of how one approaches playing the saxophone, or how one plays drums or piano. How do these things relate and how ought they be combined together, not only in the sense of what role it fills with people, but in the sense of music as an art or science, the production of sound? What's happening currently with our music and its relationship to music in general?

Archie Shepp: I am concerned about it, because I think at this point that we are actually in danger of losing a species of our music, one which is very vital: our instrumental music. I think that it is in danger of being obsolete, of being phased out. Largely because it no longer has specific relevance to dance and because of some of the factors I have mentioned before, such as the need for certain types of physical involvement with the music.

Interviewer: You mean the more abstract the music becomes.

Archie Shepp: I mean the more instrumental it becomes.

Interviewer: As opposed to vocal?
Archie Shepp: As opposed to vocal. Well, take the music of Mr. Louis Armstrong. It is not Blacks who listen to that, it is white people, primarily. The so-called "Dixieland" music, New Orleans music. It's whites who

listen. Black folks don't involve themselves in that much anymore. they don't see it as relevant. New Orleans music was basically an instrumental music. It was the beginnings of what you call jazz. So-called "jazz" is primarily an instrumental music, which produced some great vocalists. But they are called jazz vocalists because they sing like instruments.

Interviewer: Are you saying that the instrumental direction is not a bad direction, but it has tended to negate the vocal.

Archie Shepp: No. I am saying that the instrumental direction represents the creation of a meta or para language system by Black people, one which derived from the codes of the spriritual, the work song, the songs of allusion, other types of songs, such as game songs, even perhaps ritual songs. All of this carried through in the music we call jazz. Largely, that music stems from the earliest spirituals through ragtime and the blues.

Interviewer: And we are in danger of losing that?

Archie Shepp: Yes, because it's a language that does not involve either vocal music or dance. Now, I am relating this to something that happened during the Forties, when there was a cabaret tax placed on clubs that hired bands, which Max Roach told us about. It was prohibitive for singers to sing in nightclubs. People — like Billie Holiday — were affected by this during the war because they usually sang with big bands. It also meant that the dancers didn't turn out. They couldn't dance, because the club owner had to pay a highter tax, so they usually organized the shows. Firstly, they cut out the big bands and then they cut out dancing. And it was at this time that the so-called "Bebop" period begins. You have Black music beginning to occur on this level for the first time when Black folks come and check it out. So it begins to acquire the elements of what are technically called the art performances because it is no longer community in that sense, but partly one in which you go to see someone do something.

Interviewer: Not as participating...

Archie Shepp: That's right. Precisely.

Interviewer: Not as communal...

Archie Shepp: But perhaps, it was just as communal, because the African tradition was not lost. Just as when they took the drum away in slavery, the rhythms were transmitted to hand clapping and foot stomping. So with this music during World War II, some of the emphasis were merely transferred. Other types of things were brought into play, particularly by people who were sensitive to this language and this music. When we first met the Chancellor of the University of Massachusetts, Amherst, in his office, the first thing he whistled for us was Charlie Parker's *Ornithology*, which was to let us know in his own way that he was hip.

Interviewer: Won't the loss of instrumental music be significantly tragic, in that voice or vocals tend to restrict you?

Archie Shepp: But incidentally, they did develop creative dances, later on, around the bebop music. And it was called the "bop" in New York and Philly. You could dance to the music and there were dancers who were experts. But, it is a kind of dancing that you don't see much of anymore. You saw it at the Savoy Ballroom in Harlem. Much of it was very creative. It wasn't limited to just a few steps, and it entailed a lot of what we call ballroom dancing today. I really saw a lot of expert dancing at the Savoy ballroom in the style of "bop." Things that could have inspired a young choreographer today, and that so-called "jazz" music has done all along. It has been a source of inspiration to other artists, writers, painters, dancers, and poets. That's our instrumental music. Within that music there is a tradition and that tradition survives in so-called "jazz" music.

FORCE AND FREEDOM NOW SUITE: THE POLITICS OF MAX ROACH

Max Roach feels acutely the position of Blacks in North America and in the world. He identifies closely with those progressive forces that attempt to deal with social justice and racial equality. He is a committed artist and in a 1961 *DownBeat* article by Marc Crawford, he insisted,

> I will never again play anything that does not have social significance. It is my duty. The purpose of the artist is to mirror his times and its effects on his fellow man. We American jazz musicians of African descent have proven beyond all doubt that we are master musicians of our instruments. Now, what we have to do is employ our skill to tell the dramatic story of our people and what we have been through.

> Little Rock, New Orleans . . .sit-in demonstrations . . .courage of our . . .young people . . . how can anyone consider my music independent of what I am?... [a] reflection of what I feel.... music must be fresh but also it must be vital — have meaning or it's nothing....new ethics are needed if man is going to survive in an atomic age...no one can stand against change.... [People] don't have to like me or my music so long as they understand what motivates it . . . Art, real art has to come from within...get away from this idea of who is the best drummer . . . you can't rate feeling, soul . . . it's personal and individual; what's the standard? . . . conformity . . . decadence . . . TV westerns and Madison Avenue . . . suburbia and organization man.... I couldn't accommodate myself to it anymore...it was choking, stifling me . . . praise for the color of my music, prejudice for the color of my skin . . . funny if it wasn't so tragic.

FORCE

My reviews of *Freedom Now Suite* and *Force*, are meant to examine this creative aspect of Max Roach's life. As a composer and percussionist, we find this commitment in *It's Time, Members Don't Get Weary, Percussion Bittersweet, Mama, Garvey's Ghost, Man from South Africa,*

Tender Warriors, and Praise for a Martyr. The reviews speak to Max's essential commitment.

When two important creative figures meet at that juncture in history where the elements must move into another cycle, one can feel that FORCE, that ENERGY propulsion which advances time and carries us beyond the past and present into the future. Max Roach and Archie Shepp, who after working together for the past four years in the university setting, arrived at that juncture in September 1976 — when the death of Chairman Mao Tse Tung and the revolts in Southern Africa pushed them to examine that motion in history in which men, ideas, and events clash and create new realities. This historic album, FORCE, by these two giants in contemporary music, represents an articulation of conscience shaped by unyielding commitment to freedom, justice and human dignity.

Max Roach and Archie Shepp have always been at the forefront of the cultural struggle of African-Americans, as their music reflects not only the crises of the recent past, but remains an expression of the historical revolt, against slavery, racism, neo-slavery and injustice. They are immersed in the continuum of Black creative music, always bending and shaping it to the concrete reality of the American ethos. They are cultural workers who provide a spiritual force and material energy that will allow us to go forward with strength and conviction.

It is in this sense that we must examine and listen to the album FORCE. The two compositions *Sweet Mao* and *Suid Afrika '76* were written by Max Roach and both provide us evidence of his immense understanding of history. Max has moved beyond his monumental work of the sixties: the *Freedom Now Suite*. *Sweet Mao* is written in three parts: The Preparation, The March, and the Beginning (of a New Day).

The life of Sweet Mao is in essence the history of China in the twentieth century. Rare, are instances when an individual makes such a profound impact on a nation's history, but Max Roach recognizes that the two are indissolubly linked — Mao's life and the Chinese Revolution. Thus, Max attempts, in this work, to capture the essence of Mao's magnetic and majestic figure — peasant, soldier, poet, philosopher, revolutionary spokesman and leader of the Chinese people. In addition, he portrays the heroic struggles Mao experienced through the preparation, the long march and the beginning of a new day: decades spent talking and arguing with peasants, workers, miners, students, teachers and soldiers; decades spent walking the vast expanse of the Chinese countryside, organizing, founding schools, cultural centers and newspapers; decades spent encouraging dissent; decades spent, fighting the feudal landlords, the Japanese invaders, the armies of Chiang Kai Shek and finally the United States and its military allies.

To encompass the life of Chairman Mao Tse Tung and the history of the Chinese Revolution in one dramatic work is a monumental task, however, Max Roach and Archie Shepp measure up to the challenge of history. Max opens the SUITE carefully and precisely, as he sets the tone for a serious work. Archie's first statement is a blues cry for Mao and for the new China. It commands your attention, as Max begins to churn up that energy FORCE under Archie, signalling that this is not ordinary preparation: it is that motion in history which will usher in a new reality, that will mold new social relations, that will reflect a cosmic force in global politics. That FORCE will transform centuries of oppression and exploitation, making freedom and dignity accessible to those heroic people who possess the will to fight. It is the synthesis of courage and determination to control one's destiny, to sacrifice everything for future generations.

But, how does one prepare for these cataclysmic events? How did Mao prepare himself? How did Max and Archie prepare themselves? Undoubtedly, there must be some qualitative assessment of one's inner resources in order to prepare for a protracted struggle. Max and Archie attempt, throughout the work, to suggest that political commitment demands physical endurance, intellectual integrity, intense meditation, artistic vision, uncompromising courage, and an undying love for one's people.

The work suggests that there are levels of preparation and one must make a qualitative leap forward to each succeeding stage. Archie moves through the layers of FORCE, urged on by the drive of Max's rhythmic underpinning — there is the will to move, to grow, to change, to revolt to reconstruct a new ethos. Max's press-rolls heighten the tension and urgency — resembling the people's voices surging upwards, urging each other and their leaders forward. The unevenness of the tempo suggests the halting, the starting, the stumbling, the uncertainty of each move within the capsule of certainty that the people united will be victorious and will step boldly into history. As Archie grows stronger in preparation, he moves through various levels of brilliant technical execution. He is inspired by the historical event. Max emphasizes the use of crashing cymbals to provide an Eastern effect. Finally, Max makes a brief but precise statement, that the people and Mao are ready to move. The March is on.

Max recognizes that it will be a Long March, and the people are not only on the move, but history will be moved, nature will be moved, the twentieth century will never be the same again as the imperial and colonial matrix will be dismantled and new forces will march into history. It is war on all fronts, and Mao can use everyone — including the most contradictory — because the struggle will sharpen not only historical contradictions, but bring forth new ones created out by the logic and necessities of combat.

Archie signals the simple statement of the March — repeating it in many tones, colors, shades and voices. It is not a rhetorical statement, but an articulation of the affirmative precepts of historical conflict. Max controls the mood and tempo with his brilliant use of the high hat and of the drum roll. It is a propulsive energy. One knows that the pace will quicken. One feels this FORCE building. Max eases Archie into high gear, as the latter heightens the unfolding drama to the people. The March is an objective historical reality, an inevitable phenomenon. Those who continue to push forward increase in strength and determination. The ideological direction gets clearer and the trajectory only leads to victory. Max's use of the high hat indicates the people's feet, rushing to victory, exhilarated by success and by the strength of Mao's leadership, vision, integrity and tranquility. Max and Archie portray all aspects of the conflict, of the actual battles as they unfold. They are in complete control of themselves, their instruments, their message, and their technical virtuosity is phenomenal. The March is a test of endurance, stamina, strength and FORCE.

Finally, there is the beginning of a new day, a new people, a new order, a new China, — victory at one level, but movement to another. Max's opening statement is joyous, strong and affirmative. The word goes out to everyone — praises for the people's glorious victory. It swings. The mood is celebrative. It opens up cosmic interstices, so that rays of sunlight bathe the vast countryside with a warm feeling of love and unity. Max stretches out, using the cymbals with sustained effect. The rhythmic interplay is evocative. Smiles light upon the people's faces. Archie creates a delicate mood with his nuances, simple but poetic. They are gems, precious and beautiful. Go ahead Archie! Even Max laughs when he listens to the tapes again.

It's a new life, a new feeling, a new mood, but it's still faithful to the continuum, to the cultural pagentry. Everyone in the pantheon of struggle is present — but it's Archie's voice and Max's energy. Thousands of flowers are strewn in the streets. Everyone is singing and Max is riding high on the cymbals. Sweet Mao is really sweet. You cannot help but enjoy the beauty of the landscape and the glory of the people's victory.

Suid Afrika 76 is somewhat sombre in tone, dramatizing that the hour of decision is at hand. The deal is ready to go down and, once again, we are at the momentous crossroads of history. Max lays out a Pan-African statement, using the rhythmic accents of the African continent, the Americas and the Caribbean. This suggests that these cataclysmic events demand a conscious concern and involvement of Black people in the African diaspora, for it is not a Civil Rights struggle that has developed in Southern Africa, but a historical struggle for independence and the reclaiming of the land which has been stolen from African people. The rightful owners of the land have brought the rapists and their apartheid policies to the bar of history, demanding that the inequities of twentieth century politics be redressed. After Max has laid down the rhythmic chant and the complex nature of the problem, Archie enters wailing, breathing, moaning, hollering a blues line which suggests the depth of his anguish, pain and suffering. Archie glides on top of Max's multi-rhythmic statements, registering their cultural challenge to this historical reality.

This work is a gem — like the uncut diamonds and gold Blacks have dug out from the South African mines, where they toil daily. It is this exploited labor, that will pose the challenge to the latter part of the twentieth century for they will step into history as militant workers on the move. In the bass drum there is a calm, clear, steady voice, echoing the call for justice. There are no screams, no shouts, but, rather a clear and precise articulation of what needs to be done.

In *Suid Afrika '76* Max tries to create a certain feeling by using an odd meter to suggest the deformity of apartheid, and the need to redress this historical defect. At the same time, Max has to fill the void of piano and bass so that the harmonic structure will be sound and the listener would not miss them. Thus, Archie and Max have to concentrate totally, in order to think harmoniously while constructing the work, for there is no one feeding them any chords. It is like carrying out a revolutionary struggle without receiving any military or economic support from outside sources. You have to go it alone, using all your creative resources, inner spiritual strength and material base.

This two record album represents a challenge to contemporary thought. It comes at a propitious moment when young people are attempting to find meaning in twentieth century life, but feel distracted by the deflections of the plasticity of the cultural apparatus. Today, we are immersed in cosmetic decadence, and Max Roach and Archie Shepp have attempted to bring some integrity to our existence. They must be applauded for this profound statement. When you have finished listening to this album, you will be exhausted, but you will have synthesized emotions and ideas, while stepping into the sunlight of contemporary history.

MAX ROACH'S WE INSIST: FREEDOM NOW SUITE

The *Freedom Now Suite* transcends time and space, reaching out to African people wherever they are struggling for FREEDOM. Freedom of all peoples in the universe: spiritual freedom, creative freedom.

The opening of the work is an invocation of the ancestral spirit/force. It represents a cleansing and purification of the ambience – the temple of creative expression — so that the gods/orishas might be summoned to enter in and speak to the experience. It is the opening up of the universe.... For unto you a child is born....how beautiful she is....the blood of Africa molded in the Georgia clay. Max covers the diaspora. "In the land of the color line, I saw the shadow of the veil" (Dr. W.E.B. Du Bois).

Dee Dee Bridgewater begins to sing — the entonement of the spirits, those who have struggled for freedom and liberty before us. The poignancy and pathos of her voice, reflecting a spiritual strength and harmony, blending with the universe — a reaching out to the sky, to send the message of freedom to all parts of the land. The drum, the voice echo the thirst for new dimensions of existence. It moves beyond the simple war cry, the call to arms, to revolt, of Toussaint, Dessalines, Nat Turner, Cudjoe, the mountain lion, Antonio Maceo, Ganga Zumba and Shaka. It moves to the awakening of a new consciousness that will structure a new existence. Cecil Bridgewater extends the voice and connects it up with the trumpet as the call goes out. Voices rising, rising, rising up out of the earth, the cry that we are determined to be free bursting forth with the affirmation of light. A conscious and predetermined freedom, born from the categories of struggle which solidify existence.

The road is long and the preparation must be built up with cosmic intensity, yet solidly and firmly rooted in the reality of the determinants of that struggle for FREEDOM NOW! Stanley Cowell and Reggie Workman provide....Sharpeville.... The shadings of Dee Dee's voice. Max announces DRIVA MAN. He confronts our historical reality, affirms the strength and spiritual confidence that will move us beyond the instruments of oppression to the mountaintops of freedom. We transcend the oppressor spiritually and creatively, even when his institutions are geared to beat us into submission, make us slaves, beasts of burden. His instruments fail, and Billy Harper registers it in concert with the choir, for the energy of the oppressed is transferred into a creative life force that establishes new contours of freedom. Robert Ray rejoices with the voices of New Africa. The spirit cannot be killed, even though the body is shackled. Billy Harper is free and celebrates his FREEDOM NOW with the choir. Slavery has not controlled, contained, defeated or demoralized his creative spirit. He bursts through the bankruptcy of the whip, which after being used on the Blacks, emerges to turn against the white oppressor and beats the working class into cultural mediocrity.

And they killed her. Mary Turner was lynched. The Black child is ripped from her abdomen. Two feeble words reverberate from the baby's lips and echo throughout the land, FREEDOM NOW, FREEDOM NOW, the battle cry of George and Johnathan Jackson, Mark Essex and the Attica thirty-three. Dee Dee recreates the plastic experience, chronicled by Ossie Davis, the African storyteller. The dialectic of verbal and non-verbal communication unfolds, and there is a synthesis of.... FREEDOM NOW. Max strengthens the intensity of the experience, the crime against humanity. Voices of women all over the world cry out against the crime of the white lyncher.

Ancestral forces and spirits surge up out of the earth to join with the living and speak out against man's inhumanity to woman, to life, to creation. We are caught in the maddening capsule of reality: in an instant of life, there is death. The girl that was ripped out of the mother's womb will cry out FREEDOM NOW and liberate the mother and all mothers from the lyncher's rope.

Max extols the meaning of freedom thru the seven principles of Blackness – Umoja, Kujichagalia, Ujamaa, Ujima, Nia, Imani, and Kuumba – through our ancestral origins, and those values that the newly born child will express in her statements of freedom. In death there is life, a life that affirms an African existence, an African creative source distilled through the Western experiences of slavery, lynchings and struggle for FREEDOM NOW.

Max expresses a cosmological harmony with the African universe, with the diaspora as he states clearly the value structure for our existence.... principles firmly rooted in our historical experience, Umoja, Uhura Sasa. Bill Bridges expands beyond the value structure to carry the message of truth to all the people... on the block, in the churches, in the holes, in the bars, in the prisons, on the job, in the homes, wherever they might be. He is the young messenger who runs through the countryside, through the city, shouting the message of FREEDOM NOW. He carries the torch high in the air, the torch that will bring a New World into being, a world free from oppression and exploitation.

Billy Harper speaks authoritatively about the content of the message and walks with confidence behind Bill Bridges, his voice elucidating the righteous message. His statements are clear and precise. The people know that it is FREEDOM NOW and they are ready to respond to its constituent demands. Let us move forward NOW. Peace is a necessary ingredient of freedom. Reggie Workman strides elegantly as a man who knows, where he is going and what he is doing. He is in control of all the forces and elements. He is consumed by nature but not overwhelmed by it, for he is at the center of the universe in cosmological harmony with his identity, his historical responsibility and his ancestral forces.

Max then emerges to define, shape, mold, and expand the core of our cosmic consiousness. He stretches the mind to the limits of human comprehension FREEDOM DAY. Dee Dee sings it proudly. She basks in the sun and rejoices at its authenticity. It is real to her, to the choir, to all the people of the nation. The colonizer's flag has been taken down and the people's flag has risen before the eyes of the nation — Ghana, Guinea, Algeria, Nigeria, Tanzania, Guyana, Kenya, Jamaica, Trinidad and Tobago. We are all proud of freedom. The flag flaps gaily in the wind and we salute it with our heads held high and voices stretched to eternity. We have lived, fought and died for this FREEDOM NOW. It represents our historic destiny and responsibility. The daughter, torn from her mother's womb, sings thru Dee Dee's voice for she is the first to expand its meaning. FREEDOM NOW. FREEDOM NOW. The first words uttered become the first words affirmed in the Nation's Anthem, FREEDOM DAY.

Black Women Writers in the Past Two Decades: Voices within the Veil

Black women in the past two decades have made significant contributions to the body of knowledge that informs our understanding of the social process, ideology, aesthetics, and literary criticism. From Rosa Parks (who ignited the Montgomery Bus Boycott on December 1, 1955) to Assata Shakur (who continues to carry the revolutionary tradition forward, beyond her political imprisonment into exile), Black women have been at the forefront of shaping and defining the social process either through their creative vision or their indomnitable strength.

The work of Black women writers in the recent past and present provides a focus for contemporary issues. During the decade of the sixties, the emphasis of these writers was on the critical examination of the universal postulates of freedom and justice; whereas the writers since the seventies turned inward in a microcosmic fashion, raising fundamental questions with other women about the nature of their existence. In a real sense, women are talking to each other about personal matters that at first glance seem to have an apolitical tone. Yet, fundamentally their concerns challenge American society in general and male domination in particular.

It is significant to recognize that these voices within the veil have unveiled themselves, challenging both the form and content of literary undertakings with a strident tone. And this unveiling places them at the forefront of the struggle for identity, resistance and rebellion. When Sonia Sanchez wrote *We Are a Badd People*, she was insistent in her conviction that,

    now
       when i hear billie's soft
    soul/ful/sighs
       of "am i blue"
          i say

no. sweet/billie.
no mo.
no mo
blue/trains running on this track
they all been de/railed.

am i blue?

sweet/baby/blue/
billie.

no. i'm blk/
and ready.[1]

Sister Sonia had moved beyond Billie Holiday's moanful blue sounds, confronting racist American society with the conviction of Abbey Lincoln singing in *Freedom Now Suite, Mendacity and Straight Ahead.* She was indeed "black and ready," charged with her historic mission and for the past two decades Sonia Sanchez has maintained her serious political commitment.

Once Rosa Parks, Fannie Lou Hamer, Daisy Bates, Ella Baker and others had set a process in motion, with their quiet determination to confront the barriers of racial prejudice in the South, it was obvious that the floodgates of history had been opened, thereby, fulfilling Margaret Walker's dream, "Time done come to set my people free." Ms. Walker, grasped the urgency of the times and the significance of the little girls, who integrated the school system at Little Rock, Arkansas, by infusing the experience with the ancestral force of Harriet Tubman. She wrote,

I like it here just fine
And I don't want no bail
My sister's here
My mother's here
And all my girlfriends too
I want my rights
I'm fighting for my rights
I want to be treated
Just like everybody else

I like it fine in Jail
And I don't want no Bail [2]

She further accentuated the incisiveness and qualitative determination of these ordinary young women, who confronted the social order in "Street Demonstration":

Hurry up Lucille or we won't get
arrested with our group
(an eight-year old demonstrator, 1963)
We're hoping to be arrested
And hoping to go to jail
We'll sing and shout and pray
For Freedom and for Justice
And for Human Dignity
The fighting may be long
And some of us will die
But Liberty is costly
And ROME they say to me
Was not built in one day

Hurry up Lucille, Hurry up
We're Going to Miss Our Chance to go to Jail. [3]

Perhaps, the most challenging aspect of the emergence of a new consciousness in the early sixties was the radical definition of self, which Black women confronted as they moved away from the Hollywood interpretation of glamour and beauty to an affirmation of their naturalness. They struggled with the question of identity and the boldness of a self-assertion that had been negated for decades. Lucille Clifton examined *The Way it Was,* when she wrote,

mornings
I got up early
greased my legs
straightened my hair and
walked quietly out
not touching

nothing changed
  (nothing remained the same)
I walked out quietly
mornings
in the '40s
a nice girl
not touching
trying to be white. [4]

Mae Johnson extended this experience in her poem,

i used to wrap my white doll up in
an old towel
and place her upon my chest
i used to sing those funny old school songs
god bless america
my country 'tis of thee
when i was young
and very colored.[5]

This gathering of consciousness and self-assertion in the Black woman led to antagonisms within the family unit as well as in the larger society. Parents were upset with young Black women, who not only projected new conceptions of beauty, but negated the European mode. The larger society looked askance at these early warriors, who dared to be different and to define themselves outside the matrix of patterned behavior. This evoked a dialectical tug-of-war, which is one way of struggling towards self-regard, self-appraisal and self-positioning in society. Consequently, by the end of the decade of the sixties, Aretha Franklin was not only demanding RESPECT and Nina Simone was not only celebrating her "naturalness" – as a poetic extension of Gwendolyn Bennett's "To a Dark Girl" – but Mari Evans was proudly stating,

....I
am a black woman
tall as a cypress
strong
beyond all definition still
defying place

and time
and circumstance
  assailed
    impervious
      indestructible
Look
  on me and be
renewed [6]

The Black woman had moved beyond the alienating contours of her early antagonistic formation in the family, in the state, and within a certain set of politics. She had developed a self-consciousness out of the discovery of her essential beauty and the integrity of her commitment to struggle, thereby, moving Erika Huggins to write,

    i love people
    love nature
    love love
  i am a revolutionary
  nothing special
  one soul
  one life willing
      to give it
  ready to die....[7]

Central to the literary focus of the sixties was the spirit of revolt that brought dedicated, courageous women into SNCC, SCLC, CORE, RAM and the Black Panther Party. They worked, fought and died as Assata Shakur has stated:

It is our duty to fight for our
freedom. It is our duty to win.
We must love each other and
support each other. We have
nothing to lose but our chains.[8]

In a letter entitled "To my People," Assata Shakur not only declared herself a member of the Black Liberation Army, but insisted that "she has declared war on all forces that have raped our women, castrated our men and kept our babies empty bellied." In addition, she maintained that "Black people should and inevitably must determine their destinies. We must learn how to struggle by struggling. We must learn by our mistakes." She was the extension of a force created by the social conditions that permeated the sixties, out of which developed an attitude of daring. This spirit of resistance and revolt in the sixties can be contrasted with a kind of passivity and quiescense which we find in today's politics. We have moved away from the politics of confrontation to a politics of assimilation, saturated with crass opportunism and unabashed guilt, as the benefactors of the new neo-colonial order have become caretakers of the poor and the unemployed — while they enjoy the luxuries of sterile consumption. Jayne Cortez writes,

> These are the times of sterility
> of hormone shots and lobotomies
> of dehydrated funk and stagnated
> celebrities
> these are the times of solitary confinement.[9]

Of course one could view the stark contrast of Aretha Franklin's impact in 1968 when she was singing "Respect" and her 1978 wedding "a' la Hollywood."

One of the elements of the literary thrust of the sixties was the commitment of the Black woman writer to ground with the people, to move among the masses in the community whether in the South or the north and to make this experience an essential part of her subject matter. Gwendolyn Brooks wrote,

> I've stayed in the front yard all my life
> I want a peek at the back
> Where it's rough and untended and hungry weed/grows.[10]

We must note here that there was no suggestion of disdain or carricature, but rather a sense of belonging and a need to ground with her sisters and brothers. This was an exploration into the ground; a ground that fueled her existence; a ground that she could open up with dignity, for it led her to the new voices in the Organization of Black American Culture, which she helped to form, nurture and encourage. She unlocked that storehouse of creative energy on the southside of Chicago.

During the middle and late sixties, Black women writers gave support to Sonia Sanchez's plea:

Let us begin the real work
                    now
let us take back our children from
vista/
        workers   ywca/a
             sunday/schools
boy/
        girl/scouts of white/america
let us begin the work of centuries
untold.
             let us teach our children
what is to be learnnnnned bout themselves.
                    us. let us
honestlee begin
                    nation/hood
builden
             for our children.
                    with our
minds/hands/souls.
                    with our blk/visions
for blk/lives.
                    let us begin
the begin/en work now.
                    while our
children still
             remember us and loooove. [11]

This was a serious call to the Black nation and these sisters were workers in the schools, especially independent schools, with their love and creative energy. They worked hard to make these schools viable at a tremendous sacrifice to their personal advancement. They infused into the freedom schools the same enthusiasm they had given to the freedom rides and voter registration drives because they understood that education was critical to our future. Their undertaking was enormous. Yet, in spite of their efforts, by the early seventies, public school education in this country began to decline sharply and today we find 48% of Black 17 year olds functionally illiterate. I have met hundreds of Black students in the seventies and eighties who know nothing of what happened in the sixties, for their minds have been narcoticized by a bankrupt public educational system. These heroic sisters, who worked assiduously in the freedom schools and those who have continued in the more viable independent schools, saved some of our fine young minds. We owe a deep gratitude to these Black women writers who wrote especially for our young people in this period.

During the sixties, there was also a profound respect for Black men, as hero figures – Malcolm, Martin, Medgar, Paul Robeson and George Jackson, who inspired our work. But more important, we must listen to Linda Goss' lucid statement of will, as she grasps the global dimensions of our struggle for freedom and dignity,

> Revolution man Black
> listen, listen in my poem
> of love song
> song of making babies
> sons to a battle
> daughters to make sons to a battle

> Revolution man Black
> before you go
> and win the battle
> leave in me a seed
> your son
> your daughter to produce a grandson.

> Revolution man Black
> when you come home
> winning the battle
> you will see you in our son
> and you will plant more seeds in me
> make brave warriors and fertile daughters.[12]

Sarah Wright's poem to Paul Robeson ("Until They Have Stopped") is also a powerful statement about Black women's concerns for the injustices heaped upon them by capitalism and imperialism.

Until they have stopped filling my lungs
with tear gas in Alabama, U.S.A.
And vomiting gas in Vietnam – knowing that
to rob a person of will is to rob them of life,
Until they have stopped disgracing the languages
of the peoples of this globe
By calling these murderous attacks "humane" – and
out-and-out war "deterrant activity"
Until they have stopped this
 assault to my
natural intelligence,
I will not desist from saying, "No!"

"No!" to the would-be destroyers of my mother's milk,
Full of earth and determination and broken fingernails –
Hurting to the quick from digging and groveling and
Making this and that do when she knows by the
standards of her Christ
Nothing else would do except
A more equitable distribution of the wealth of this
earth.
Until they stop the necessity of millions of mothers
All over this earth from having to feed children on
Fairy tales as a substitute for food
Until they stop! I will not desist from saying "No!"
For no fairy tale will do when the belly bleeds
from the claws of hunger.[13]

At this time Black women writers talked about their male counterparts with conviction, even when they were critical about their involvement in drugs and reactionary political behavior. Sonia Sanchez's "answer to yo/ question of am I not yo/woman even if you went on shit again" and "chant for young brothas and sistuhs" were straight forward and poignant statements from a Black woman, who dealt with a situation directly but not negatively. She confronted Black men but did not put them down like

Mr. Louisiana Hot Link and especially Beau Willie Brown in Ntozake Shange's "For Colored Girls Who Have Considered Suicide When the Rainbow is Enuf."

The literary writers of this decade were constantly absorbing and returning to the community with their consummate strength. They gave much love and hope, as they walked together. From Angela Davis to Imani Kazana, these sisters have committed themselves to the freeing of George Jackson, Ruchell McGhee, Ben Chavis, the Wilmington Ten, and thousands of political prisoners unjustly persecuted in the penetentiaries throughout this country. These women have stood by Black men, walking tall, "coming a little closer and stating where they are from." They have never been afraid to project Mari Evans' beautiful statement "Speak the truth to the people."

> Speak the truth to the people
> Talk sense to the people
> Free them with reason
> Free them with honesty
> Free the people with Love and Courage and
> Care for their Being
> Spare them the fantasy
> Fantasy enslaves
>
> Speak the truth to the people
> To identify the enemy is to free the mind
> Free the mind of the people
> Speak to the mind of the people
> Speak truth.[14]

And then we moved into the seventies.

To understand something new requires that we make ourselves ready for it. It entails the shaping of a new form. The challenge of the seventies was in understanding not only the day to day reality of Black women, but our status as a people and the role we are to play in the shaping of the 21st Century. At one level, we are faced with the dictates of the commodity market, in which Black female (and male) writers are being promoted by the publishing and entertainment industry in a way that is quite different from the sixties. During the earlier decade, the poets and writers had to go out among the people selling their books, reading their poems, and singing their songs because the cultural apparatus was not prepared to market *Mississippi Goddam* or *The True Import of the Present Dialogue Negro vs Black*. However, there are certain Black writers whose work have now become the central focus of today's dialogue.

The emphasis has changed as Black women explore critical problems in their interpersonal relationships, especially their experiences with Black men as they reflect on their roles in the Nation of Islam, SNCC, SCLC, US, Spirit House, the Black Panther Party and the many Black student unions across the country. What has been the nature of that experience juxtaposed against their heroic work in the struggle for freedom? As Black women turn inward, they see the Black man as a complex, difficult, weak, stumbling, opportunistic person. They don't find the father that Margaret Walker wrote about in *Epitaph for my Father*,

> Yet I have known
> A noble prince-like man for all my life,
> For he was humble in his dignity
> Composed and calm in every storm of life,
> Harsh poverty could not debase, demean
> His deep integrity. He rose above the fray.[15]

They don't find these men, because 52% of Black women are heading households with children and no fathers.

Ms. Louise Little asks her son Malcolm X when he visited her at an insane asylum in 1952 "where have all the people gone?" Ms. Georgia Jackson asked me in 1972 when I visited her home in Pasadena, California "Where have all the Black men gone." Well, we know that they are being shot down everyday in the streets of this country. The homicide rate, for Black men between the ages of 15 and 35, is alarmingly high. They are being incarcerated in the prisons and insane asylums. They are being lobotomized culturally and physiologically at an early age in the public school system.

But in the decade of the seventies, the substantive issues raised by Black female writers – who are searching for meaning in a plastic, consumer society – must be seriously examined. Ntozake Shange writes,

> we deal wit emotion too much
> so why don't we go on ahead and be white then/
> and make everthin dry and abstract wit no
> rhythm and no reelin for sheer pleasure/yes
> let's go on and be white/we're right in the
> middle of it/no use holdin out/holding onto
> ourselves/lets think our way outta feelin/
> lets abstract ourselves some families and
> maybe tonite/I'll find a way to make myself
> come without you/no fingers or other objects
> just that which isn't spiritual evolution
> cuz its empty and godliness is plenty is
> ripe and fertile/thinkin wont do me a bit
> of good tonite/i need to be loved/and
> haven't the audacity to say
> where are you/and don't know who to say
> it to.
>
> i've lost it
> touch wit reality.[16]

And this becomes a position, which we must deal with, for our young people have lost touch with reality as they become absorbed into the illusions and fantasy of the disco-world and the crippling numbness of the televised message.

Stephany deepens this feeling of alienation, when she raises the question,

> Who is not a stranger still
> even after making love
> or the morning after?
> the interlude of sleep again divides
> it is clear again where one body
> ends and the next begins.

Think to think at each encounter,
we will be strangers still
even after making love
and long conversation
even after meals and showers
together

and years of touching.
It is not often that the core
of what I am is lost in longing

and is less often filled.
I understand my clinging
to the thought of you.[17]

Toni Morrison stretches this argument even further in *Sula*,

> The men who took her to one or another of those places had merged
> into one large personality: the same language of love, the same
> entertainments of love, the same cooling of love. Whenever she
> introduced her private thoughts into their rubbings or goings, they
> hooded their eyes. They taught her nothing but love tricks, shared
> nothing but wrong, gave nothing but money. She had been looking
> all along for a friend, and it took her a while to discover that a lover
> was not a comrade and could never be – for a woman.

It is obvious, that in these statements and in the fundamental concerns of *Sula* and *Meridian* (Alice Walker), there is an attempt to come
to grips with the hurt and pain of sexual exploitation, alienation and
emptiness. And Sonia Sanchez writes in Poem No. 7 in of *Love Poems*,

when he came home
from her
he poured me on
the bed and slid
into me like glass.
and there was
the sound of splinters.[18]

This is an experience which is at the heart of our coming to grips with the meaning of relationships and the conflicts that exist in our social order. These women are searching for clarity; but, at the same time, the cultural apparatus has begun to manipulate these antagonisms with Marlena Shaw singing *Little Boy Get Lost*, Linda Clifford's *Runaway Girl*, Tina Turner's *What's Love Got to do With it*, and Janet Jackson's *What Have You Done for Me Lately*. The lyrics of these songs dramatize the conflict and encourage disunity in the community.

However, there remains the positive attitude of Cheryl May, a seventeen year old poet who writes with a great deal of optimism. She sees possibilities in the continuum, in her poem entitled "Meaning Revolution,"

> And they said it means bloodshed
> But, I think it means change
> "Cause he didn't even know me
> I just said please
> And he standing there
> in windbreaker and tennis shoes
> kinda dug my black need
> And Gave me
> three pennies
> and a nickel————————change
> So I could ride the bus home.[19]

Finally, the call which Angela Davis made to us in the early seventies, looms larger in significance as we begin to close out the twentieth century. It is absolutely necessary that our writers, scholars and activists begin to put their stamp on what has taken place in the twentieth century. We must delineate and define what took place at the turn of the century when we moved from the South to the North, when we began to come to grips with the "Betrayal of the Negro," when we reflect on the migratory experience through the writings of Margaret Walker and Zora Neale Hurston, when we begin to deal with the horrors of lynching through the work of Ida B. Wells, the "quicksands" of identity struggle through Nella Larsen and Georgia Douglass Johnson, the explosions of war, technology and urbanization through Margaret Walker, integration and protest through Lorraine Hansberry, Gwendolyn Brooks, Paula Marshall, and Ella Baker, student demonstrations through Margaret Walker, Sonia Sanchez and Carolyn Rodgers, violence and revolt through Nikki Giovanni, Pearl Cleage, Johari Amini, Jayne Cortez, Mari Evans, Sarah Fabio, Alicia Johnson and June Jordan, and alienation and separation through Toni Morrison, Ntozake Shange, Alice Walker and Gayle Jones.

This body of critical literary analysis must be seriously examined, in hope that a careful summation might be passed on to future generations. Angela Davis has issued this historic challenge in her statement:

> We, the Black women of today, must accept the full weight of a legacy wrought in blood by our mothers in chains. Our fight, while identical in spirit, reflects different conditions and this implies different paths of struggle. But as heirs to a tradition of supreme perserverance and heroic resistance, we must hasten to take our place, wherever our people are forging on towards freedom.[20]

NOTES

1. Sonia Sanchez, "Liberation/Poem", *We A BadDDD People*, p. 54.

2. Margaret Walker, "Girl Without Bail," in Duley Randall, ed., *The Black Poets*, pp. 156-157.

3. Ibid., Walker, p. 156.

4. Lucille Clifton, The Way It Was, *Good News From The Earth*, p.3.

5. Mae Johnson, "Memories," Arnold Adoff, *Black Out Loud: An Anthology of Modern Poetry by Black Americans*, p. 48.

6. Mari Evans, "I Am a Black Woman," *I Am A Black Woman*, p. 12.

7. Ericka Huggins, "I Love People," in Angela Davis', *If They Come in the Morning*, p. 111.

8. Assata Shakur, "Women in Prison: How We Are," *Black Scholar*, Vol. 9, No. 7, April 1980, p. 56.

9. Jayne Cortez, "These Are The Times," *Scarifications*, p. 21.

10. Gwendolyn Brooks, "A Song In the Front Yard," *Selected Poems*, p. 6.

11. Sonia Sanchez, "Let us Begin the Real Work(for Elijah Muhammad, who has begun)," *We A BaddDDD People*, p. 65.

12. Linda Goss, Revolution Black Man," Orde Coombs, *We Speak as Liberators, Young Black Poets*, p. 61.

13. Sarah Wright, "Until They Have Stopped, *Black Out Loud*, p. 125.

14. Mari Evans, "Speak The Truth to the People," *I Am A Black Woman*, p.91.

15. Margaret Walker, "Epitaph For My Father," *October Journey*, p. 24.

16. Ntozake Shange, "For Colored Girls Who Have Considered Suicide/ When The Rainbow Is Enuf," p. 25.

17. Stephany, "Who is Not A Stranger Still," in Dudley Randall, *The Black Poets*, p.331.

18. Sonia Sanchez, "Poem No. 7, *Love Poems*, p. 42.

19. Cheryl May, "Meaning Revolution," *Howard University Hilltop Review* (March 1971), p. 6.

20. Angela Davis, "Reflections on the Black Woman's Role in the Community of Slaves," The Black Scholar: The Black Woman, Vol. 12, No. 6, (November/December, 1981), p. 15.

PART THREE

THE EDUCATIONAL IMPERATIVE:
TOWARD THE RECONSTRUCTION
OF THE BLACK WORLD

III. THE EDUCATIONAL IMPERATIVE

INTRODUCTION

At no time has the responsibility of the Black professional been as great as now. And this responsibility has been betrayed by the decisions of some Black professionals and the omissions of others. Some have directly sold us out for personal rewards and advancement; others have remained silent in the face of exploitation and oppression. Black independence (cultural, political, and economic) remains a serious challenge that educators must confront. Black professionals have to deal with the problems affecting Black people as a social responsibility. They cannot stand at a distant horizon and gaze at the people's suffering and plead for objective analysis. They have the responsibility of intelligence, which should compel them to develop their people as an independent force on the world stage.

Education must reflect the unification of our cultural, social, political, and economic perspectives and values. The problem of educating African Americans has been the attempt to measure Black people against a standard outside of our cultural context. The Western powers during the twentieth century have intensified "specialization" in their educational and training activities. They have programmed people's minds through isolated forms of language where there are few, if any, common bases for effective communication. This takes away a sense of solidarity or unity and produces cold, alienated people without human values.

The experiences of Black people, conditioned through oppression, require an entirely different design for information and knowledge input. We must develop new educational learning systems, which are applicable to large numbers of mis-educated people — who continue to live under conditions of economic deprivation — and which take into account our cultural, political, social and economic needs.

PART THREE - *Introduction*

Our brains analyze, synthesize and store knowledge and facts selectively on the basis of social value judgements. We learn only in proportion to the values we place on new information and knowledge as it supports our needs. These values and needs become the organizing factors in perception and take place on a subjective level of ordering. Parameters often are unconsciously projected through culture and consciously through the environment. One's environment (school, education, home) usually helps to classify knowledge in a way that makes it more assessable. Thus, if the environment is discriminating, constraining and self-defeating, that is what will be learned. Therefore, educators must establish a wider cognitive domain from which Black people can operate to expand our knowledge and redefine our place in the world.

Black progress will depend on Black people collectively understanding the facts (our consciousness level), mastering our resources, and supporting our collective development. We will begin to solve our problem of subsistence living and achieve advancement for all our people when we realize that the critical component for Black development is education.

CULTURE AND THE UNIVERSITY COMMUNITY

> When [Herr] Goebells, the brain behind Nazi propaganda, heard culture being discussed, he brought out his revolver. That shows that the Nazis — who were and are the most tragic expression of imperialism and of its thirst for domination — ...had a clear idea of the value of culture as a factor of resistance to foreign domination.
>
> — Amilcar Cabral, *Return to the Source*

In any discussion of culture, one must recognize that culture is born, of necessity, out of the disagreements of men and women in societal relationships. It reflects both intra-group as well as inter-group antagonisms. Because culture brings one to that secret awakening in which individuals strive to realize their destiny, the salvation of culture is bound with the salvation of humanity. And, it is disagreement which heals our inadequacies. Therefore, the great thing is to arrive at the painful realization that each one of us has limitations, which are inherent in human nature. But, no one can disagree with another unless he/she holds fast to the truth that he/she defends and which can be challenged. This essay is presented in the spirit of disagreement, challenging critically ongoing activities in various university communities. Futhermore, it is precisely because political, cultural, military and technological problems are interconnected that any aesthetic principle, any work of art, any cultural manifestation, or any intellectual discourse will have political and philosophical implications.

Jacques Stephan Alexis, before he was imprisoned and assassinated by the Duvalier government in Haiti, wrote:

> What is culture, in fact, if not, on a general level, the product of that tendency which impels men to organize the elements of their knowledge of the universe and of the society in which they live, to organize them collectively in relationship to the past and the present and to recompose an image of them which is vaster than the apparent one, an image which is projected in their psychisms, in their acts, in their comportment and in all their production? When societies enter

upon the process of forming a people or a nation, culture becomes
something more complex, richer and more varied. One might say that
in this case culture is a community of psychisms, of tastes, of
tendencies, of concepts, which expresses itself in all fields of human
activity, a community formed by history, more or less clearly defined,
more or less stable, a community resulting from a psychic heritage and
exteriorizing itself by works of beauty and reason, in variable relation
with the development of the productive forces and the social
relationships of the society which produces it. [1]

With this in mind, we can realize that culture embraces the whole
life of a people from the beginning of its formation, its gradual constitution, down to its modern organization. In this process, culture evolves as
an incessant happening whose origins are lost in the darkness of time and
whose prospects fade into the mists of the future. This formulation of the
notion of culture should provide the foundation for an examination of
contemporary North American culture and the intellectual communities
that sustain the imperatives of the existing ethos by their approaches to
entertainment and education.

As I moved around the country during the past fifteen to twenty
years, the familiar question on campuses or in the street, "What's happening?" seemed to elicit a patterned response, "Nothing." There appeared
to be a lull in activities, as though young people in the seventies and
eighties had by-passed the sixties and were nostalgically floating in the
fifties. In addition, the educators in these communities were apparently
battle-worn, and, at times, they were unable to cope with issues raised in
American society during the sixties.

Of course, I have recognized that after periods of great emotional
stress in the larger society, *the nation* has turned to the cultural apparatus
to manipulate the sensibilities of its citizenry and to "cool things out."
Historically, we can find evidence of this prevailing attitude, for after the
challenges of the great issues of the latter part of the nineteenth century,
we have seen in the twentieth century the great flowering of popular
culture as films, radio, Broadway musicals, dance, sports, music, literature, theatre and advertising expanded the base of the commodity market.
For example, in the 1900s it was "ragtime," the "cakewalk" and

vaudeville; in the 1920s it was the Charleston, the Cotton Club and the Broadway musical; in the 1950s, it was the twist, American Bandstand, "rock and roll," Marilyn Monroe and John Wayne; in the seventies it was the discotheque, SoulTrain, sports spectaculars, electronic music, horror movies and Roots. But there is a much more chilling effect when one observes that the lull on campuses does not reflect a turning inward, a search for the creative self, a type of woodshedding perhaps, but rather a negation of reality and a refusal to believe that one could summon up the energy to engineer productive change.

In order to exist, individuals must realize their essence by the increase and expression of vital force. For Max Roach in his album, "Force," is creative energy in motion. But when the automatic response "nothing's happening" is systemic, it is clear that these respondents have been made into mere zombies living in a cosmetic bubble. There is no "force" in their lives, no creative motion, and one can see that they are in a death-trap in terms of shaping the future. The "I can get high with a little help from my friends" syndrome remains prevalent.

The distinction between true and false consciousness, real and immediate interest, is still meaningful, but it has become blurred in the larger society by the availability of consumer items, which suggest freedom of choice. Free choice among a wide variety of goods and services does not signify freedom, if these goods and services sustain social controls over the life of toil and fear — that is, if they sustain alienation. Our concern, at this point, is *how much we consume and not what we consume.* Likewise, the compelling force in the cultural super-market is the attractiveness of the pre-packaged commodity projected as creative work in wrappings that are as as attractive as they are useless to our development. We are locked into a Kleenex-type culture. Thus, in the entertainment world today, we look at not what has been said and done, but rather at how slick or attractive it has been presented so as to affect our subliminal perceptions. Of course, this means that pleasure can be adjusted to generate submission resulting in the atrophy of our mental organs. We can stay on "cloud nine" in our "pipe dreams," and even when Gil Scott Heron comes to the campus community, we rememmber "the

Bottle," but forget quickly the messages of "Watergate" and "Johannesburg."

We must, therefore, determine ways to use our mental equipment when we attend musical, theatrical and dance productions mounted on college and university campuses or when we view art exhibitions and/or commercial films like *Network, Rocky Rambo, Trading Places, 48 hours, or Do the Right Thing*? Also, we must determine how to examine the relationship between entertainment and learning in our experiences. Entertainment can be one of the most effective modes of learning in the university community and it could provide an organic link between the ivory tower and the real world. However, to accomplish this linkage, there must be more than a casual exchange between the educational institution and the artist. There should be mutual interest and concern for the dynamic aspects of the creative process and not a feigned distance based on services performed or consumed.

To teach the contemporary world what is behind the ideological and material veil and how it can be changed, the artist must link the spectator's identification with the events on stage. There shoud be an attempt to provide distance and reflection beyond empathy and feeling for the work performed or witnessed. You should not strive to get "high" on Max Roach's or Archie Shepp's technique or musical virtuosity, but rather you should attempt to comprehend the language and logic of their message; you should try to synthesize its implications so that the experience goes beyond the emotive to the cognitive, in order that all the semantical and/or linguistic possibilities of the creation might be clearly understood. This is "FORCE." The mind must not be blown by Max Roach's *Freedom Now Suite*. It must be nurtured by the essential truths of the message and moved to higher levels of responsible action and work.

On the other side of the coin, if we turn to entertainment *qua* entertainment, we would discover the exploration of the violent, the erotic and the sensual, which can provide immediate gratification. But, in a technological society, a mechanical state of containment can easily be contrived to induce these conditions of institutionalized desublimation, music by Musaz and the disco sound. For example, in today's music

Down Wit OPP, Comfort Zone, and *Ain't Too Proud To Beg* are only minor musical modes consumed by young people. In the seventies, a university outside of Washington, D.C invited the Jimmy Castor Bunch with his live apes and monsters on stage, together with Kool and the Gang and Parliament Funkadelics one week; while Kizz and Greatful Dead were invited the following weekend. In this environment, the music of the soul becomes the music of salesmanship. Commercial value, not truth counts. On it centers the rationality of the status quo and all alien rationality is bent to it. Thus, the common denominator of culture is the most salable canned commodity.[2] Students absorb this as educational institutions become places of comfort and leisure, with thousands of consumers benefiting from expanded cultural budgets, gala homecoming affairs and diffuse entertainment activities. They have become centers of well-being, even for the oppressed minorities and the response remains, "the community is too well-off to care."

A college student is not only an individual to whom books are necessary, he/she is also a person whose reasoning, however elementary it may be, affects and directs his/her life. Definitive or not, this can be a viable concept and an important tool for examining the student's relationship to culture and the consumer society. In the forties and fifties, for example, college students were interested in buying clothes and being part of the latest fashions. Their dormitory rooms were modestly furnished. There was a great emphasis on reading so they built personal libraries. Today, students spend less money on clothes (since dungarees and levis have been in vogue for the past ten years), even less on books, but most on compact discs, television sets, stereo equipment, VCRs, herbs, posters, mobiles and other gadgets for their rooms. They are more visually oriented as a result of television and film, and they are deeper into popular music. The technology of popular entertainment has changed their lifestyles, tastes, and consumer habits, for they are attracted by new sounds and images. Herbert Marcuse writes in *One Dimensional Man*:

> the so-called consumer economy and the politics of corporate capitalism have created a second nature of man which ties him libidinally and aggressively to 'the commodity form.' The need for

possessing, cosuming, handling and constantly renewing the gadgets, devices and instruments, engines offered to and imposed upon the people for using these wares even at the danger of one's own destruction, has become a 'biological' need in the sense just defined.[3]

This means that the import/export trade of culture on campuses demands a rapid turnover of new experiences, acts and information. The university has become a center of popular consumption, with agents and managers of the cultural apparatus gearing their products to this specific market. A whole entourage of popular artists, speakers, writers, etc. vie for this expanding market and gear their message to its needs. Agents recognize that students do not have to leave downtown to go uptown, rather students can have all their entertainment brought to the campus, cash-on-delivery, Las Vegas style.

Our advanced technological society is rapidly making objects of most of us, and subtly programming us to conform to the logic of the system. To the degree that this has happened, we have become submerged in the "culture of silence," artistic silence and political silence. There are loud noises all around us in electronic media, but very little has emerged as a distinctive, creative character in the nation at large, especially in the university community. There is cultural sterility and/or academic mediocrity. Actually, there is not even space for evoking conscience or a spirit of inquiry against the oppressive elements of reality. Consequently, the increasing use of drugs and alcohol in the schools, reinforced by electronic music, violence and eroticism in image-making and the alienation experienced in finding relevance to one's intellectual development have all contributed to the style of participation at cultural events. At a Bob Marley concert on a certain campus, the audience was more concerned with "getting high" and "tripping out" than with dealing with the message of the music. This ambivalence extends from Jimi Hendrix's concerts to Public Enemy's events in the Terror Dome. On another occasion, at a recent Natalie Cole concert, the emphasis was on fashion, style, "getting down" and "getting over." The insanity of indifference to the whole absolves individual insanities in the cosmetic experience and turns cultural mediocrity into a rational enterprise.

One of the important aspects of culture in the national synthesis is the myth-making capability of the apparatus in the diffusion of bourgeoise ideas. In the cultural agenda of the university community, the architects of entertainment build in success models so that one can measure artistic accomplishment with financial rewards or social prestige. However, even beyond that, there are several myths that are constantly propagated: (1) the myth that anyone who is industrious can become an entrepreneur and can be successful in the larger society, (2) the myth of the equality of all people, (3) the myth of the universal right to educational opportunity, and (4) the myth of private property as fundamental to personal human development.

All these myths and many more, vital to the socialization process, reach their highest level of articulation in the university community. Thus, the cultural agenda is organized to project certain commercial achievements in society, where emphasis is placed on the artist's ability to attract large audiences. But at the same time, we tend to overlook these myths — whose internalization by students remains essential to their effective control both as consumers and aspiring professionals. These young people are the targets of patented bites of propaganda as part of their cultural diet. They are socialized to be passive consumers, attracted to the glitter of the flea market. In this situation, reality is nullified and alienation is intensified; the more alienated people are, the easier it will be to divide them and keep them divided.

Just as it is necessary to divide the people in order to preserve the status quo, and, consequently, the power of the dominators, it is equally essential, both in the university community and the society at large, for the oppressors to keep the oppressed from perceiving their strategy. So, the oppressors must convince the oppressed that they are being defended against the demonic actions of marginals, disrupters, radicals and "enemies of God." To divide and confuse the people, the destroyers call themselves builders in the brave pursuit of humanization and accuse the true builders of being disruptive and destructive. (History, however, always takes it upon itself to modify these designations). There is an official need to control the environment and manipulate consciousness through culture and the effective distribution of scarce resources. This manipulation encourages opportunism. It can also be a significant instrument for deflecting creative energies. In this manner, you can reduce people to a manageable, unthinking agglomeration and "cool them out." This was the efficient Nixon strategy of the early seventies that was brilliantly executed by Gerald Ford after the former's dismissal. Also, we observed what President Jimmy Carter had in store in the remaining years of that decade. Ronald Reagan and George Bush have encouraged cultural passivity by using subliminal images of patriotism and ethnocentrism, while pushing the nation further into debt.

Manipulation of the sensibilities, like the conquest, whose objectives it serves, attempts to anesthesize the people so they will not think. In the seventies, just as today, we were locked into the disco sound and the making of the Frankenstein monster. *Rambo* and *Rocky, Jaws* and *King Kong* became important entertainment outlets. *Charlie's Angels* were national heroines paraded by *Time* Magazine as television superwomen. *Fear of Flying* was popularly consumed. Through it all, we hardly recognized elements of fascism creeping under these grotesque distortions of reality. We applauded *Death Wish* and *Taxi Driver* as the ultimate expression of our innermost feelings and *Last Tango in Paris* was discussed as high art.

But Johnathan Jackson, before his death, wrote to his brother George,

> Consciousness is the opposite of indifference, of blindness, of blankness. Consciousness is knowledge, recognition, foresight; common experience and perception; sensibility, alertness, mindfulness. It stirs the senses, the blood; it exposes, it suggests; it will objectify, enrage, direct. There are no positive formulas for a thing so complex. We have guidelines only to help us with its growth. This means that after we are done with our books, they must be put aside, and the search for method will depend on observations, correct analysis, creativity and seizing the time! [4]

I wonder if this type of incisive perception could have found him a place in the sun of any university campus, or if like Charlie Parker, "he had already played his music, tomorrow." Charlie Parker, in an interview in Paris with Julio Cortazar, once said,

> Because of the way things were at home, time never stopped, dig? From one fist fight to the next, almost not stopping for meals. And to top it all off, religion, aw you can't imagine. When the man got me an alto saxophone, you'd have laughed yourself to death if you'd seen it, then I think I noticed the thing right off. Music got me out of time, but that's only a way of putting it. If you want to know what I think, really, I believe that music put me into time. But, then you have to believe that this time had nothing to do with...well, with us, as they say.[5]

When Charlie Parker played *Now is the Time*, he was playing tomorrow. I wondered what it would have been like if Bird and Jonathan had stepped on any university campus together at age sixteen — that would be *Force*.

But today, it becomes difficult to realize this dream, for the cultural apparatus has successfully produced stereotypical students and the effect is to reduce them to caricatures. The modern minstrels of the acid rock generation are caricatures of the nineteenth century and then, to top it off, we have imitators of the imitators in both black and white face. This synthetic cultural solution can be aptly labeled "Koolade," and not even "Gatorade."

The disco sound, which was so successfully merchandised, created a new attitude in dance. House parties were passe'; units of friendship were disrupted; and alienated dancers invaded the dance floor, supposedly free of their inhibitions, but quietly imbibing the grotesqueness of their distorted motions, by the illusions of light, sound and motion. The technology eliminated the creative spontaneity of dance and the celebrative, ritualistic expression we enjoyed as we watched excellent dancers. The disco madness was even televised on wide screens in certain discoteques. You could boogie to "Dr. Funkenstein" and see yourself on television — "Disco baby, you so fine, girl you ought to be on T.V."

George Jackson discussed this reinvention of Frankenstein in his brilliant political tract, *Blood in My Eye.* He wrote:

> Frankenstein's need for a servant was an expression of his diseased ego, so he created a demented ugly creature, pathologically strong and huge. He censored the beast's activity by making him underintelligent. He erected institutions flexible enough to keep the giant working, but rigid enough to forestall any growth of his mental facilities. A brain was grudgingly attached to the beast to provide a way for it to act. The beast was content to watch the creator flourish. He lived through his creator. And when he finally saw himself as he was, he went mad.[6]

George was not looking into any surrealistic glass bowl. He was dealing with the *now* in American society, August, 1971, two weeks before he was brutally assassinated. George maintained that these Frankenstein monsters walk the streets daily. Yet, it is difficult to recognized them because they do not belong to any race, class, color, sex or creed. They are products of a dis-eased culture.

This cultural agenda, after it has been tested on the streets and validated at the educational institutions, then becomes exportable to foreign consumers, especially in the Third World countries. Imperialism of the soul follows the cultural invasion of the multi-national giants. So we have salsa in Colombia and Venezuela, soul in Nigeria and Ghana and rock in Brazil and Japan. Morever, when Muhammad Ali was fighting in Zaire or in the Philippines, we overlooked the tremendous political implications of the C.I.A's covert program in Angola, as well as direct military and economic support for Presidents Mbotu and Marcos, whose governments are infected with corruption. I am quite certain that while the majority of the people in the "free" world were digging "the Thrilla in Manilla," the heroic people of Angola, Mozambique, Guinea Bissau, Vietnam and Cambodia were checking the contradictions. But Muhammad Ali made millions of dollars for Columbia Motion Pictures with his movie, *I Am the Greatest*. It was shown on several campuses throughout the nation. In addition, Francis Ford Cappola's multi-million dollar epic film, *Apocalypse Now*, shot on location in the Philippines, was intended to rewrite the history of the Southeast Asian war with gross distortions, in the same way that *Glory* was flawed in its restating of nineteenth century history.

These are important projections; for, we are faced with a problem of visual illiteracy since we are bombarded by false images. Cultural conquest leads to the cultural inauthenticity of those who are invaded; and the invaded begin to respond to the values, standards and goals of the invaders. Cultural invasion is on the one hand an instrument of domination, and on the other, the result of domination.[7] Homes and schools, nurseries and universities, exist not in the abstract, but in time and space. Within the structures of domination, they function largely as agencies that prepare the invaders of the future. It is in this sense that the cultural life of the university community and its institutional imperatives, prepare the technicians and the managers for that cultural penetration.

The students who design, promote and shape cultural programs on campuses must not install themselves in a mirage, for this can very easily happen through films, theatre, dance and music at the popular level: the mirage can become a social reality for them. They should analyze, discuss and understand fully *Dog Day in the Afternoon, Woman Under the Influence, Network, Rocky,* and *One Flew Over the Cuckoo's Nest.* They should examine *Car Wash* and *House Party* as entertainment qua entertainment. They should study the response of Michael Schultz, the director of *Car Wash,* who argued that he made the movie simply to make people laugh, and if anyone wanted a message, they should go to Western Union. He argues that his function as a film-maker is not to provide messages for society. His concern was simply to make folks laugh and be happy — with unemployment ranging from 7.9% officially to 40.9% unofficially and inflation taking a bite out of every penny. I guess that's something to laugh about, as you "work and work and work your fingers to the bone . . . at the Car Wash," as the lyrics of the hit tune from the sound track emphasize. There is a message in *Car Wash* and it is loud and clear: this is the place where the unemployables will find their Hollywoodized destiny — at the Car Wash — for they have been systematically miseducated in the public school system and they will end up with service jobs as the scrap heap of urban society. This is twentieth century neo-slavery with the "boogie" and the "hip hop"instead of the earlier "cakewalk" on the automated plantations.

In this situation, a society can become the most avid consumer of the myths it creates. Sometimes society can also forget that it created the consumer and that it is responsible for the notion that its citizens are the most interesting people in the world. We have done that, especially since World War II, through culture, and yet there is *Hearts and Minds*, the documentary film *Puerto Rico*, the *Ugly American*, the assassinations of John F. Kennedy, Martin Luther King, Jr., Robert F. Kennedy, Malcolm X, Fred Hampton, Emmett Till and remember Attica! Of course, there is also Boston, Massachusetts or *Mississippi Burning* and the landmark experience of Attorney Landsmark.

Perhaps, the medium that has tremendously affected our cultural and aesthetic sensibilities in contemporary society has been television. We are products of television and film, and, as such, we belong to a visual age. However, television is the product of the dialectic between fact and fiction, between reality and entertainment. The governing contradiction in this medium is that while television does its best work in channeling reality to mass audiences, the economics of television demand that most of the money, time and corporate energy be spent on entertainment, usually on a very crude level. Even public television is faced with this dilemma and the Public Broadcasting Corporation is sometimes referred to as the Petroleum Broadcasting Corporation with some deference to its major sponsors.

A cursory examination, for example, of C.B.S.'s *Person to Person* program, which was produced in the fifties, should have indicated that this represented the exploitation of the voyeuristic appeal of the medium. From there on in, it meant that the line between private and public life and/or death became very thin, exploring all of its complex and sordid realities. John F. Kennedy's death and later Lee Harvey Oswald's became the logical extension of this reality. The $64,000 quiz program, in spite of all its unethical practices, dominated the television ratings from 1956 to 1958 and was able to present contrived reality as entertainment very successfully. Finally, by the early sixties, the concept of the media event, (i.e., reality especially staged for television), had become an established political and communicative tool (from the Kennedy/Nixon debates to the

Carter/Ford debates). Thus, the institution of televison has had a profound impact on nearly every aspect of American life from political campaigns and consumer attitudes to social rituals and early childhood education.

It is precisely this medium of televison that has influenced us to accept certain leadership, by projecting specific people in society — many of whom have been invited to the campus communities as activists, intellectuals and/or entertainers. It helped to project Black Power (Stokely Carmichael) feminist power (Gloria Steinham), religious power (Billy Graham) and reactionary power (Bill Buckley). Talk shows and news programs have brought key personalities to the forefront, from Edward R. Morrow and Barbara Walters to Oprah Winfrey and Arsenio Hall. By the sixties, television had established itself as the center of the American experience. It had become the main channel for the dissemination of advertising, the main forum for political discussion, and, to a large extent, it determined how public politics was acted out. Today, more North Americans learn news from television than from the print media, and television has also become the main stage for historical events, such as Richard Nixon's visit to China, the Persian Gulf War, and the present crisis of Central government in the Soviet Union. Young people are the children of a television age. Students have been bombarded by its messages in the university centers, spending more time looking at the "boob-tube" than even attending classes. Therefore, students who are involved in mounting cultural programs must begin a serious examination of visual literacy and visual illiteracy, as a result of the expansion of film and television in the twentieth century. The novel and the printed word were nineteenth century phenomena. Today, it is film and television. However, they must also recognize the attempt to make their minds inelastic through the saturation process of distorted images and synthetic information.

A Columbia Records business executive, Clive Davis wrote:

> Men in the music business do not easily make futuristic judgements. Nor, in the strictest sense are they expected to discover "artists." They are paid to recognize talent and then turn this resource into profit. The quest for artistic excellence and sometimes for showmanship and virtuosity, is, bluntly stated, a search for profit.[8]

This is at the core of the entrepreneur's approach to culture. His sole concern is to spot emerging artists, nuture them and then launch, merchandise and showcase them. This is a very interwoven and complicated apparatus with large companies like Capitol Records understanding the social and economic implications of Nat King Cole in the fifties and Natalie Cole in the seventies. Furthermore, Clive Davis maintains that "time is the key in launching an artist." He writes,

> The executive must know the ingredients of musical excitement, and be able to feed the potential for consumer success. It is dangerous to be too progressive or too far ahead of your time, but it is far more disastrous to lag behind it. The difference can be as subtle as defining what is coming...what is arriving. When an artist or musical trend has arrived you must be fully in place. Errors in judgement can cost millions of dollars, careers, prestige...points on the stock market.[9]

There is the same phenomenon in the publishing business *The Fire Next Time*, *The Autobiography of Malcolm X*, *Soul on Ice*, *Black Power*, *The Wretched of the Earth*, *The Prison Letters of George Jackson*, *Beloved*, *Color Purple*, *Song of Solomon*, and *Roots*, all captured a thriving and expanding market in the sixties and seventies. Black Power and the search for identity, opened up a new market in the cultural apparatus and provided new levels of consumption in literature, theatre, poetry, music, dance and the graphic arts. In the seventies, this was further expanded in the Black exploitation film market. In the university community, there was an increasing demand to connect up with the work of these artists. Books were like cross-over records, and soon the authors, poets, and specialists in this genre were in demand by young students as educators and/or entertainers.

This type of demand created certain schisms in the campus community, which had been wedded to classical art and the shopworn pedagogy of European art appreciation and art history courses. For example, in the colleges of arts and humanities, popular culture, and expecially entertainment, was never taken seriously, and its impact on the North American cultural ethos was rarely examined. Few professors attended or actively participated in the design of these popular creative outpourings and there developed a knowledge gap between rival constituencies on the campuses. However, students pressed on in their desire to come to grips with critical issues in contemporary society and by the end of the decade of the sixties, this frightened the establishment. Therefore, the strategy of Richard Nixon and others who control the cultural apparatus was to check mate this burst of creative energy. The media used nostalgia and distortions to push the students back into the doldrums of the fifties. Of course, the Nixon administration received ample support from reactionary elements on campuses, who wanted to quiet things down so that the institutions could be more manageable. Expanded budgets for cultural affairs solved this problem in part, while educational mediocrity became endemic to academic life. There was a passive acquiescence to mediocrity and non-involvement.

In no arena is the struggle between the various ethnic communities more sharply defined than in culture. The knives get sharpened, when one tries to deal with these matters in educational institutions, for there are many highly sophisticated ways to express European cultural hegemony. The battles can be long and difficult. Puerto Ricans, Chicanos, Asians, American Indians, Blacks and students from Third World Nations know this struggle intimately.

Ethnic differences are the very essence of cultural diversity and national activity; but they must not be based on stereotypes. The archetype is the most valid expression of creative integrity. However, in North American life, the pervasive attitude of cultural superiority among whites remains a problem. Likewise, it is embedded deeply in the mores and folkways of university life. Albert Murray in the *Omni-Americans* writes,

> The obsessive preoccupation of the white people of the United States with the folklore of white supremacy makes one thing all too obvious: White Americans do not take the priviledged status of white people for granted. They work at it. They pretend that it is natural to their social inheritance . . .and their films, television programs, literature and art work — expand and project that folklore.[10]

In other words, Archie Bunker is for real; there is never any casual indifference in the ideas projected to targeted audiences as he reflects white working class racism, chauvinism, and cultural arrogance. Certainly, the struggle for political and aesthetic liberty is nothing, if not a quest for freedom to choose one's own way or style of life. Morever, it should be equally obvious that there can be no such thing as human dignity and nobility without a consummate definitive style, pattern or archetypal image. Once again, it is in the area of Black music that we discover some virtue. Of course, this is not to suggest a total exclusion of the other arts, but, music makes the point a little more graphically. The Black musician in North American society has been a humanizer of chaos from the spirituals, such as *Steal Away*, to John Coltrane's *A Love Supreme* and Stevie Wonder's *Songs in the Key of Life*. The musician develops an aesthetic equipment for living in which the improvisation of experience is the central element in the dymnamics of his/her life. Musicians constantly improvise on central themes, turning disjunctures into continuities. For instance, he/she is not disconcerted by intrusions, lapses, shifts in rhythms, intensification of tempo, but rather, is inspired by them to higher and richer levels of spontaneous improvisation and creative solutions. Stevie Wonder in *Sir Duke* sings: "But just because a record has a groove don't make it in the groove." There is a key to this, which Black students miss because as they attend these educational institutions, they lose that sense of improvisation and become stylized, pasteurized and even homogenized. They miss the historical beat. But the great tragedy is that this happens to Black faculty and administrators as well, and they do not seem able to glean any understanding of the musician's metaphor. No self-respecting Black musician would ever be guilty of following the stock arrangements of white song writers as precisely as Black educators and leaders adhere to the Tin Pan Alley programs of white social technicians.[11]

Therefore, we must begin to realize that when Black musicians perform or sing by ear, it is not because they cannot read music. Rather, it is because in the very process of mastering reading music, they have found it inadequate for their immediate purposes. Therefore, they take their creative spirit to the next level. At times, they even move beyond their own creations to another level of musical creation, viz in the manner of Miles Davis, John Coltrane and Stevie Wonder. As students and educators, we should learn from these serious Black musicians in our approach to education — as we take classical instruction and radical thought beyond the West's traditional level of pedagogy into the area of creative solutions for human betterment and everyday problems. We should approach learning not with reverence, fear or arrogance, but with discipline and humility, conscious that the expansion of our creative sensibilities would be useful for the enrichment of life and the service of humanity.

How do white students and faculty deal with this phenomenon on their campuses and how can they benefit from a clear understanding of this creative process? Again, in the area of music, the question is raised, "can white people really play Black music?" whenever there are complaints about the inauthenticity of the white musician. The answer is, "of course, they can," but this is qualifiable, and the qualification must be taken very seriously. White musicians can play Black music if they are good enough musicians and respects the medium as they would any other art form. If they develop the same familiarity with Black music's idiomatic nuances, the same love for it, and humility before it as good Black musicians do, why not? But certainly not if white musicians are really ambivalent about Black music, not if they hang around with it for a while and then withdraw and allow themselves to become the "white" hope, not if white musicians prostitute Black music, not if they allow their publicity to convince them that they are superior to the masters they are still plagiarizing.[12]

Black music contains the most comprehensive rendering of the complexities of the Black experience in North America. It is in this music that the Black artist tells the epic nature of our experience. Yet, Black music has not been legitimately included into the cultural matrix of the university community. Black music is still the step-child of music depart-

227

ments, which often pretend that they are embarrassed by its presence. There is a kind of cultural paternalism here. James Baldwin writes, " For a tradition expresses after all, nothing more than the long and painful experience of a people, and it comes out of the battle waged to maintain their integrity, or to put it more simply, out of their struggle to survive." Furthermore, Ralph Ellison states that:

> The blues is an impulse to keep the painful details and episodes of a brutal experience alive in one's aching consciousness, to finger its jagged grain and to transcend it, not by the consolation of philosophy but by squeezing from it a near-tragic, near comic lyricism. As a form, the blues is both autobiographical and collective chronicles of personal and group catastrophe expressed lyrically.[13]

I would suggest that the feminists and supporters of the women's movement study seriously the works of Bessie Smith, Billie Holiday, Abbey Lincoln, Dinah Washington, Nina Simone and Aretha Franklin on the cultural front and examine the lives of Sojourner Truth, Harriet Tubman, Assata Shakur, Ida B. Wells, and Angela Davis on the political front.

However, we have seen blues singers invited to campuses and treated as though they were beer hall entertainers. The neglect by Black students or the mistreatment by white students of these creative giants is appalling. Whether it is the Preservation Hall Orchestra, Willie Dixon, Big Mama Thornton, or Muddy Waters, the attitude of students is one of paternalism, sentimentality, or outright disrespect. These artists are treated as relics of a golden age, and their genius for poetic lyricism is by-passed, except as resource material for rock artists, such as the Rolling Stones, The Greatful Dead, or the Beatles, and folklorists or ethnomusicologists like Alan Lomax, Charles Keil and Paul Oliver.

In the movie *The Graduate*, the old man tells Dustin Hoffman to check into the plastics industry. The message here is that he is steering him into future economies. Faculty members should be able to tell students something about tomorrow and the challenges of the twenty first century. Radical professors should point out to their constituencies that even though revolutions in the twentieth century succeeded through the will, strength and determination of the people, (the mass of the population), these struggles only advanced because the leadership was technically proficient to select the most vulnerable targets and use the most efficient weapons. Who else is supposed to clarify such things if not teachers and intellectuals? They should instruct students in the military brilliance, technical virtuosity, political courage, discipline and intellectual integrity of people like Lenin, Mao-Tse Tung, Chou En-Lai, Amilcar Cabral, Agostinho Neto, Frantz Fanon, General Sampang, General Giap, Ho Chi Minh, Che Guevarra and Fidel Castro. These men were not only exceptional leaders, but men of tremendous technical competence in their respective disciplines. Either, we are prepared to produce leaders in our intellectual communities, whose presence and ingenuity would affect changes in society, or tenure is a rip-off for mediocrity, do-nothingness and intellectual sterility. The university must not become obsolete. Radicals and progressives, rather than fight for tenure, should struggle to develop the great minds of tomorrow.

For Third World students, this question of technological development becomes even more critical. It was in 1968 that I first stated,

> The technological input of the last century, coupled with the need of Black people here and in the diaspora for rapid industrialization for increased productivity and improved living conditions, demands that our educational planning focus on the development of technical skills, undirected by a progressive political vision. Technology brings about a systematically applied approach to how we organize knowledge about physical relations for useful purposes. There can be no economic growth in Black communities and African nations without application of technology to land, labor, capital and education, now or in the future.[14]

I believe that this argument is still valid. We will not be able to solve the problems in the Sahel by begging for foreign aid; we cannot wait for President George Bush to solve the problems of the Black and poor who are unemployed and might even be unemployable as a result of miseducation, automation, and economic mismanagement; we cannot prevent the exploitation of the Black artist without the development of the technical and managerial infrastucture to support the work of Nina Simone, Diana Ross, and Marvin Gaye; we cannot develop Cuba, Brazil, Puerto Rico, Jamaica, Trinidad, Angola, Mozambique, Guinea Bissau, Harlem, Watts or Roxbury without technically skilled and competent people. Humanitarianism, paternalism, and social welfarism will not solve the problems of economic development. It is necessary, therefore, for us to train our people as quickly as possible to produce sytematically, through established and creative logical processes, man-made hardware useful to the improvement of the quality of life in decaying cities and developing nations.[15] Students must make optimum use of available resources and skills, as we move into the twenty first century.

In the entertainment field alone, students must recognize that compact discs and video discs are now available; there is cable juke-box, Dial-a-Party, which is an extension of the disco world; there are video cassettes; and the march of microprocessors that will bring about tremendous changes in the technology of entertainment. In the critcal areas of energy, for example, we must begin to prepare students to study solar electric power, nuclear power with the elimination of radioactive leaks, ocean gradient power in which nutrients are extracted from agua culture, cellulose conversion, gene splicing and geothermal energy. Also, there are important areas in metallurgy, oceanography, astrophysics, acoustical engineering and medical engineering.

If university education cannot lead young people to the advanced sectors of contemporary society, while at the same time develop the critical consciousness necessary to change the character of society and the present misuse of the earth's resources, then we are wasting time — grooving on an empty "pipe dream." Entertainment and education should, therefore, inject creative energy into students' lives so that they can acquire the knowledge to move forward progressively, and if the faculty or administration negates its responsibility to meet this challenge, students should struggle for better leadership and/or take the institutions to court in a class action suit for miseducating them. The institutions of higher learning have a public responsibility to provide students with knowledge, in the same way that public school sytems are responsibile for educating young people properly. (There is a case, in the California courts, in which some parents are suing the public school system for the miseducation of their children.)

Finally, there is a need for a unified front of progressive students, (organized systematically) to achieve specific objectives that will result in the emergence of a creative cultural ethos on campus and throughout the country. There must be a connecting of the struggle around tasks that are clearly defined and attainable. But this effort to unify different segments of the student body should not be based on sloganeering. If students are to unite, they must first cut the umbilical chord of magic and myth that binds them to the world of oppression; the unity that will link student groups must be of a different nature than what has been projected by the cultural apparatus. To achieve this indispensable unity, cultural action must form a vital part of the process. Cultural work should clarify to student constituencies their objective situation, which binds them to the plastic bubble, visible or not. From there, they can expand their political and educational tasks to prepare them for tomorrow.

I will close, with Frantz Fanon's incisive statement to young Afrika, which is applicable to young America: "Every generation must out of its mission, fulfill it, or betray it."[16] The message is clear. The future is ahead; and the future is now. Only young people with courage and conscience can bring it to its fullest flowering. David Diop bites the bullet, when he writes, *Challenge To Force*:

You who bend you who weep
You who die one day just like that not knowing why
You who struggle and stay awake for other's rest
You with no more laughter in your look
You my brother with face of fear and anguish
Rise and shout: NO!![17]

NOTES

1. Jacques Stephan Alexis, "Of the Marvellous Realism of the Haitians," *Presence Africaine:The First International Conference of Negro Writers and Artists, Paris*, (September1956), p.254.

2. Herbert Marcuse, *One Dimensional Man*, (Boston: Beacon Press., 1966) p.57.

3. Ibid., p. 11.

4. George Jackson, *Blood in My Eye*, (Baltimore: Black Classic Press, 1990) p. 22.

5. Julio Cortazar, "The Pursuer in Blow Up," *Hopscotch*, p. 56.

6. George Jackson, *Blood in My Eye*, p. 92.

7. Paolo Soleri, *Matter Becoming Spirit*, p. 34.

8. Clive Davis. *Inside the Record Business*, p. 1.

9. Ibid., p. 2.

10. Albert Murray. *The Omni Americans*, (New York: Avon., 1977) p. 70.

11. Ibid., p. 93.

12. Ibid., p. 191.

13. Ralph Ellison, *Shadow and Act*, (New York: Random House, 1972) p. 90.

14. Acklyn Lynch, "Blueprint for Change," p. 10.

15. Ibid., p. 12.

16. Frantz Fanon, *The Wretched of the Earth*, translated by Constance Farrington (New York: Grove Weidenfeld, 1988) p. 167.

17. David Diop, "Challenge to Force," in *Hammer Blows*, p. 47.

BLUEPRINT FOR CHANGE

The decade of the nineties demands that Black educators begin to examine seriously the future of higher education for Black people, especially in institutions like Howard University, Southern University, Morgan State College, Hampton Institute, North Carolina A & T, etc., that must serve the interest of our community. In the sixties, critical questions were raised about the organization, form and content of Black education as students, faculty and administrators embarked on a search for relevancy. Earlier in the decade, Black students engaged in a serious political struggle to dramatize the social inconsistencies of the American nation state. These students also attempted to raise the level of consciousness among Black people in the rural South and the urban centers in the North and West. In every instance, Black students were in the vanguard of the struggle and many endured the pain and anxiety of this liberating experience. At every level of confrontation, the involved students were criticized severely. However, today, we have dramatic changes in the American social order, which resulted from the courage and indomitable will of these Black warriors who held their ground and boldly heralded a new day dawning.

Black colleges and universities must now come to grips with the serious questions posed in the sixties. They must begin to provide the leadership in Black education that students demand. It is in this vein that I am suggesting a total reorganization of academic life, so that it may be structured to address the challenges of the future. Black educators, must be bold in recommending and effecting change. This change should provide a philosophical direction that redirects our creative energy to building of our communities, people, and our nation.

My principle recommendation is to eliminate the college of liberal arts, which is now a moribund institution and an environment that encourages frustration and disillusionment. Liberal arts colleges might have been valid up through the decade of the fifties, but the imperatives of contemporary technology compel us to question their usefulness and the viability of their educational potential. Liberal arts graduates are lost in a sea of uncertainty, for they are not equipped with specific skills that are useful to contemporary society. They know too little about anything to be functional or productive, and very often the graduates of our liberal arts colleges feel estranged from the Black communitites that they should serve. They are then compelled either to go on to professional (or graduate) school or endure a life of continued mediocrity. In fact, they are nothing but functional illiterates, stripped of any ideological direction or positive commitment and constrained by their lack of deeper understanding of the essence of Black culture.

It is already evident that we are facing major change in the world's economy. The graduates of Black colleges and universities have a mandate to shape the new economies of the Black poor in America and in the Third World, where the majority of their "foreign" students come from. The political matrix of social and economic life is changing fast in a global context, and knowledge has become the central capital, the cost center and the crucial resource of existing economies. At Black Colleges and Universities, we are still training Black students for old technologies shaped by outdated assumptions of liberal arts education. Black students are not prepared to enter the lead sectors and productive processes of the national and global economy. Our failure to produce the new Black men and women of power and knowledge will add to the effective domination of the Black World. It is urgent that we re-examine our educational resources and direction. We cannot bequeath this legacy to future generations since confrontation remains a reality of the struggle for independence.

All educational practice implies a theoretical stance on the part of the educator. This stance, in turn, implies an interpretation of men and women and the world. The assumptions of our liberal arts colleges are primarily european (greek philosophical principles ajoined with Judeo-Christian social ethic) and include the shaping of this cultural imperative to the American socius. Through this educational experience, we have been locked into a dehumanizing structure that shapes our dependency and alienates us from our true nature. Therefore, as we confront reality in our search for freedom and independence, we must recognize that there is no other road to our humanization but an authentic transformation of the existing dehumanizing structure. In order for us to move out of this level of intransitive consciousness (dehumanization), we have to inform our analysis with a careful examination of our historical condition. Also, we must take advantage of the real and unique possibilities that exist in our cultural experience–possibilities that are useful to the transformation of social reality.

We shall deal with the transformation process by taking the best of African heritage in terms of the essence of life. But this will be basic to the ethos of Black people in America. The retention of Africanisms will be understood as it undergirds our peculiar collective ethos and provides us with historical continuity. However, we will not become rooted in the past, for our pressing concern is the ordering of the present and the shaping of the future. The past will inform us historically of our spiritual experience in the struggle for freedom in the face of unparalleled adversity. We will capture the strength of the experience and walk boldly on the stage of history as defiant Black creators. We cannot take lightly the untold legacy handed down to us as a result of the untold suffering of our ancestors — who were ripped off from Africa, who suffered the horrors of the Middle Passage, who endured the beastiality of slavery, and who have continuously fought valiantly for freedom and independence. This is a rich legacy of pain and triumph, and it urges the present to carry the banner forward to a resolution of problems posed as a result of this Black experience. Black educators, have a responsibility to unfold this legacy in the tradition of W.E.B. Dubois, Carter Woodson, Mary Mcleod Bethune, E. Franklin Frazier, Rayford Logan, Ida B. Wells, Richard Wright, Assata Shakur, Sterling Brown, Martin Luther King, Jr., Malcolm X, George Padmore, C.L.R. James, Aime' Ce'saire. Frantz Fanon, Kwame Nkrumah, Julius Nyerere and Se'kou Toure'. But also we have the deeper responsibility to provide answers for our people to the perplexing problems these men and women have encountered in their struggle for freedom and independence.

Therefore, we must reorganize the educational structure of Black colleges and universities into arenas of study that will be useful to nation-building. I am proposing a six year educational program with a terminal degree: Master of Arts, Science and Technology (MAST). The first two years will be spent in a School for Black Culture, and the next four years will be spent in a Technical Institute.

The School of Black Culture will shape the attitude, involvement, discipline, commitment and perspective of the student with a consistent ideological direction. Students will participate in learning centers engaged in the study of art, architecture, education, religion, history, science, mathematics and Black family life, while appreciating the multifaceted aspects of each problem in our historical evolution and the many ways that Black people have attempted to resolve these problems. In addition, the students will develop concrete skills in mathematics, science, verbal and non-verbal communication, symbolic logic and analysis. There will be established an effective dialogue between students and faculty in the galaxy (satellite learning centers), as emphasis will be on ideological commitment, discovery, and creativity. Student will be involved in discovering what they already know, ordering, storing, and synthesizing this knowledge with new knowledge in an integrative process, and then using it creatively for understanding and shaping reality. In the galaxies, faculty members will teach various disciplines, thereby allowing for a free interchange and flow of creative thought in the work and in the cognitive dimensions of the learning process.

At the end of two years, a review board will examine the student's projected area of technical concentration. The student's choice of study should be aligned with demonstrated potential. The curriculum design should provide him/her with the necessary expertise. The decision-making process of the review board and the planning of the student's career should be carefully organized with the final determination of technical concentration made within three months of the student's appearance before the Board. At the end of this three month period, the student will join an Institute, where he/she will participate in a four year program designed to prepare and sharpen technical proficiency.

The following Institutes will represent advanced level learning centers:

1. Institute of Mathematics and Natural Sciences
2. Institute of Creative Expression - Black Art
3. Institute of Communications and Information Systems
4. Institute of Education
5. Institute of Social Engineering and Systems Managers
6. Institute of Global (Multi-national) Studies and Revolutionary Processes
7. Institute of Geopolitics, Military Science and Armaments Technology
8. Institute of Engineering and Computer Technology
9. Institute of Oceanography and Marine Science
10. Institute of Transportation and Delivery Systems
11. Institute of Materials Technology
12. Institute of Agronomy, Agricultural Science and Technology
13. Institute of Urban Planning, Evironmental Systems, Ecology and Ecosystems.
14. Institute of Health Sciences
15. Institute of Business and Economics
16. Institute of Law, Public Administration, and Policy Planning

These institutes will be designed in concentric circles that will overlap and provide a free flow of knowledge through cross-fertilization of ideas, interdisciplinary research, and joint project and program planning. The Institutes will not function as isolated, compartmentalized units of knowledge, work, and instruction, even though they will be administered separately by their respective governing boards.

In addition to the above Institutes, there should be a Center for Black Thought and Creative Expression, and a Center for Research in Applied Science and Technology, as well as a Center for Social and Economic Research. The work of these research centers will undergird and sharpen the intellectual life of the Institutes. The research centers will deal with concrete problems confronting contemporary Black society, performing three distinct but interrelated functions. The work will be diagnostic, evaluative and explanatory. The centers should be engaged in short-term, service-oriented research relating to Black life and problems in Black intellectual thought, as well as original research in science and technology useful to the Black World. As the innovators of tomorrow, Black people must invent and build new gadgets and techniques.

The technological input of the last century — coupled with the Black world's need for rapid industrialization, increased productivity and improved living conditions — demands that our educational planning focus on technological institutes. Technology brings about a systematically applied approach to how we organize knowledge about physical relationships for useful purposes. There can be no economic growth in Black communities and nations without the application of technology to land, labor, capital and education, now or in the future. It is necessary, therefore, for us to train people as quickly as possible to produce systematically, through established and creative logical processes, manmade hardware to improve the quality of life in Black communities.

At all levels of work in the Institutes, students will be aware that every measure of education and science will relate to public service values and, therefore, will move away from productivity for profit and individual gain to productivity for the enrichment of the flow of life. The student will also understand the direct relationship between theory and practice (work and study will be merged). Emphasis will be on extending the humanistic values developed, examined and re-examined in the School of Black Culture. Members of the Institutes will be engaged actively in the liberating process, as they represent the catalyzing agents of social change.

In the Institutes, we will be concerned not only with the technological expertise acquired, but the development of the whole person consciously participating in the collective life of the community as this reflects his/her social function. In this educational experience, the chains of oppression and alientation will be broken, as the students regain their true nature, manhood and womanhood through liberated work, study, and the expression of their proper human condition through Black culture and art.

Students will engage in a four year study program in the respective Institutes. On successful completion of the program, the student will be awarded a Master of Arts, Science and Technology (MAST) degree. Third year students from various Institutes will be organized in specific project teams to design, build and administer a concrete and identifiable service to address the need of a Black community, whether it is in Mississippi, Newark, Guyana, or Nigeria. For example, students will work on the construction of an irrigation system, health system or communication system, as requested by a specific community following discussions between the community and the university officials. This specific aspect of the student's training will be narrowly focused and professionally designed–so that students can come to grips with team work and the execution of a project outside of the University community– but integrated with theoretical and training. This third year program will extend from six months to one year. On the students' return to the University, the team will be responsible for providing university officials with a documented report of its work and its progress. This report will be discussed, analyzed and concretized for its theoretical and practical implications. It can become the basis of a thesis paper presented to the governing board of the Institute as one of the requirements for graduation. This will necessitate that each team member reporting to respective Institutes will use some aspect of the project design for thesis work.

This educational experience will be concerned with developing leaders, innovators, discoverers, creators and liberators. Our students will become the architects of change and the engineers of growth and development. I firmly believe that education involves discovery and creativity. Black students must discover (1) themselves and those societal factors which influences their behavior, (2) their creative potential and the cognitive processes which influence their intellectual development, and, (3) their cultural autonomy and the correct response to its constituent demands. This discovery on the part of Black students will then lead them to maximum use of their creative energies in the service of Black people. It will also allow students to explore their creative potential as well as new arenas of thought and analysis so that they will be better prepared to meet their future responsibilities. Finally, in our immediate educational experience, the Black student in the learning centers and Institutes will be prepared to serve Black communities not in a sentimental petit-bourgeois fashion, but rather as scientists, technicians, or administrators, whose political commitment and positive attitudes will focus on eliminating the critical problems of hunger, disease, poverty, illiteracy, drug addiction and political powerlessness.

This reorganization of Black colleges and universities represents a program of action. We must liberate ourselves from the stultifying aspects of liberal arts education. Even when we try to impose a sugarcoating of blackness on white education, we are still trapped in the cobwebs of assumptions upon which American education has been built, and which the cultural apparatus manipulates to colonize and mystify our minds. In the liberal arts college our students simply glide into classrooms of despair and walk on the enchanted quagmires (quicksands) of frustration and irrelevancy. The constructs of thought and the messages of the classroom are essentially informed by European intellection and historiography. We must liberate ourselves from the corruptive chains of Western imperialistic society which infuse our present educational experience. We must cut the umbilical cord which ties us subjugatingly to white European, Judeo-Christian society and its philosophical and cultural imperatives. Finally, we must liberate ourselves from the sorcery (magic) and phantoms (ghosts) of underdevelopment that is the immediate expression of neo-colonialism.

Black colleges and unversities are not organized for or around work. They are organized around play and the broadening of the cultural orientation and social exposure of the individual student. This is the reason for party life, Greek fraternities, sororities and narcotics addiction in an education process crusted over with a smattering of knowledge in the liberal democratic tradition (with emphasis on social sciences, humanities and fine arts). Furthermore, there is a spillover from undergraduate life and the morals of its make-believe superficial world to our professional schools, where students engage in similar functions and lifestyles.

This reorganization will compel us to look closely at inept administrators, non-progressive faculty and trifling students. If there is a thorough shake-up in our university and college communites, a serious ideological perspective and commitment demonstrated, and a marked increase in the level of productivity, serious Black faculty, adminstrators and students will come to Black universities and colleges. We must seize the time and realize that many potential nation-builders are frustrated in white institutions and they will come to Black institutions if there is a modicum of seriousness projected. Unfortunately, those who work at Black colleges and universities are our worst public relations people. The *Towards a Black University* Conference, which was held at Howard Unversity in the Fall of 1968, graphically taught me this sad lesson. Black people came to Howard Unversity with hope and left in despair. Black educators wake up — a new day is dawning.

We must develop a new frame of reference that projects an Africanity (Blackness) shaped by new guidelines, new values, new goals, new structures, new thoughts, new forms and new images. We must turn over a new leaf; we must work out new concepts; we must try to set afoot new women and men. The present is a time for struggle. The future is ours. A liberated people, with liberated minds remain fundamental to our educational experience.

AT THE DAWN
OF ANOTHER DAY

Sun Ra writes, "If you are not a reality / Then whose myth are you." Toni Cade Bambara at the writer's conference held at Howard University in the mid-seventies stated, "it is the duty...the responsibility of the writer representing an oppressed people...to make revolution irresistable." This statement remains a serious challenge to writers and cultural workers around the world. In the eighties, only a few artists have attempted to meet that challenge. What essentially has happened in the cultural ethos that has blunted the creative process?

Several of us are braiding and unbraiding the same question, but how do we look upon reality as a landscape? What do we see at the dawn of another day, in this last decade of the twentieth century? Furthermore, what do we refuse to see in order to obfuscate reality, so that one might collaborate with official society? Is everything really everything and is everything MELLOW-D. Have people done enough, expecially our leaders and artists, to save us as well as themselves? Are we committing cultural suicide by crossing over or is there a genuine struggle to preserve our cultural patrimony?

Where do writers fit into this matrix? I am not simply talking about survival, because, we, as a people, have been survivors. I am talking about the existence of the entire group and the quality of its life force — not merely the individual, but the collective Black experience.

What we cannot speak about we usually pass over in silence, but that silence echoes with a deafening roar. Yet, one can observe clearly a continuum of trajectories functioning in the cultural apparatus. The issues of resistance and collaboration in the Black creative process, especially in the written word must be addressed. How we participate in these exercises is evident in our daily actions.

One's imagination could be perched on the precipice of doubt, but it is the compelling force of one's action, which eliminates doubt and identifies the political agenda, conscious or unconscious. To solve the paradox, to speak about that which we must remain silent, about those things, which we have carefully swept under the rug or kept hidden in the closet, is to compel us to hear ancestral voices — only to be replaced by further unanswerable questions. These voices replace but do not cancel each other out. What role have we played in collaboration or resistance? What is "the price of the ticket" and how is it expressed in the literary work? Are there any safe harbors and disguised modes of expression? Are we above ground or underground? Are we inside the barricades or outside the barricades? What are the elements of the discourse, the terms of the discourse and the mode of discourse, which must be translated to our people? Who is really setting the agenda, the Black agenda?

Perhaps one needs a few markers to recognize the path, to remember the way. Ayi Kwei Armah suggested "the way" in *Two Thousand Seasons* and *The Healers.* Toni Cade Bambara gave us *The Salt Eaters* and Toni Morrison looked hauntingly in *Beloved*, dramatically portraying the collective surge for freedom by the brothers in the chain gang, who were about to be suffocated by the mud slide,

> It started like the chain-up but the difference was the power of the chain.
>
> One by one, from HiMan back on down the line, they dove, Down through the mud under the bars, blind, groping. Some had sense enough to wrap their heads in their shirts cover their faces with rags put on their shoes. Others just plunged, simply ducked down and pushed out, fighting up, reaching for air. Some lost direction and their neighbors, feeling the confused pull of the chain, snatched them around. For one lost, all lost. The chain that held them would save all or none, and HiMan was the Delivery. They talked through that chain like Sam Morse, and, Great God, they all came up. Like the unshrived dead, zombies on the loose, holding the chains in their hands, they trusted the rain and the dark, yes but mostly HiMan and each other. [2]

In another sphere, there have been the strident claims of Martin, Malcolm, Mandela and Marley for a *Redemption Song.* We must also recall Duke Ellington's *A New World A Coming*, Max Roach's *Freedom Now Suite* and Margaret Walker's *Jubilee.*

One never gets to know the meaning of things until they are detailed out or peeled off like the petals of a flower. Humanity has been stripped of everything but voices, some eloquent, some strangulated. And as we walk along those two paths, we must strip the eloquence down to its essentials for there is *No Easy Walk To Freedom* (Nelson Mandela). Also, we must recognize that the strangulated voice might yet whisper simple truths before vomiting up the putrid after effects of the historic compromise, drowning in the blood of its ruptured aneurysm. The strangulated voice will declare "I truly overrated their invincibility, their absoluteness, their geopolitical power, their ethic and aesthetic. Conversely, I totally underestimated our potency and our humanity." "They are not gods and our people will be free" said the *Three Men By The River* (Rene Marques). They understood that, as a conquered people, "You must kill the God of Fear only then you will be free."[3]

It is only through the critical study of the Black question that you will discover the answer to the Black question. We have to emancipate ourselves before we can emancipate others. And this a frightening responsibility because we are aware of the shackles that bind us to self-hatred and self-destruction. We know the escape routes and the subterranean channels to anonymity and self-gratification. We know the bleakness of uniqueness and the seduction of compromise as we became *The Spook Who Sat By The Door* (Sam Greenlee) or the "Only One On The Bloc" (Malcolm X). The responsibility of the Black writer is to push the discourse to justice. The questioning has created emptiness, and this is necessary in order that a new interrogation — virgin, free and compelling — might see the light of the sun.

Sister Pearl Cleage has confronted us in *Mad at Miles* with the antagonistic relationship between Black women and men, with the disturbing disintegration of the Black nuclear family, and with the character of physical and psychological violence imposed on Black women by Black men. She heightened the drama of increasing sexual abuse and, as she lay bare the raw, naked truth, she demanded "what are we going to do about it?" She insisted that we talk honestly and purposefully so that in the end we will know how to find dignity in the imbalance of the question.

We must not get boxed into answers that paralyse us and lead us down a path of self-destruction. George Jackson in an interview in August 1971, shortly before he was assassinated in San Quentin prison, argued that we should re-open the question of the Black man and woman. He demanded a critical examination of our principle contradictions as we engage in rigorous political analysis. Assata Shakur was also very critical of the leadership of the Black Panther Party on this question.

For quite some time, I have tried to establish the linkages between literature and history, literature and ideology, literature and propaganda, literature and publishing. Like any other cultural artifact, creative writing always comes under the close scrutiny of the state. Writers are heard or silenced, jailed or exiled, committed to insane asylums or starved to death. William Carlos Williams wrote "the pure products of America go crazy," and Duke Ellington extended the argument when he said "madness in great ones must not go unwatched." But creative minds are essential to the identity of the state and its evolving ethos. It is the writer's brilliance and mastery of images through words, which inform the pedantic musing of teachers. History and literature teachers would not have jobs if their work wasn't fueled by creative writers and thinkers. Some of these academicians, catechists and interlopers are very boring people, a fact that we all know, even though we must live with them.

The state watches its creative writers carefully. They are dangerous people. Ngugi wa Thiongo, Wole Soyinka, Miguel Hernandez, Nazim Hikmet, Dennis Brutus have all been sent to prison for their opposition to the state. Herr Goebbels knew how dangerous artists were and he instituted absolute control over their creative product. Joseph Stalin did the same thing. Many leaders in the cultural apparatus, among the political elite, pay specific attention to what progressive artists are saying. Who are these wordsmiths and what are their tools?

Words are but the surface appearance of the deeper echoes of songs, of dance and their eternal rhythms. Words are necessary, you must hear them. But there are times when it is not important to listen closely; only their resonance is necessary, their concrete existence and deeper urges are awakened. Then, they can reach a conclusion and this conclusion is not cold logic but a soothing warmth or fiery response. Anyone listening to Sterling Brown, Toni Morrison, Sonia Sanchez, Margaret Walker, Alice Walker, Amiri Baraka, Ntozake Shange, Linton Kwesi Johnson or Mutabaruka can hear the echoes in their voices. It is clarity, a precision and a passion for truth, which we find in their use of language. It reminds me of Bird, Trane, Billie, Abbey, Max, Miles or Monk, "Straight, No Chaser."

In Zora Neale Hurston's *Their Eyes Were Watching God,* she writes

There is a basin in the mind where words float around on thought...and thought on sound and sight. Then, there is still a depth of thought...untouched...by words, and deeper still a gulf of formless feelings untouched by thought. [4]

Nanny entered this infinity of conscious pain again on her old knees. Towards morning she muttered, 'Lawd, you know mah heart. Ah done de best Ah could do. De rest is left to you.' She scuffled up from her knees and fell heavily across the bed. A month later, she was dead. [5]

Listen closely and you will hear Ma Rainey, Bessie, Billie, Mahalia, Dinah, Abbey, Nina, Aretha and Bernice Reagon in Nanny's cry. The Black writer must preserve the word, the coinings, shadings and musicality that will bring out the Nommo force, which undergirds the integrity of the continuum as well as the continuity of resistance. The word must deal with the *Future In the Present* (C.L.R. James), while clarifying the lessons of the past. The word must elevate, celebrate, be as bodacious as Larry Neal portrayed "Shine."

Today, our young people are deep into Rap Music, Hip Hop, the word which moves globally carrying the message from Trenchtown to Soweto, from South Bronx to Brixton, from Bed-Sty to Watts. Many of these young Rap artists are expressing an urgency in their music as they present a critique of repressive urban society. They are scratching and searching for a new language of revolt, a heightened consciousness to "fight the power" (Public Enemy), while elected officials continue to compromise with official elites. I and I are downpressed by the collaborators and when Sister Olive Senior (Jamaican poet) asks in "City

Poem," "why did you damage the statue of the national hero?" The reply from I and I came sharply, "because I have plenty damage insides me. You want to see my scars?" [6]

Rap artists like Public Enemy, Boogie Down Productions, Ice T, X-Clan and Big Daddy Kane demand resistance. They adopt an iconnoclastic, irreverent and confrontational posture. How can one have reverence for Western civilization and Judeo Christian ethic, while living in the tenements of South Bronx or Brooklyn, while living in abandoned cars and run-down shacks like *Kaffir Boy* (Mark Mathabane) in Alexandria and Soweto or like *Child of the Dark* (Carolina Maria de Jesus) in the favelas of Rio de Janeiro and Sao Paulo? Kenneth Clarke at the end of his book *Civilization* writes,

> The trouble is that there is still no center. The moral and intellectual failure of Marxism has left us with no alternative to heroic materialism, and that isn't enough. One may be optimistic, but we can't exactly be joyful at the prospect before us. [7]

Rap music is also a language of helplessness, of feeling the need to scratch one's way out of an aborted reality. However, it also demands profound social and political change in the Black world. This shouted language knots itself up as a language of frustration and contortion, the choppiness, drumming, acceleration, lusty repetitions, slurring of syllables, allegories, hidden meanings and gestures, all of these elements represent a verbal delirium, which condenses, phrase by phrase, the tragedy and urgency of this historic moment. These young artists are anchored in Marley, Malcolm and Mandela. Many of the cultural purists and academicians dismiss them as marginal, faddish and youthful aberrations, in the same way that they dismissed Birdman and Locksmen in earlier periods. However, Quincy Jones had to hook up with Ice T and Big Daddy Kane to get "back on the block," since Michael and Janet "done crossed over."

The Rap artists are like the urban maroons coming out of the "Hills" and connecting with the children of the collaborators, who lost their moorings when they moved to suburbia and exurbia. In the coming decade, Rap lyrics will have an enormous impact on literature and on how young people will use words, sound and music. It has already impacted on dance and dress styles. It will push us into the stark reality of marginalization and social dislocation, after our journey through Naomi Madgett's "Exits and Entrances:"

> Through random doors we wandered
> into passages disguised as paradise
> and out again, discarding,
> embracing hope anew, discarding again:
> exits and entrances to many houses. [8]

We must deal with these social ambiguities. We must move beyond the petrified and fossilized language of "collaborationist logic" (Kiarri T-H Cheatwood).

A writer creates out of the depth of his or her experiences. It is the same for musicians, dancers, sculptors, painters and Rap artists. The creative imagination is anchored in experience. However, everything depends on how one shapes the context of that reality how the bitter/sweet memory informs the creation and recreation of its energy and style. The writer searches for a moral center, an ordering of the experience which allows him/her to live within the word.

James Baldwin, in *The Evidence of Things Not Seen*, points out that we have people in urban centers with scarred knees and fractured psyches wandering around the streets homeless and poor. The journey marks the end of that long march from community to isolation. Edward Kamau Brathwaite writes in "Springblade:"

> the city asphyxiates itself
> it has eaten too many sons and
> daughters
> it has burnt too many hopes. [9]

But, how do we come to grips with the deferment of the private vision, when it crumbles into public pain as the city becomes an artificial dance serenaded by icy institutions? We see old men and women with sunken eyes sitting on corners waiting for a morsel of hope and young people lining up at soup kitchens, glass-eyed and looking for a hot meal. The despair widens as the economy recedes into cyclical recession and hopelessness converges on main street.

> It is the
> living skulls of men
> Empty and dented
> Tin pan
> shells of men
> That I must weep for now
> As I wept then (Wayne Davis, "Royal Jail")[10]

Kalamu ya Salaam extends the metaphor in "Iron Flowers: A Poetic Report on a Visit to Haiti,"

> congealed into too many urban areas
> our people idly littering stolen
> streets, oh
> these spaces are so bitter
> Africa has had
> to walk so many rough waters.[11]

Public Enemy raps "Welcome To The Terrordome" as we shuttle between the homeless in the subways, at Grand Central Station, at Madison Square Garden and Wall Street, where junk bonds change fortunes. But, we have sent a so-called volunteer army to Saudi Arabia to defend feudalism and slavery of African people in Arab nation states run by kings, princes and emirs. Are the homeless and unemployed related to the soldiers who went to the Middle East to preserve democracy and oil "rites"? Who is endangered at this historic moment, those on the streets, in the subways, in the desert or maybe some others? Abbey Lincoln reminds us that with the increasing marginalization of the middle and working classes that "the people in the houses don't have long."

Our people have been battered in the recent past both internally and externally. They continue to search for corners and everyday survival. They demand responsibility, but the ethical bases for improved human relationships are not examined within the framework of propaganda and the diminished quality of life which leads to isolation and alienation.

We turn in an accusatory tone to the violence of the Other — urban gangs, drug dealers, terrorists, etc. — while constantly being bombarded by the horrors of the state through "law and order," justifiable homicide, COINTELPRO activities, and an ongoing state of siege. Despite our complaints, we continue to avoid the consequences of our legitimating principles. Moreover, we stand outside ourselves, claiming innocence and powerlessness, while allowing state terror to be expanded by the official elite. How do creative writers distance themselves from Jonestown, the Atlanta children's murders, Attica, Wounded Knee, the invasions of Grenada and Panama and Operation Desert Shield? How do we become preoccupied with who won the latest Pen Literary Award or Pulitzer Prize? How can there be business as usual in our daily lives when hunger, dislocation and terror stalk the streets? Are these the inevitable result of things unspoken? One is always in the position of having to decide between amputation and gangrene. We argue that injustice is commonplace, but this doesn't allow us to be complacent. We must fight these injustices with all our strength. The fight begins in the heart. But, do we find ourselves repressed by a dangerous and reverberating silence? The story is told compulsively in symbols and signs, in hieroglyphics and graffiti. Prince calls it "the sign of the times."

I cannot conceive of any Black urban youth, who, by the age of thirteen, has not been permanently scarred by the psychic damage of the culture of violence, despair, alienation and atrophy. We recognize young men and women growing into stunted maturity. And the wonder remains that, rather than so many being ruined, there are still those who survive and can flourish. Mark Mathabane etches in *Kaffir Boy* the pain and struggle of his mother's determination to afford him a passport to knowledge:

> Stay in school...stay in school
> For you my children, I'll sacrifice
> my life...
> Tears came to my eyes, when I heard that. [12]

When we observe the constant horrors in Central and South America, the untold suffering of the Intifada and Palestinian people on the West Bank, the political carnage in Liberia and Somalia and the unending strife and pain in Southern Africa, we must reflect on Martin Carter's work:

> This is the dark time my love
> It is the season of oppression, dark
> metal and tears
> It is the festival of guns, the carnival
> of misery
> Everywhere the faces of men are strained
> and anxious. [13]

We feel the prophetic words of Gabriel Garcia Marquez in *One Hundred Years of Solitude*, when he writes "a people who have lost the memory of their history will be condemned to a hundred years of solitude...to make the same mistake again." But you can't condone; you can't be silent on whether or not you will participate in the bloodbath in central America, the Middle East or South Africa. Do we really believe that we will be spared by the gods and the ancestors for our collaboration in imperial designs? There must be some price to be paid for this ticket. Minister Malcolm X said in the sixties that we were fighting the wrong people in Southeast Asia. General Colin Powell, who was born in Harlem and grew up in South Bronx, argues differently. Today, we must ask ourselves seriously, are we the *buffaloes* or are we the *buffalo soldiers*?

The nation state acts as a protagonist and as the embodiment of the creative vision. It is a projection of the global horror in *Rambo* and *Apocalypse Now*. America has decided to become a hired gun, protecting demcracies from South Korea to Kuwait. What a travesty. What a historical paradox. Maybe this irrefutable logic will lead us in the decade of the nineties to send American troops, the majority of whom will be Black and Brown to the Soviet Union to preserve democracy and Gorbachev's vision.

It is clear that the nation state has a role and we must ask, "what is that role?" How must writers deal with this reality? What is it that saps our spirit and deadens our imagination, while death ravages the ecology, the aesthetic, the streets? Why is there silence among many Black writers? Are we mainstreaming or mainlining? Are the voices of resistance becoming fainter? Are the ranks becoming thinner and thinner? Perhaps, we must keep asking, how does all of this affect me, my future, my image as Mars Blackman, Jesse B. Simple, or even Miles...Ahead? And please don't forget Junebug, who will be graduating tonight. The Black elected officials, athletes and entertainers are caught up in the same image game. The shadow Senator leads the pack in IMAGE processing and packaging.

Robert Stone, in his *Children of Light* deals with a society high on drugs, stupefied by alcohol and dazzled by celebrities. George Clinton, Dr. Funkenstein, sings "here is a chance to dance our way out of contradictions." However, popular entertainment, which we consume daily, deepens the pathology among young people, leading them through bizarre experiences and freakish behavior. Literature, films and videos are saturated with violence and insanity. At a very early age our children are given G.I. Joe and Nintendo games as Christmas gifts. Later on, they are seduced by soap opera and freaked out with pornoflicks and horror movies. Jayne Cortez warns us that,

These are the times of sterility
of hormone shots and lobotomies
of dehydrated funk and stagnated
celebrities. These are the times of solitary
confinement. [14]

Yet, we expect these young people to assume mature postures and enter into adult relationships of love and sexual responsibility, of gentleness, kindness, reciprocity and whatever is out there at the end of the rainbow with all of its *Nappy Edges, Disappearing Acts, Invisible Men* and *Hanging Judges.*

Can we drink the *Water from an Ancient Well* (Abdullah Ibrahim) or do we remain addicted to today's technology? Will it be too difficult to *Return To Our Native Native Land* (Aime Cesaire) or to John Coltrane's *A Love Supreme*? Will we remain on the auction bloc available to the highest bidder for our creative work or will someone put on the tombstone of an unmarked grave, "Beloved" or "No more auction bloc for me"? "My memory stammers; but my soul is a witness," writes James Baldwin. We must search for a map of the Black world, as well as a map to our interior, because just for the sake of living, we must not lose the reasons for living.

In several conversations in certain circles, I have heard some persons argue that we have lost a generation of young people who were born after April 4, 1968. Is that what Dr. King died for? Some parents maintain that these young adults have lost their memories. But who is to blame, the children or the adults? Something must have happened in Atlanta, the evidence of which we still have not seen. Dr. W.E.B. DuBois predicted in *The Education of Black People: Ten Critiques, 1906-1960* that integration would bring a loss of memory,

> When we become equal American citizens what will be our aims and ideals and what will we have to do with selecting these aims and ideals? Are we to assume that we will simply adopt the ideals of Americans and become what they are or want to be and that we will have in this process no ideals of our own?
>
> That would mean that we would cease to be [Blacks] as such and become white in action if not completely in color. We would take on the culture of white America doing as they do and thinking as they think.
>
> Manifestly, this would not be satisfactory. Physically it would mean that we would be integrated with Americans losing, first of all, the physical evidence of color and hair and racial type. We would lose our memory of [Black] history and those racial peculiarities which have long been associated with the [African]. We would not try to develop [Black] music and art and literature as distinctive and different, but allow them to be further degraded as they are today. [15]

Dr. W.E.B. DuBois could not have been more correct. He analyzed events and interpreted occurrences in a manner that few people were capable of doing at that time. Today, young students come into my class and they have hardly read any Black literature, two books at best, perhaps *Native Son, Invisible Man* or *Color Purple*. They don't know anything of Elizabeth Catlett, Charles White or Romare Bearden. They know very little about Alain Locke, Dr. DuBois, Sterling Brown, Langston Hughes, Lorraine Hansberry, Gwendolyn Brooks, Muddy Waters, Blind Lemmon Jefferson, Paul Robeson, Mahalia Jackson, Count Basie and Art Blakey. What a predicament in 1991. How did this happen so dramatically in the past twenty years, even though there has been more information available and accessible? The tragedy is that our young people don't really know about Black people's creative work and they have been systematically sidetracked, derailed. Moreover, what is even more pathetic is that many attend classes not even caring about the fact that they don't know their own culture and history. Many of them came from nurturing institutions called homes, schools and churches, which taught them how not to care and how to be cold and unfeeling. They have lost their memory and they are tied to a posture of indifference, not one of resistance and self-defini-tion. They are not anchored in any concrete historical reality. They are floating on the fragility of the present, buoyed by high levels of consump-tion. Many of these young people already belong to the revolving door and recycled world. They are among those who drop in and out of the public school system, junior colleges and universities. This increasing social dislocation has led William J. Wilson, Jr. to identify them as *Truly Disadvantaged* and Douglas Glasgow to label them as the *Black Under-class.*

However, the children of the Black "overclass" also got run over at Virginia Beach, when they tried to "do the right thing" and "fight the power." These young people are emotionally "downpressed" trying to "box" with the American Dream like Shelby Steele, Thomas Sowell, Ralph Ellison and Albert Murray. They are still in a daze being raised by parents who took them to Footlockers rather than bookstores, and who didn't insist that they read Black literature, having abandoned them to private and public schools, which sanitized and homogenized their im-agination and disconnected them from a "Dream Variation" on a cold

January day. They celebrate Dr. Martin Luther King's birthday, but they completely forget the people's revolt on April 4 and 5, 1968.

There is historical amnesia when one refers to Martin's 1967/68 statements:

> We must recognize that we can't solve our problem now until there is a radical redistribution of economic and political power....America is deeply racist and its democracy is flawed both economically and socially. The Black revolution is much more than a struggle for the rights of Negroes. It is forcing America to face all its internal flaws...racism, poverty, militarism, and materialism. It is exposing evils that are rooted deeply in the whole structure of our society. It reveals systemic rather than superficial flaws and suggest that radical reconstructon of society is the real issue to be faced....The whole structure of American life must be changed. [16]

How do we hear this today after engaging in war with Iraq, and with economic recession as an ugly reality? What would Martin, and Malcolm have said today if they were alive? Young people know Martin through his "I Have a Dream" speech at the 1963 March on Washington. They are searching desperately for Malcolm's voice but with little appreciation for his organizational accomplishments, intellectual discipline, vision, sagacity, wit, sacrifice, love, inner beauty and uncompromising sense of political integrity. These young men and women are searching for Malcolm beyond the red, black and green, beyond wearing medallions, beyond slogans and posters captioned "By Any Means Necessary." But, there is no one at home, in school or in church to analyze critically this great figure for them, whether it is a parent, teacher, politician or preacher. They are still getting Malcolm and Martin from a distance — not close up inside the literature, but, rather from *Eyes on the Prize* or *Do The Right Thing*. Martin and Malcolm have become celluloid images, frozen in time, and they are not connected up with George and Jonathan Jackson, Assata Shakur, Toni Cade Bambara, Angela Davis, Frantz Fanon, Amiri Baraka, Amilcar Cabral, Steve Biko, Winnie and Nelson Mandela, Walter Rodney, Maurice Bishop, Duke Ellington, Charlie Parker, Thelonius Monk, Archie Shepp, Abbey Lincoln, Max Roach, Charles Mingus, Paul

Robeson, Nina Simone, John Coltrane, Dizzy Gillespie, Bob Marley, The Mighty Sparrow, Miriam Makeba, Henry Dumas, Ed Love, David Diop, Askia Muhammad Toure', James Baldwin, Sonia Sanchez or Jayne Cortez.

The collaborators tell their young children "these are not dark times my love. This is not the season of oppression. We have come a long way from the sixties. We don't need any more of that racial and radical stuff. We have intergrated into the American mainstream. We are no longer 'spooks who sat by the door.' We sit around board tables in the Councils of War, on trilateral and multi-lateral commissions, and even in the White House. We must see ourselves as heroic individuals. Forget all that Black talk. This is the period of Eddie Murphy's *Coming To America* and *Arsenio Hall's Late, Late Show*. It is no longer *Guess Who's Coming To Dinner*. We have gone past the *Middle Passage* and now we are in the corporate corridors, the centers of power, and, by the way, we are having the members of the board over for dinner Saturday night. So please, none of that Black stuff." It all sounds like the soap operas but the situation is for real. Jayne Cortez reminds us,

> If you get caught up with soap operas
> Things and events will start passing
> you by. [17]

We are in a period of stasis. With economic recession at our doorstep and thousands of workers having been laid off, "rigger mortis" has set in and many of us are one paycheck away from bankruptcy. Time runs like a broken river, dragging along uprooted trees and scattered branches. We have yet to bury some of our dead properly and privately, and the ranks keep getting thinner. Gustavus Aquiano, a slave in 1789 wrote in his *Narratives*, "I must learn to navigate through this experience that would otherwise kill me." The time that we are in now is a time of disease and terror, corruption, social malaise, isolation, political indecision, cowardice and ideological bankruptcy in the Old World as well as the New World — on both sides of the waters. The writer must continue to deal with his/her reality. You can't escape it. There are no safe harbors.

James Joyce once said "history is a nightmare from which I am trying to awaken," but Sam Cooke sang,

> I was born by the river in a little
> old tent...and just like the river
> I've been running ever since...It's
> been a long time coming...but I know
> a change is gonna come.

What type of change? For the better or for worse? Revolutionary change, passive reforms, or is it simply a change of diapers, clothes, contact lenses, hair styles, cars, congressmen, senators, mayors, governors, political parties or presidents? What kind of change? "I know a change is gonna come." But tell me what kind of change is it going to be. In the final analysis, We have to be responsible for that change through our collective work and action.

Larry Neal wrote,

> We bear witness to a profound change in the way we now see ourselves and the world. And this has been an ongoing change...a steady march to a collective sense of who we are and what we must be about to liberate ourselves. Liberation is impossible if we fail to see ourselves in more positive terms for without change we are slaves to the oppressor's ideas and values. Ideas and values. Ideas and values that attack the very core of our existence. Therefore, we must see the world in terms of our own reality. [18]

This is the way to go and Brother Larry is quite correct. Ayi Kwei Armah in *Two Thousand Seasons* says, "We are not a people of stagnant waters. We are remembers of the way." [19]

We must move beyond our present divisions by continent, class or gender, vertically or horizontally. In the New Testament, Matthew wrote, "Every kingdom divided against itself is a wasteland....And no city or house divided against itself will stand." We should pay heed to this prophetic statement in the Black world, whether we are in South Africa, South Carolina or South Bronx. We must take hold of the circumstances surrounding our lives and empower ourselves to change our present reality. We cannot afford to lose time, because to lose time is to lose everything. Remember, Bird wrote, "now is the time."

NOTES

1. Toni Cade Bambara, Panelist - Writer's Conference, Howard University 1976

2. Toni Morrison, *Beloved* (New York: Dutton, 1991) p. 110.

3. Rene Marque's, "Three Men By The River," *Caliban: Towards A Discussion of Culture in Our America*, Vol. XV. No. 1/2 (Winter/Spring 1974) A Special Issue. The Massachusetts Review, ed. Roberto Marquez, p. 87.

4. Zora Neale Hurston, *Their Eyes Were Watching God (New York: Harper Collins, 1990), p. 24*.

5. Ibid., p. 25.

6. Olive Senior, "City Poem", ed. Pamela Mordecai, *From Our Yard, Jamaican Poetry Since Independence*, p. 216.

7. Kenneth Clark, *Civilization*, p. 347.

8. Naomi Madgett, "Exits and Entrances," ed. Erlene Stetson, *Black Sister, Poetry By Black American Women 1746-1980*, p.128.

9. Edward Kamace Brathwaite, "Springblade," *Third World Poets*, pp. 34-35.

10. Wayne Davis, "Royal Jail," Gordon Rohlehr, *My Strangled City: Poetry in Trinidad 1964-75*, *Caliban*, Vol. II, No. I, (Fall/Winter 1976) ed. Roberto Marquez, p. 24.

11. Kalamu ya Salaam, "Beyond The Boundaries. (meditating on the Meaning of Life)," *Inn Flowers: A Poetic Report on a Visit to Haiti*, p. 26.

12. Mark Mathabane, *Kaffir Boy*, (New York: Dutton, 1987) p. 176.

13. Martin Carter, "This is the dark time my love," *Poems of Resistance*, p. 35.

14. Jayne Cortez, *Scarifications* (New York: Bola Press, 1973) p. 21.

15. Dr W.E.B. DuBois, "Whither Now And Why," *The Education of Black People, Ten Critiques. 1906-1960* (New York: Monthly Review Press, 1973) pp. 149-151.

16. David Garrow, *The F.B.I. and Martin Luther King Jr: From Solo to Memphis* (New York: Viking, 1983) pp. 214-215.

17. Jayne Cortez, *Scarifications*, p. 25.

18. Larry Neal, *Visions of A Liberated Future* (New York: Thunder's Mouth, 1989) p. 136.

19. Ayi Kwei Armah, *2000 Seasons* (Chicago: Third World Press, 1987) p. 94.